Young Man Thoreau

THOREAV

·1970·   ·BASKIN·

Richard Lebeaux

Young Man Thoreau

University of Massachusetts Press
Amherst, 1977

Grateful acknowledgement is made to the following publishers for permission to reprint copyrighted material. Basic Books, Inc. for material from "Youth: Fidelity and Diversity," by Erik H. Erikson in *Youth: Change and Challenge,* edited by Erik H. Erikson, © 1961 by the American Academy of Arts and Science, © by Basic Books Publishing Co., Inc., New York. A. C. Cain, I. Fast, and M. E. Erickson, "Children's Disturbed Reactions to the Death of a Sibling." Reproduced, with permission, from the *American Journal of Orthopsychiatry,* copyright © 1964 by the American Orthopsychiatric Association, Inc. Duke University Press for material from Joel Myerson, "More Apropos of John Thoreau," *American Literature* 45:105, 106. Copyright © 1973, Duke University Press. Faber and Faber Ltd. for material from Erik H. Erikson, *Identity: Youth and Crisis,* copyright © 1968 by Faber and Faber Ltd. Harcourt Brace Jovanovich, Inc. for material from Kenneth Keniston, *The Uncommitted: Alienated Youth in American Society,* copyright © 1965 by Harcourt Brace Jovanovich, Inc. Harvard University Press for material from *The Journals and Miscellaneous Notebooks of Ralph Waldo Emerson,* vol. v, edited by Merton M. Sealts, Jr., copyright © 1965 by the President and Fellows of Harvard College; and for material from *The Journals and Miscellaneous Notebooks of Ralph Waldo Emerson,* vol. vi, edited by Ralph H. Orth, copyright © 1966 by the President and Fellows of Harvard College. The Johns Hopkins University Press for material from Henry David Thoreau, *The Collected Poems of Henry Thoreau,* edited by Carl Bode, copyright © 1964 by The Johns Hopkins University Press. Alfred A. Knopf, Inc. for material from Walter Harding, *The Days of Henry Thoreau,* copyright © 1965 by Alfred A. Knopf, Inc. New York University Press for material from *The Correspondence of Henry David Thoreau,* edited by Walter Harding and Carl Bode, copyright © 1958 by New York University. Reprinted by permission of New York University Press. W. W. Norton & Company, Inc. for material from Erik H. Erikson, *Identity: Youth and Crisis,* copyright © 1968 by W. W. Norton & Company, Inc.; and for material from Henry David Thoreau, *Cape Cod,* arranged with notes by Dudley C. Lunt, copyright © 1951 by Dudley C. Lunt. By permission of W. W. Norton & Company, Inc. Ohio State University Press for material from Nathaniel Hawthorne, *The American Notebooks,* edited by Claude M. Simpson (Centenary Edition of the Works of Nathaniel Hawthorne, vol. viii [Columbus, Ohio: Ohio State University Press, 1972]), pp. 354, 369. Princeton University Press for material from Maurice R. Stein, *The Eclipse of Community: An Interpretation of American Studies,* copyright © 1960 by Princeton University Press; Expanded edn. 1972; Princeton University Press paperback, 1972, pp. 265–66. Reprinted by permission of Princeton University Press. The Thoreau Society, Inc. for material from the *Thoreau Society Bulletin:* "The Fire at Fairhaven Bay," 32 (July 1950); and from Raymond Adams, "Thoreau and His Neighbors," 44 (Summer 1953).

To Ellen and My Parents

Contents

Acknowledgements

There are those who heard or who have read "The American Scholar" whose lives have never been quite the same afterwards. I consider myself one who was inspired by Emerson. He was an educator in the best sense of the word. Similarly, I have had teachers in my academic career who have inspired and influenced me greatly—whether or not I got to know them personally. This book can in part be traced back to such teachers.

I could not have asked for a more spirited and knowledgeable introduction to Thoreau than I received from Professor Reginald L. Cook in his American Literature Survey at Middlebury College. His enthusiasm for Thoreau—and, more generally, for literature and ideas—first ignited my interest in that "traveller in Concord." Although there was a long hiatus—or "moratorium"—between my first exposure to Thoreau and the first serious research for this work, Professor Cook's lively and loving introduction kept the fires of my interest burning and provided me with the impetus to "travel much in Thoreau."

At Harvard I enrolled in the Graduate School of Education's section of Erik Erikson's "Human Life Cycle" course. Listening to Erikson, himself a "great man," I gained new perspectives on human development and the human condition. His learned, sensitive, and wise lectures led me into his writings and aroused my concern for how best to interpret the lives of "great" men and women—and how we may all gain richer perspectives on our own lives. I was further benefitted by having Dr. Robert Coles as my section leader in Erikson's course and as teacher in another course combining literature, psychology, and education. His integrity, open-mindedness, warmth, humility, compassion, and intellectual style have ever since served as models for me. Though I did not know it at the time, my experience with Erikson and Coles would intersect with my curiosity about Thoreau. The eventual outcome of that intersection would be this book.

In the Department of Sociology at Brandeis University I had the good fortune further to study Erikson with Professor Gordon Fellman, who not only helped clarify for me psychoanalytic-sociological theory but who also provided me with a fine example of how to combine humane concerns with a commitment to teaching and scholarship. While reading Erikson at Brandeis, I came upon Walter Harding's *The Days of Henry Thoreau;* the facts of Thoreau's life, so well-documented and clearly presented by Harding, leaped out at me and demanded an interpretation—particularly of young man Thoreau. During this first stage of excitement, my conversations with Professor Fellman were of much value.

In the American and New England Studies Program at Boston University I had the opportunity, under the guidance of Professor Norman Pettit, to pursue in depth the study of Thoreau and to become more familiar with the New England context. At the dissertation stage I benefitted greatly from Professor Pettit's thoughtful suggestions and encouragement. I am also grateful to Professor Richard Bushman for his close reading and perceptive criticisms of the text; moreover, I owe a debt to his "Community Studies" seminar, "Social Change in Concord," and to all the students in that seminar, for providing me with useful insights. Professor Cecilia Tichi's constant support and counsel have been profoundly appreciated.

My thanks also to Professor William Vance for his advice and for giving me the opportunity to work on an "Eriksonian" approach to literary study in his Whitman seminar; to Professor Herbert Moller, in whose "Historical Thought and Method" seminar I had the chance to become better acquainted with psychohistorical inquiry; to Professors Rudolph K. Haerle, Jr. and Norman Schwartz, who gave me a valuable and memorable initiation into sociology and anthropology at Middlebury College; and to Mrs. Anne McGrath, Curator of the Thoreau Lyceum. My conversations with graduate student colleagues at Boston University—particularly with Paul Wright, who also read and commented on parts of the text—helped greatly. I "tried out" many of my ideas on students in my "New England Writers: How Is A Life To Be Lived?" courses, and they made several constructive comments. I am sure that, in one way or another, students in all the courses I have taught have made a contribution to this book.

I wish to express my deep appreciation to all those who read the manuscript of this book for the University of Massachusetts Press, including Professor Leo Marx, Dr. Robert Coles, Professor Raymond Gozzi, and Professor Walter Harding. Their astute suggestions and encouragement have helped immensely. I am, of course, indebted to the guidance of Ms. Leone Stein, Director of the University of Massachusetts Press, and the members of the Press staff.

Finally, my deepest gratitude to my wife Ellen, who has helped me over many snow-capped mountains.

East Lansing, Michigan
September 1976

Introduction

The development of Thoreau's identity—from David Henry, son of John and Cynthia, to Henry David, sojourner at Walden—was a long, complex, and painful process; it was by no means a fully self-assured, stately march to the beat of a different drummer. The period between Thoreau's graduation from Harvard in 1837 and the beginning of the Walden experiment in 1845 was a time during which he was struggling to define his identity, when he was in the process of becoming—and almost *not* becoming—a "great man" in American literary and cultural history. What can be seen is the fatefully prolonged adolescence and troubled early adulthood of a gifted and sensitive young man: facing dilemmas of identity, vocation, and relation to parents, siblings, and community; searching for models and finding a "great man" to emulate and an ideology to embrace; seeking satisfactory forms of intimacy; engaging in a rivalry with the brother he deeply loved; seeking to establish his own home and become his own man; sensing his potential for greatness and fearing he would never realize that potential; traumatically confronted with, and profoundly influenced by, the death of his brother; enduring an extended "winter of discontent" before coming into his own—as writer and as "great man"—at Walden Pond and in *Walden*. The "inner" man was not identical to the "outer" man or, for that matter, to the "larger-than-life" figure who has become such an integral part of our cultural tradition.

In order to understand the "identity crisis" of this complex person who called on his readers to "simplify," it is necessary to show Thoreau growing up in—and subject to the promises, conflicts, and limitations of—a particular era, culture, and community. Moreover, in order to get to the roots of Thoreau's identity and identity confusion, it is necessary to pay considerable attention to his family background and childhood experiences. In a very real sense, an inquiry into this background provides the foundation upon which is constructed the interpretation of young man Thoreau in the period from 1837 to 1845.

Thoreau's writings—particularly the *Journal, Correspondence*, and early poems and essays—help us to understand the person. They show us that Thoreau was a human being—extraordinary and praiseworthy, but also beset by conflict, confusion, and insecurity. Indeed, were it not for his conflicts and weaknesses (which he often transformed into strengths), he would not have become the writer of such classic works as *Walden* and "Civil Disobedience." By humanizing Thoreau, by recording his struggles and setbacks, it is hoped that his achievements will be appreciated all the more—they were not come by simply or easily. The ways in which we "front the essential facts" of the "historical" Thoreau can tell us much, not only about confronting other historical and literary figures, but also about how we can come more fully and compassionately to terms with other human beings in our lives—and with ourselves.

Recently, many scholars have acknowledged the inadequacies of previous attempts to understand Thoreau's life and personality. In his *Thoreau Handbook* (1959), Walter Harding argued that until we have "a detailed, factual account of his day-to-day life," we "cannot hope for adequate interpretive biographies." [1] Harding himself answered that need for a "detailed, factual account" with *The Days of Henry Thoreau* (1965), to this day the definitive factual biography (with severe—and intended—limitations as an interpretive work). His careful investigation of Thoreau's day-to-day life has made it possible to connect more closely the outward events of his life with the writings—and to present a more concrete and convincing picture of the period from 1837 to 1845.

Since *The Days of Henry Thoreau*, there has yet to be published an adequate interpretive biography. Moreover, no recent biographer has fully incorporated the findings of Raymond Gozzi's extraordinary Freudian thesis, "Tropes and Figures: A Psychological Study of David Henry Thoreau" (1957). Gozzi focuses primarily on the "unconscious," "determined and driven" [2] Thoreau, on the childhood and family experiences that shaped his personality, later life, and writings. One of his major discoveries, the ramifications of which he explores with great meticulousness, is that Thoreau had an "unresolved Oedipus complex." We are given an insightful analysis of "figures of speech" and imagery from a Freudian viewpoint. Gozzi is admirably humble about his findings, even remarking that "after some half-dozen years of reading, studying, and writing about Thoreau, . . . a satisfying comprehension of him eludes me still." [3] He also acknowledges that "psychological studies of Thoreau produced by non-Freudian students . . . would be very different" [4] and that there is still need for a study of the unconscious *and* conscious Thoreau. In a perceptive essay, "The Half-Hidden Thoreau" (1962), [5] Carl Bode suggests that investigations of Thoreau's "unconscious life," while certainly "controversial," can enhance significantly our understanding of the man and his work. Bode devotes much attention to presenting and commenting on Gozzi's hypotheses, and he examines the proposition that the main characteristic of Thoreau's unconscious "was a marked Oedipal complex which aborted his emotional life but richly informed his writing." [6] An earlier psychological portrait by David Kalman, "A Study of Thoreau" (1948), makes use of the concepts of Dr. H. A. Murray and (with reservations) Freudian vocabulary. Though Kalman's paper contains some valuable insights, it is too sketchy as it appears in the *Thoreau Society Bulletin,* and it seems obsessed with "pathology": psychoanalytic jargon is used in such a way as to make its subject a clinical "case" rather than a living, creative, and partially self-determined person.

In *Consciousness in Concord* (1958), Perry Miller presents Thoreau in an exceedingly unsympathetic way; there is little compassion or empathy in his account. Thoreau is seen as a "Byronic egotist" who rejected the responsibilities of the human community, a person who "strove to transcend not only experience but all potential experience," [7] a lone pilgrim on a "perverse pilgrimage." Miller takes a condescending, moralistic view of his subject. Rather than trying to explain the underlying sources and causes of Thoreau's so-called "perverseness," he is usually content to condemn the symptoms. He offers us penetrating insights into (and insults of) Thoreau, but he fails to provide us with corresponding insights into himself, into the reasons why he responds to Thoreau as he does. He does not seem to have honestly confronted the ways in which his own consciousness (and "unconscious") serves as a prism for perceiving Thoreau. The biographer's personal rage and discomfort is not dealt with. Instead of facing what he might have in common with his subject, Miller presents himself as essentially different from, and morally superior to, Thoreau. Miller's denial of common bonds with Thoreau, his "objectification" of the subject, makes his analysis suspect—though not without a pithy richness. Yet Miller did do something that needed to be done—he went beyond veneration and sought to understand the "historical" Thoreau.[8]

In contrast to Miller's work, Sherman Paul's *The Shores of America: Thoreau's Inward Exploration* (1958) examines Thoreau's "inner life" with sympathy and with careful, yet inspired, scholarship. It is one of the few studies, moreover, that has emphasized the various ways in which Thoreau's thought developed and changed over the course of a lifetime. Nevertheless, Paul—although deeply and laudably sensitive to his subject's emotional difficulties and crises—stops short of using psychological or psychoanalytical insights and seems a bit too intent on portraying the Thoreau of the late 1850s and early 1860s as having fully resolved his conflicts. Also worthy of mention as, in part, a developmental study—and one which focuses on a specific period in Thoreau's life—is Leo Stoller's *After Walden: Thoreau's Changing Views on Economic Man* (1957). As the title indicates, Stoller limits his discussion to certain issues, but he manages to suggest a wide-ranging, if debatable, interpretation of the post-Walden Thoreau.

In recent years two critics, Leon Edel and Quentin Anderson, have commented on the deficiencies of previous interpretations and suggested directions for further study. Both critics argue that our very vision of Thoreau's life and personality must be revised. Edel speaks in *Henry D. Thoreau* (1970) of "a crisis of identity so fundamental that Thoreau rescued himself only by an almost superhuman self-organization to keep himself, as it were, from falling apart." [9] In his conclusion Edel remarks, "A much deeper history of Thoreau's psyche may have to be written to explain his tenuous hold on existence in spite of the vigor of his outdoor life: his own quiet desperation, his endless need to keep a journal ('as if he had no moment to waste,' said his friend Channing), and his early death of tuberculosis at forty-five in Concord during the spring of 1862." [10] Throughout his monograph, Edel seems intent on debunking myths and stressing certain biographical facts (such as Thoreau's accidental setting on fire of the Concord woods in 1844); generally, Edel's stance toward his subject is unsympathetic, even hostile—somewhat reminiscent of Perry Miller's stance in *Consciousness in Concord*.

Quentin Anderson, in the July 4, 1971 lead article of the *New York Times Book Review* ("Thoreau on July 4"), speaks eloquently of the need for a Thoreau scholarship liberated from a "cultish" stance:

> We have seized on his "Walden" persona, ignoring (for this purpose) the "Journal" and the letters, to make a figure who would fulfill our fantasy, answer to our emotional need. On this abstracted persona most current Thoreau scholarship depends. Readers are licensed to do with books what they will, and we may say in defense of those who have used "Walden" for solace that Thoreau invited the reading most have given it. If we haven't accorded it historical meaning, it is in part because, in "Walden," Thoreau offered himself and danced away so that our pursuit of him is a ballet of the American imagination circling about the time when we most nearly possess the whole world, the undifferentiated

world of childhood. The passionate attachment to this image of Thoreau substantiates the presence of a cult with roots in the past. But critics, scholars, and historians have a distinct mandate they have failed to carry out in Thoreau's case.[11]

It behooves us to see Thoreau as a "complex and tortured man," even if this is not what we want to see. (He is so complex a man that estimations of his "happiness" are often wildly at variance; Harding, like Henry Seidel Canby in *Thoreau*, tends to see Thoreau as "the happiest of the whole Concord group," though he does admit that "the whole question needs further study.") [12] Surely, if we are to de-mythicize our study of Thoreau, we must explore in much greater depth the *Journal* and *Correspondence* as well as the private content of his more public efforts, such as *A Week on the Concord and Merrimack Rivers*, *Walden*, *The Maine Woods*, *Cape Cod*, and essays concerning politics and nature.

Young man Thoreau is in many ways a particularly appropriate subject for an Eriksonian study, in a similar vein to *Young Man Luther* and *Gandhi's Truth*. *Young Man Luther*, after all, follows Luther "through the crisis of his youth, and the unfolding of his gifts, to the first manifestation of his originality as a thinker," and concludes with his emergence into historical "greatness." [13] Unlike Luther or Gandhi, Thoreau was not a world shaker in his own time, but he can legitimately be considered a "great man" who emerged onto the stage of history when he went to Walden Pond and wrote *Walden*, when he spent a night in jail and subsequently wrote "Civil Disobedience." Indeed, the essay on "Civil Disobedience" had a profound influence on Gandhi— and later on Dr. Martin Luther King, Jr.—and thus can be said to have had a profound influence on history. *Walden*, of course, has been accorded a special place in our cultural and literary history. While there will always be some who disagree, it is surely not too bold to suggest that Thoreau has had an important impact on the twentieth century, that his "presence"—in large part based on his "Walden" and "Civil Disobedience" personae—is still strongly felt. He maintains the power to change, even transform, people's lives.

An Eriksonian study of Thoreau is an important advance over a strictly Freudian study. Though Erikson owes a great debt to Freud, he attempts to see human personality in a more holistic and flexible way. His approach takes into account the conscious self as well as the "unconscious." He does not perceive a person as wholly "determined and driven" by his childhood experiences; a human being grows, changes, and matures while at the same time remaining his mother's and father's child. Erikson speaks of the dangers of "originology"—that mode of analysis which attempts to explain fully (and thereby "reduces") human experience and personality by referring back to infantile and childhood "origins." [14] It is, then, justifiable to build on—as well as to revise—Gozzi's findings in the light of a truly developmental and epigenetic approach that does not focus exclusively on the first stages of life, that instead grants to every life stage its own importance, integrity, and meaning. Erikson's insights into the particular dilemmas (and opportunities) of adolescence and young adulthood—he is, of course, widely known for such concepts as "identity crisis" and "psychosocial moratorium"—can help us to understand more fully the critical 1837–1845 period in Thoreau's life.

There are additional advantages to the Eriksonian approach which should be mentioned here. For instance, the use of Erikson's life-stages does not stress a priori the "pathological" nature of the person being studied; in fact, many of Erikson's concepts apply explicitly—to a greater or lesser extent—to "normal" persons as well as to "cases." Erikson himself is well aware of the dangers of "reducing" a "great man"—or a gifted artist—to "patienthood." Along these lines, it must be recognized that Thoreau's "gift," his "genius," cannot be reduced to, or fully explained by his problems, conflicts, or "neuroses." [15] While this study will attempt to shed some light on the sources of Thoreau's creativity, I believe that the origin of any person's creativity will probably always remain something of a mystery.

Erikson's mode of analysis, furthermore, incorporates and takes seriously historical, sociological, and cultural factors. He does not see persons (as Freudian psychoanalysts often do) living in a sort of psychological vacuum—Freud himself not having taken fully into account the time-bound aspects of his formulations. In Erikson's work, he is deeply interested in how his subject is influenced by—and indeed, influences—culture, social structure, and history. His studies have attempted to show how personal needs and conflicts are related to the supra-personal, how identity is related to "ideology." As earlier indicated, this work will try to explore how Thoreau's personal development intersected and interacted with the supra-personal.

One fruitful way to organize and conceptualize a study of Thoreau's life and personality is the use of Erikson's "life-cycle" model. Erikson hypothesizes a series of "stages," or developmental "crises," which a human being must encounter over the course of a

lifetime. In each stage there are issues which must be adequately resolved if one is to grow in a constructive fashion: "Each successive
step, then, is a potential crisis because of a radical change in perspective.
Crisis is used here in a developmental sense to connote not a threat or
catastrophe, but a turning point, a crucial period of increased vulnerability and heightened potential, and therefore, the ontogenetic source
of generational strength and maladjustment." [16] As identified by Erikson, the eight stages are conceptualized as follows: trust vs. mistrust;
autonomy vs. shame, doubt; initiative vs. guilt; industry vs. inferiority;
identity vs. identity confusion; intimacy vs. isolation; generativity vs.
stagnation; integrity vs. despair.[17]

It is important to point out that these issues are not resolved in an
"either-or" sense but rather, as Robert Coles has said, in a "both-and"
sense—"with tone or emphasis all important." [18] As Erikson is very careful to stress, a person does not simply "resolve" each issue and then
move on to the next. Each stage, each "life-crisis," builds on the previous stages; thus by employing Erikson's approach, it becomes possible
to discuss the ways in which experience had its *cumulative* effects on
Thoreau and how he *continued* to struggle throughout his life with
issues first encountered in earlier developmental stages. It should be evident that no stage can be considered entirely independently of other
stages. For instance, issues of identity may be closely linked to issues of
intimacy; a person defines himself partly by the people and things to
which he chooses (and chooses *not*) to be close. Someone who carries
with him a strong sense of mistrust acquired in the first developmental
stage is not likely to escape feelings of isolation and despair in later
life.

Emerson once remarked, "To me . . . the question of the times resolved itself into a practical question of the conduct of life. How shall
I live?" [19] Thoreau confronted this question with great intensity and
courage. He sought to answer it in his own life and through his art,
and he passed on what he had learned about living—his wisdom—to his
own generation (few of whom paid heed) and to those yet to come.
Thoreau clearly has limitations as one who, by his words, thoughts, and
deeds, can guide or lead us today. For instance, I have deep reservations about his relative disinterest in, and apparent devaluation of,
human relationships and "social facts"; [20] our fulfillment and very
survival depend in large part, I believe, on our sensitivity to the needs
of other people, our respect for their experience and aspirations, our
willingness to put into action our care and compassion, and our recogni-

tion that, as human beings having so much in common on this miraculous and threatened planet, we need each other.

While Thoreau certainly cannot tell us how to solve all our contemporary problems, it is important that we consider how he may speak constructively to us. In "Life Without Principle" he asked, "How can one be a wise man, if he does not know any better how to live than other men?—if he is only more cunning and intellectually subtle? Does Wisdom work in a treadmill? or does she teach how to succeed by her *example?* Is there any such thing as wisdom not applied to life?" [21] Whether or not we agree with most of his specific answers to the dilemmas of the human condition, a consideration of Thoreau should at the very least lead each of us to ask, "How shall *I* live?" And perhaps confronting directly that most crucial of questions will help lead us to the wisdom we so much need in our time.

Practically, the old have no very important advice to give the young, their own experience has been so partial, and their lives have been such miserable failures, for private reasons, as they must believe, and it may be that they have some faith left which belies that experience, and they are only less young than they were. I have lived some thirty years on this planet, and I have yet to hear the first syllable of valuable or even earnest advice from my seniors. — Thoreau, *Walden*.

Men are pleased to be called the *sons* of their fathers—so little truth suffices them, —and whoever addresses them by this or a similar title is termed a poet. — Thoreau, *Journal*, I

"The Age of Revolution"

Characteristically, David Henry Thoreau may not have attended his own commencement-day exercises at Harvard on August 31, 1837.[1] Had he decided to brave the crowds, toasts, and speeches, he might have had the opportunity to hear his fellow townsman, Ralph Waldo Emerson, deliver his noontime "American Scholar" address to the Phi Beta Kappa Society. The address, Thoreau would have recognized, spoke profoundly to him and to other well-educated, sensitive, questing adolescents growing up in what Emerson called "the age of Revolution."[2]

Erik Erikson has told us that adolescence is a period of "identity crisis," and so it was—fatefully so—for Thoreau. Moreover, it seemed to Emerson that America was still in its adolescence, confronted with both the "fear and hope"[3] of identity-definition.[4] While political independence had been won sixty years before and had been reaffirmed in the War of 1812, the young nation was still in the process of breaking away socially, culturally, and spiritually from the parent country. Speaking to and for his "own platoon of people,"[5] Emerson gave the clarion call to a non-political revolution: "Our day of dependence, our long apprenticeship to the learning of other lands, draws to a close."[6] Such "seekers" as Emerson knew that they could not depend upon the learning of the Old World to determine what kind of "adult" America would become. After all, had not Wordsworth, a kindred spirit to

Emerson's platoon of intellectuals, warned against following the Old World's example? He had lamented, "The world is too much with us late and soon, / Getting and spending we lay waste our powers," and "Rapine, avarice, expense, / This is idolatry; and these we adore: / Plain living and high thinking are no more." Those people in America devoted to the ideals of "plain living and high thinking" were wary of their countrymen who were jumping on the band-wagon of material-istic "progress" before they knew where it was destined to go. Such "progress," although not without promise, was dangerous if accepted without reflection or if it became the dominant criterion of human progress. The "revolution" advocated by Emerson was neither com-mercial nor industrial; rather it was a revolution of the intellect and spirit. "The revolutions that impend over society," he said in "Lecture on the Times," "are not now from ambition and rapacity, from im-patience of one or another form of government, but from new modes of thinking."[7]

Emerson and his idealistic brethren felt that America's adolescence should not be ended prematurely; the nation should not become a mir-ror image of England or emulate Old World modes of thought. New England, with its "City Upon a Hill" heritage, should seek to become truly *new*. Just as an adolescent often needs a "moratorium"[8] during which to experiment with different identities, to feel his way around before final commitment, so did America in 1837 need to experiment, reflect, and avoid a headlong rush into adulthood. In 1837 it remained possible to believe that America could resist an adulthood dominated by industrialization, capitalism, and commercialism. The machine was chugging into the garden ever so slowly,[9] and business had not yet be-come "big business." For a brief, breathtaking moment it must have seemed to some "plain living and high thinking" men that the machine's gears could be locked into place and commerce could be subordinated to the human spirit. Indeed, Thoreau voiced these hopes in a Class Day conference at Harvard on "The Commercial Spirit" (August 16, 1837):

> We are to look chiefly for the origin of the commercial spirit, and the power that still cherishes and sustains it, in a blind and unmanly love of wealth. Wherever this exists, it is too sure to be-come the ruling spirit....
>
> Let men, true to their natures, cultivate the moral affections, lead manly and independent lives; let them make riches the means and not the end of existence, and we shall hear no more of the commercial spirit.... This curious world which we in-

habit is more wonderful than it is convenient; it is more to be admired and enjoyed than used. The order of things should be somewhat reversed, the seventh should be man's day of toil, wherein to earn his living by the sweat of his brow; and the other six his Sabbath of the affections and the soul, —in which to range this widespread garden.[10]

In his 1844 review of Etzler's "The Paradise within the Reach of all Men, without Labor, by Powers of Nature and Machinery," Thoreau would argue that mechanical progress should be (and could be) subordinated to moral progress:

> The chief fault of this book is, that it aims to secure the greatest degree of gross comfort and pleasure merely.... Undoubtedly if we were to reform this outward life truly and thoroughly, we should find no duty of the inner omitted. It would be employment for our whole nature; and what we should do thereafter would be as vain a question as to ask the bird what it will do when its nest is built and its brood reared. But a moral reform must take place first, and then the necessity of the other will be superseded, and we shall sail and plow by its force alone. There is a speedier way than the "Mechanical System" can show to fill up marshes, to drown the roar of the waves, to tame hyenas, secure agreeable environs, diversify the land, and refresh it with "rivulets of sweet water," and that is by the power of rectitude and true behavior.[11]

As Thoreau's comments would suggest, the sociocultural situation was not purely "Adamic":[12] Adam had taken his first bite of the apple, but he had not yet fully swallowed or digested it.

This was indeed an era of fluidity, of experimentation and reform movements, of "freedom's ferment."[13] Emerson and his "platoon" hoped that the fermentation progress would yield a sweet, invigorating cider. However, their hopefulness was accompanied by deep apprehension that America's bright promise was all too quickly fermenting to vinegar, that the young nation had already gone too far in defining itself in an unsatisfactory fashion. "The Americans have little faith," Emerson complained. "They rely on the power of a dollar; they are deaf to a sentiment."[14] In "Lecture on the Times," he identifies with the "purists" whose spirit "casts its eye on Trade, and Day Labor, and so it goes up and down, paving the earth with eyes, destroying privacy and making thorough-lights."[15] Emerson speaks of "this great fact of

Conservatism, entrenched in its immense redoubts . . . which has planted its crosses and crescents, and stars and stripes, and various signs and badges of possession, over every rood of the planet." [16] This "entrenched" conservatism is associated in Emerson's mind with "material might" [17] and moral-spiritual shallowness. The commercial system, "purists" feared, was rapidly expanding and solidifying; it emphasized pecuniary success, "physical gratification," [18] and competition rather than love and spiritual fulfillment. "I content myself," Emerson remarks in "Man the Reformer,"

> with the fact that the general system of our trade (apart from the blacker traits, which, I hope, are exceptions denounced and unshared by all reputable men) is a system of selfishness; is not dictated by the high sentiments of human nature; is not measured by the exact law of reciprocity, much less by the sentiments of love and heroism, but is a system of distrust, of concealment, of superior keenness, not of giving but of taking advantage.[19]

The purists were disturbed not only by the prospect of the "commercial spirit," but also by the rise of the "mob," of mediocrity, of a cult of social conformity. Jacksonian democracy was by no means an unadulterated blessing. Tocqueville reported that Americans loved equality more than liberty; to be equal to, or the same as, one's neighbors took precedence over autonomy or self-definition. The power of public opinion could outweigh the voice of the individual.[20] Emerson was deeply critical of such conventionalism:

> In America, out-of-doors all seems a market; in-doors an airtight stove of conventionalism. Every body who comes into our houses savors of these habits; the men, of the market; the women, of the custom. I find no expression in our state papers or legislative debate, in our lyceums or churches, especially in our newspapers, of a high national feeling, no lofty counsels that rightfully stir the blood. I speak of those organs which can be presumed to speak a popular sense. They recommend conventional virtues, whatever will earn and preserve property; always the capitalist; the college, the church, the hospital, the theater, the hotel, the road, the ship of the capitalist,—whatever goes to secure, adorn, enlarge these is good; what jeopardizes any of these is damnable. The 'opposition' papers, so called, are on the same side. They attack the great capitalist, but with the aim to make a capitalist of the poor man. The opposition is against those who have money, from those who

wish to have money. But who announces to us in journal, or in pulpit, or in the street, the secret of heroism? [21]

Emerson knew that the quest for identity—on both individual and cultural levels—could be agonizing, particularly in an increasingly conformist, materialistic society. To be "Man Thinking" in an ever more "divided or social state" [22] did indeed require a special kind of heroism. "The young man," says Emerson, "on entering life, finds the way to lucrative employments blocked with abuses. The ways of trade are grown selfish to the borders of theft, and supple to the borders (if not beyond the borders) of fraud." Moreover, a young man of "genius and virtue" is not likely to find such "employments" as society offers "fit for him to grow in, and if he would thrive in them, he must sacrifice all the brilliant dreams of boyhood and youth as dreams; he must forget the prayers of his childhood and must take on him the harness of routine and obsequiousness. If not so minded, nothing is left him but to begin the world anew, as he does who puts the spade into the ground for food." [23] In "The American Scholar," we get the distinct sense that he is thinking of his own prolonged adolescence when he depicts the plight of the idealistic, identity-seeking scholar or artist who wishes to "begin the world anew":

> Long he must stammer in his speech; often forego the living for the dead. Worse yet, he must accept—how often!—poverty and solitude. For the ease and pleasure of treading the old road, accepting the fashions, the education, the religion of society, he takes the cross of making his own, and, of course, the self-accusation, the faint heart, the frequent uncertainty and loss of time, which are the nettles and tangling vines in the way of the self-relying and self-directed; and the state of virtual hostility in which he seems to stand to society, and especially to educated society. [24]

His soon-to-be protegé, Thoreau, would discover the painful truth of this description when he returned from the "anything is possible" atmosphere of Harvard to the confines of his native village. [25]

Erikson hypothesizes that identity becomes an overriding concern in eras of social transformation; Hendrik Ruitenbeek says that in such an era, the question "Why can't I do what I want?" in part gives way to "What do I want?" and "Who am I?" [26] Therefore, it makes great sense that the age in which Thoreau grew up and whose atmosphere he imbibed was "bewailed as the Age of Introversion." [27] When there is a perceived plurality of choices and few "taken-for-granteds," it is much more likely that the individual will become self-conscious and, in some cases, self-critical if he does not resort blindly to "other-direct-edness." Emerson would say, in retrospect, that "the young men were born with knives in their brains, a tendency to introversion, self-dissection, anatomizing of motives," that the key "to the period appeared to be that the mind had become aware of itself." [28] Like Hamlet, who endured an excruciatingly and ultimately fatally prolonged adolescence, the identity-seekers of 1837, those young men of "genius and virtue" were, indicates Emerson, "infected with Hamlet's unhappiness, —'Sicklied o'er with the pale cast of thought.' " [29] But, he continues, there is also pleasure and promise in prolonged adolescence:

> Is it so bad then? Sight is the last thing to be pitied. Would we be blind? Do we fear lest we should outsee nature and God, and drink truth dry? I look upon the discontent of the literary class as a mere announcement of the facts, that they may find themselves not in the state of mind of their fathers, and regret the coming state as untried; as a boy dreads the water before he has learned that he can swim. If there is any period one would desire to be born in,—is it not the age of Revolution; when the old and the new stand side by side, and admit of being compared; when the energies of all men are searched by fear and by hope; when the historic glories of the old can be compensated by the rich possibilities of a new era? [30]

From Emerson's point of view, there is a deliciousness and delight in standing at the crossroads. As he observes in "Self-Reliance," "Power . . . resides in the moment of transition from a past to a new state." [31] In "Lecture on the Times," he compares living in the "age of Revolution" to sailing on a "wondrous sea":

> Here we drift, like white sail across the wild ocean, now bright on the wave, now darkling in the trough of the sea;—but from what port did we sail? Who knows? Or to what port are we bound? Who knows! There is no one to tell us but such poor weather-tossed mariners as ourselves, whom we speak as we pass, or who have hoisted some signal, or floated to us some letter in a bottle from far. But what know they more than we? They also found themselves on this wondrous sea.[32]

Viewed in this light, the inability to commit oneself to action could become a virtue. Emerson remarks that the reforming movement, while "sacred in its origin," is "in its management and details, timid and profane." [33] The "student," on the other hand, may remain devoted to "the sacredness of private integrity": [34]

> I must get with truth, though I should never come to act, as you call it, with effect. I must consent to inaction. A patience which is grand; a brave and cold neglect of the offices which prudence exacts, so it be done in a deep upper piety; a consent to solitude and inaction which proceeds out of an unwillingness to violate character, is the century which makes the gem. [35]

"The genius of the day," exclaims Emerson, "does not incline to a deed, but to a beholding." [36] The time for decisive action, for firm commitment to adult identity, thus could be justifiably postponed:

> There is a sublime prudence which is the very highest that we know of man, which, believing in a vast future,—sure of more to come than is yet seen,—postpones always the present hour to whole life; postpones talent to genius, and special results to character.... As the farmer casts into the ground the finest ears of his grain, the time will come when we too shall hold nothing back, but shall eagerly convert more than we now possess into means and powers, when we shall be willing to sow the sun and the moon for seeds. [37]

As the years advanced, Emerson must often have felt—as the United States entered upon an adulthood of capitalism, industrialism, predominant commercialism, and Civil War, and as he himself became a member of the adult "Establishment" [38]—that it was far more gratifying and exhilarating to stand and "behold" at the crossroads, to drift on the "wondrous sea," than to take any one path or sail into any one port. It was preferable to be born *and* to die in an "age of Revolution," a "moment of transition." To take one road or choose one port, as an individual or as a nation, meant relinquishing options and dreams. Was it not better, he must have asked himself, to prolong personal and national identity-choice as long as possible so as to protect against a frustrated, limited, paunchy adulthood? Could not the "age of Revolution" be held in a sort of suspended animation—at least until an acceptable adulthood could be found? For what age would follow the age of Revolution? Born into this transitional time and partaking of its spirit, Thoreau would be one who felt especially strongly that he would prefer a prolonged adolescence, an infinitely extended moratorium—not only for himself but for his society—to an adulthood which would limit choice and destroy visions of greatness and heroism.

Although conflict between generations occurs in all but the most traditional and authoritarian of societies, it was unusually intense in this "age of Revolution." Emerson describes Thoreau's generation as being "not in the state of mind of their fathers"; fathers were questioned, challenged, thought of as failures by their sons. The traditional order had broken down into "the party of the Past and the party of the Future; the Establishment and the Movement."[39] Many American fathers were perceived by their sons as somehow diminished—as conformists, business failures, spiritual failures, out of touch with the times,[40] or too captivated by the "commercial spirit" of the times. Emerson says of the era: "Children had been repressed, kept in the background; now they were considered, cosseted, and pampered. I recall the remark of a witty physician who remembered the hardships of his own youth; he said, 'It was a misfortune to have been born when children were nothing, and to live till men were nothing.' "[41] At the time when Emerson rose to speak of the American Scholar, of young men of "genius and virtue" who must "begin the world anew," the "founding fathers," as Quentin Anderson has so acutely observed,[42] had passed from the scene: Jefferson and John Adams in 1826; DeWitt Clinton, 1828; Monroe, 1831; John Randolph, 1833; William H. Crawford, 1834; John Marshall, 1835; Madison, 1836. Another "father," President Van Buren, was blamed by many—however unfairly—for the Panic of 1837, thus casting a shadow on the capacities of all fathers to lead. Tocqueville noted the decline in strength of paternal authority in the home.[43] Furthermore, as Emerson indicates, the "popular religion of our fathers had received many severe shocks from the new times";[44] in his 1838 Harvard Divinity School Address, Emerson audaciously put himself in the position of challenging all the fathers of the church and, indeed, the very conception of God as father. He referred to his "conservative" elders as a "generation of unbelievers."[45] Andrews Norton, a conservative Unitarian, gave a "Discourse on the Latest Form of Infidelity," but such revolutionaries as George Ripley and Theodore Parker (and Emerson himself) had the temerity to refute vigorously Norton's pronouncements. There is much evidence to support the idea that fathers and authority figures no longer claimed the deference or obedience (or even respect) they once could.[46]

Whether an 1837 Harvard graduate decided to join the "Establishment," to gain membership in the emerging bourgeois-commercial-capitalistic order, or to join the "Movement," to rebel against that order and create something really new, he put himself in the position of challenging or potentially surpassing the father. Many young men

sought a more prosperous and prestigious life for themselves than their
fathers had had. The opportunities were certainly there for those ambitious persons who wished to seize them. Other young people (those
stressed in Emerson's "Historic Notes" and inspired by "the American
Scholar") were determined to reject the learnings of their "faithless"
elders and the society their "Establishment" peers and elders were
building. Whichever path a young man took, guilt was likely to be a
disturbing companion. Erikson explains that we become aware "of the
inexorable succession of generations" at the same time in childhood
during which we develop "the propensity for intense and irrational
guilt." "To better the parent," he says, "thus means to replace him; to
survive him means to kill him; to usurp his domain means to appropriate the mother, the 'house,' the 'throne.' " [47] To be more successful
than one's father (even if the father seems to encourage the son to be
more successful than he) can thus evoke "intense and irrational guilt"
rooted in childhood. Furthermore, in "attacking and criticizing society," a "Movement" adolescent is "at bottom attacking his own father
and all that father stands for";[48] once again, guilt accompanies the
"devaluation" of the father. On a conscious level, either surpassing or
challenging the father may lead a young man to believe he has hurt,
or wants to hurt, his elder. Therefore, in a culture characterized by a
sense of the "failure of the fathers," [49] the experience of guilt among
the young and rising generation may be unusually widespread and
excruciating.[50] Because of his culture's "devaluation" of the father and
his personal sense of his own father's failure, Thoreau would have to
contend all the more strongly with feelings of guilt.

It was, then, increasingly difficult for many sons to model themselves after their parents. For adolescents growing up in an age of
transition, the loss of the father as model could only serve to aggravate
and intensify crises of identity. Questioning youth had to search for
substitute fathers, alternative models, new leaders and meaningful
ideologies, "great men"; indeed, Thoreau's formative years were
marked by a cultural preoccupation with "great men"—perhaps to fill
the vacuum created by the perceived absence of great men in nineteenth-century America. For gifted and sensitive young men like
Thoreau, easy answers to questions of identity were not forthcoming.
As Thoreau would later remark in *Walden:*

> Practically, the old have no very important advice to give the
> young, their own experience has been so partial, and their lives
> have been such miserable failures.... I have lived some thirty

years on this planet, and I have yet to hear the first syllable of valuable or even earnest advice from my seniors. They have told me nothing, and probably cannot tell me any thing, to the purpose. Here is life, an experiment to a great extent untried by me; but it does not avail me that they have tried it. If I have any experience which I think valuable, I am sure to reflect that this my Mentors said nothing about.[51]

By taking on the difficult task of becoming his own father, Thoreau—a very "special" man[52]—would be responding not only to the failures of his own father, but would also be confronting the identity dilemmas of a generation of sons.

Concord: Choice and Limitation

During Thoreau's formative years, New England towns such as Concord were in the process of defining and redefining themselves.[53] For Concord and its inhabitants, there were less givens, more choices to make, than there once had been. Indeed, Thoreau's development into a questioning, questing, often ambivalent young man could not fully be explained without reference to the fact that there were fewer taken-for-granteds than previously. A selection of topics debated in the Concord Lyceum—established in 1829—suggests some of the issues and choices encountered by concerned Concordians, who were growing more aware of the outside world and more conscious of the need to define local, regional, and national identity:[54] "Would it be expedient to establish an infant school in Concord?"; "Are religious controversies beneficial?"; "Would it be expedient for the U.S. to purchase Texas?"; "Ought provision to be made by law for support of the poor?"; "Is it expedient to form a county temperance society?"; "Is the Union threatened by the present aspect of affairs?"; "Ought New England to encourage emigration to the West?"; "Would it be an act of humanity to emancipate at once all slaves?"; "Does the pulpit or the bar afford the greatest field of eloquence?"; "Are contributions to the poor beneficial to the community?"; "Is it expedient to establish a savings bank in town?"; "Ought there to be a law compelling parents to send their children to school?"; "Is the community benefitted or injured by the present credit system?"; "Is the present banking system beneficial?"; "Is the territory of the United States, with her natural domain, already too large to insure permanent prosperity?"

Religion itself, which had been the rockbed of unity in the town's early years, was undergoing an identity crisis as Thoreau grew up in Concord. No longer could religion bring everyone in the town together. Dr. Ezra Ripley, the long-time minister and "father-figure" of Concord, was himself being challenged. Under his aegis, the Concord First Parish Church had become Unitarian—abandoning the doctrine of the Trinity and following the benevolent lead of William Ellery Channing and his movement.[55] In 1828 the conservatives of the town, under the leadership of Deacon White, split with Ripley's church and established the Trinitarian Society. The parish poll tax was still collected with town taxes; however people could no longer be forced to go to church.[56] In 1833 Massachusetts passed an amendment separating church and state. These upheavals caused problems in many families, where husband and wife found themselves on opposite sides of the religious fence.[57] The strong-willed Cynthia Thoreau had also split with Dr. Ripley, but later she decided to return to the First Parish. Thoreau himself would "sign off" from the church in 1841. When Ripley died on September 21, 1841—to be succeeded by Barzillai Frost —another distinguished "father" had passed forever from the scene. Some had found his leadership wanting, and Frost was even less likely to satisfy his townsmen; Emerson's 1838 Divinity School Address had portayed him as a representative of "corpse-cold Unitarianism," as having "lived in vain." [58] A new creed, whose most eloquent spokesman was Emerson, challenged more than one particular sect; it challenged organized religion itself. Not only was there more controversy in religious matters; church membership was declining. Secularization was setting in.

Whereas the earlier community had been organized around the institutions of church and family, other organizations were beginning to make claims on the time and commitment of Concordians. People began to define themselves not only by the primary groups into which they were born but also by the secondary groups they voluntarily joined. Political parties—Whigs and Democrats—fought for the allegiance of town members; undoubtedly many townspeople identified themselves with one or another of the parties. It is quite likely that the vehemence of political rhetoric served as a substitute for religious ardor. A Female Charitable Society was organized in 1814, dedicated, in their words, to "relieving distress, encouraging industry and promoting virtue and happiness among the female part of the community." [59] Mrs. Cynthia Thoreau was an active member of the society. Among other organizations which townspeople could use as reference groups were the Temperance Society, the Corinthian Lodge of Masons, the Concord Light Infantry and the Concord artillery, the Anti-Slavery Society, the Concord Lyceum, and the Library.

Henry Thoreau had been born in 1817 on a farm on Virginia Road in Concord, where his family was residing temporarily with Cynthia's mother. His father was a storekeeper by trade rather than a farmer. Thus, Thoreau was one of many in his generation who was to discover that farming was by no means the only occupation or way of life in early nineteenth-century New England. The self-sufficient family farm, for which each family member performed vital economic functions, was declining in numbers. Fewer young people expected that they would spend their entire lives on a farm. Ascribed status was giving way to achieved status and possibilities of upward (and downward) mobility in an expanding commercial order. Thoreau's father had no farm to hand down to his son; like many others of his generation, Henry could not depend upon patrimonial inheritance to determine his identity.

While Concord as a whole contained "about 850 male inhabitants, two-thirds [of which] were boys, and of the remaining men, all but a hundred were farmers," [60] the *village*—into which John Thoreau moved his family in 1823 (after a five-year period in Chelmsford and Boston) and where he took up pencil-making—was becoming increasingly commercial. Sanborn describes it as it was in 1823:

> The schoolhouse, town-house, and church were not far from the "Milldam" ... at first a footway over the dam which made the millpond for this nonchalant miller.... A daily stage-coach ran through, from the westward as far as Keene, to Boston, and Concord itself supplied a local coach or wagon to take the townspeople through Charlestown, or over the Cambridge turnpike, to the city; while wagons, chaises, and long lines of market-wagons went and came by the same roads. New Hampshire and Vermont sent their rural products to market by teams that "baited" at the three taverns as they went down to Boston with their loads, or returned with "dry goods," "West India goods," and groceries, from that port of entry. Everything in the village bespoke of commerce and the mechanic arts, for every kind of mechanic had his shop or bench there.[61]

If in 1823 the village "bespoke of commerce," it spoke of it even more loudly in subsequent years. The center of town was forever modified by the draining off of the millpond, the widening of Main Street, and the selling of lots by the Milldam Company—an early capitalistic venture.[62] The change in the village center symbolized the movement away from the traditional crafts and light industry to business and services. The tanyard, for instance, was replaced by a general store, later to become a drugstore.[63] The informal system of paying off debts by providing services declined, as a more rational and orderly money economy took firm hold. Such concerns as the Middlesex Mutual Fire Insurance Company, the Concord Bank, and the Middlesex Institution for Savings were all housed in the village center before Thoreau graduated from Harvard. With the new institutions came merchants, bankers, lawyers, and insurance men.

As Concord village became more and more a market center for farmers in the outlying areas, the split between village and town became increasingly obvious. The well-to-do tended to cluster in the prestigious residences at the village center. Indeed, when the Thoreau family moved into the Parkman House on Main Street in 1837, it must have been conceived by Mrs. Thoreau as something of a social triumph.

It was becoming ever more apparent to townspeople that there was a "big world out there." If Concord was not cosmopolitan, it was, as Richard Bushman suggests, at least moving from isolation to provinciality. Rapidly improving transportation and communication brought town and urban centers closer together. New businesses, banks, and industry often had extra-local connections. The volume and diversity of imports—foreign and domestic—increased in the 1820s and 1830s; relatively less was being made in Concord. Newspapers carried some national and regional as well as local news. Advertisements told the townspeople what the new, popular styles were in the urban centers. Storefronts began trying to attract customers with conspicuous displays of their wares. People were beginning to define themselves by what they bought; even in the early days of commercialization, there was a measure of conspicuous consumption. It became possible to be more fashionable, up-to-date, by consuming what the "big city" had produced.[64] Exposure to the outside world, then, brought with it exciting—though often bewildering—new opportunities for town- and self-definition.

Industry as well as commerce increased Concord's diversity. As suggested by a drawing of J. W. Barber's (engraved by J. Downes), there were trees and gardens in the center of Concord. Industry had by and large moved out of the town center as business came in. However well the garden image was maintained in the village and among the well-to-do, the machine was invading the periphery. Not until

1844 would the machine (in the form of the railroad) roar through Concord, disturbing a dreamy Hawthorne in a nook of the woods called "Sleepy Hollow"[65] and intruding irrevocably into the daily lives and consciousness of townspeople. Even before 1844, however, Concord had begun to experiment with industry—though not on the scale of Waltham and Lowell. Calvin Damon bought a large mill in 1834 in West Concord, and before long it became a factory village called Damondale.[66] Other factories—for shoes and lead pipes—had been established around 1820. Along with the factories—and later with railroad construction—came a group of "outsiders" into the town, among them Irish immigrants. The town's population would never be as "pure" as it once had been. Ruth Wheeler maintains that Concord of the 1820s and 1830s was "too small to have strata. Few were poor and none were rich."[67] To the extent that this *was* true, it was becoming less true with the introduction of factories, working men and women, servants, immigrants. With these new people, it became less possible to assert that there was no class structure, no inequality of wealth, status, prestige, and power—no matter how hard the village population, by insulating themselves residentially from those different from them, tried to keep up the illusion. In *Walden*, Thoreau would make it abundantly clear that there were disparities of wealth and status in Concord, that the presence of such people as Irish immigrants belied any claims that the town remained homogeneous.

Perhaps the most urgent identity-choice for a young man or woman in Thoreau's generation was whether or not to leave Concord. While many persons were coming into the town, others were leaving. Women often married professional men from outside the community. Some men went to the exciting, glittering, opportunity-filled urban areas such as Boston or New York. But probably the most significant exodus was that of western emigration. Ruth Wheeler informs us that in Thoreau's formative years "every family lost at least half its boys to the frontier."[68] Emerson observed in his "Historical Discourse" on Concord (1835):

> Of late years, the growth of Concord had been slow. Without navigable waters, without mineral riches, without any considerable mill privileges, the natural increase of her population is drained by the constant emigration of the youth. Her sons have settled the region around us, and far from us, their wagons have rattled down the remote western hills. And in every part of this

country, and in many foreign parts, they plough the earth, they traverse the sea, they engage in trade and in all the professions.[69]

To those farming (or potentially farming) in rocky New England, the storied fertile valleys of the west must have been inviting indeed. No doubt numerous New Englanders and Concordians feared that they would be losers in agricultural competition with the west. Many may have left because their farms, or the farms of their fathers, were failing. Others were attracted to the west for the more general reason that they perceived greater opportunities there—in the "wide open spaces" where rich, fertile land could be acquired cheaply. During the Panic of 1837, when Thoreau first confronted the dilemmas of earning a living, there must have been heavy pressure on young people to leave their native towns.

The young men and women of Concord were exposed to an unprecedented range of choices of identity, occupation, reference group. Concord was no longer a "folk community" in which the path of one's life was foreordained or taken for granted. New choices provided new possibilities for fulfillment, but they could also lead to confusion and dismay. Growing up in a town which was in many ways becoming more open and diverse, Thoreau would experience both the heightened promise and the identity confusion associated with an increasingly pluralistic community.

It remains to be explained, however, why Concord, for all its diversity, was regarded by Thoreau as ultimately limited and limiting, why he seemed so dissatisfied with what the town had to offer.[70]

On September 12, 1835, Emerson gave his "Historical Discourse at Concord" on the occasion of the town's bicentennial—a time when heritage is invoked to inspire citizens and remind them of the perceived ideals and virtues of the founders.[71] In his speech Emerson reminded Concord's inhabitants that the town "was settled by a party of nonconformists, immediately from Great Britain."[72] He spoke of the courage, perseverance, faith, and frugality of Concord's settlers; the "planting of the colony," he said, "was the effect of religious principle."[73] If the town's "nonconformist" religious heritage was something of which to be proud, so was its unique Revolutionary heritage. "The Revolution," Emerson observed, "was the fruit of another principle, —the devouring thirst for justice." He conjured up the imagery of "embattled farmers":

In these peaceful fields, for the first time since a hundred years, the drum and alarm-gun were heard, and the farmers snatched down their rusty firelocks from the kitchen walls, to make good the resolute words of their town debates.... Those poor farmers who came up, that day, to defend their native soil, acted from the simplest instincts.... They supposed they had a right to their corn and their cattle, without paying tribute to any but their own governors. And as they had no fear of man, they yet did have a fear of God.[74]

Emerson concluded his oration by expressing his hope that his townsmen would remain true to the spirit of their ancestors. Yet, even while delivering his address, he must have been aware—as young Thoreau was—that the "commercial spirit" was becoming a more dominant force in Concord than either the "religious principle" or the urge for independence.

It was in Concord village, where Thoreau spent much of his childhood and adolescence, that the "commercial spirit" was most apparently becoming the "ruling spirit." In his chapter on "The Village" in *Walden*, he would bemoan the commercial character of Concord: "Signs were hung out on all sides to allure him; some to catch him by the appetite, as the tavern and victualling cellar; some by the fancy, as the dry goods store and the jeweller's; and others by the hair or the feet or the skirts, as the barber, the shoemaker, or the tailor." [75] At the same time that Concord was intent on invoking its heritage of principled, pious "nonconformists" and "embattled farmers," Thoreau— who early in his life had come to value purity and staunch independence[76]—could see that the town was becoming less autonomous, more dependent on the outside world. No longer was Concord primarily a town of isolated, self-sufficient, courageous farmers. The growth of interrelationships and interdependencies among towns and cities led to increased standardization and uniformity in many areas of life. Concord was coming to rely more and more on material goods, fashions, values, institutions, and technological innovations not native to the town or true to the spirit of its ancestors. Concomitant with the diversity of choices offered by the outside world was a perceived diminution in *self*-reliance. The coming of the railroad in 1844 was perhaps the most obvious example of that loss of autonomy which accompanied the intrusion of the outside world. As Thoreau would say in *Walden:* the "startings and arrivals of the cars are now the epoch of the village day. They go and come with such regularity and precision, and their whistle can be heard so far, the farmers set their clocks by them." [77]

Closely related to Thoreau's feeling that Concordians were becoming overly dependent on the outside world was his sense that, in the vacuum created by the decline of traditional standards, men and women were coming to rely too heavily on the opinions and standards of their neighbors rather than seeking to be autonomous.[78] Living as he did in the village center, he was only too aware of the extent to which social propriety and conventional behavior were valued over personal authenticity. People were afraid to confront directly the problems of identity definition; moreover, they were afraid of social disapproval, of being unlike their neighbors. Surely such people, Thoreau must have thought, could not be considered as brave and heroic as their ancestors. Only through truly *individual* definition of identity and behavior could men achieve autonomy. Therefore, while Thoreau's struggle against dependence was in large part a response to his personal situation,[79] it was also a response to what he perceived as the increasing dependence of Concordians on everything but themselves.

In a far more general sense, Thoreau objected to the predominant "commercial spirit" in Concord because it valued materialism over purity, piety, and spirituality. The "religious principle," the devotion to the ideal of a "City Upon a Hill," upon which Concord—and all New England—had been founded had been betrayed. As Stanley Cavell has observed, Thoreau identified deeply with the Puritans "not only in their wild hopes, but in their wild denunciations of the betrayals of those hopes, in what has come to be called their jeremiads." [80] In *Walden* he would speak passionately of the town's "dirty" —impure and profane—institutions.[81] He was predisposed against materialism (and conventional notions of success) long before he went to Harvard,[82] and the revolutionary experiences he imbibed during his college years made him even more dissatisfied with the "commercial spirit" and the accompanying decline in piety.

Although Concord offered a wider range of identity and career choices than it had before, the range was still too narrow for a young man like Thoreau who was seeking a life of the spirit, who had read *Nature* and "The American Scholar" and valued moral heroism. Sherman Paul has observed that Thoreau's college education suited him most specifically for "the clergy, the law, business, and, at last resort, teaching." Yet none of these entirely "fit his character," and therefore (as Paul quotes the younger Henry James), there was a "terrible paucity of alternatives" in New England towns like Concord for such people as Thoreau.[83] For reasons to be explored later,[84] Thoreau could not leave Concord; he was in too many ways emotionally attached to it. Thus he returned after college to a town which seemed to him limited both vocationally and spiritually.

Not only did Concord fail to provide him with a completely satisfying calling, but it also demanded that he adopt *immediately* a vocation and identity which were not fully acceptable to him. Young men who chose to stay behind rather than go west or to the city were expected to take their places immediately in the adult community. Apart from a college education—which in some sense delayed adulthood—there was no institutionalized period of moratorium whereby a young person could postpone commitment and experiment with various identities. As far as is known, there were no delinquent or deviant peer groups with which a youth could identify in order to resist what the adult world demanded of him. Tocqueville commented suggestively, "In America, there is, strictly speaking, no adolescence: at the close of boyhood the man appears and begins to trace out his path." [85] Beset by identity confusion and the sense that Concord did not offer him fulfilling alternatives, Thoreau was in need of a prolonged adolescence. Because he could not leave, he had to create a moratorium for himself in a community which demanded conventional behavior, hard work, and adulthood from its young men.[86]

Moreover, for those young and old who stayed behind, it frequently became necessary to justify the decision. Erikson points out that the sedentary inhabitants of many established towns felt threatened by the seemingly adventurous strangers who passed through "bragging of God knows what greener pastures." The townspeople had the choice of either leaving for the frontier themselves or remaining where they were and "bragging louder." Thus the knowledge that some people *were* boldly setting out for the frontier, with its exciting opportunities and unknown dangers, compelled those who did not leave to be "defensively sedentary and defensively proud." [87] It is likely that "town boosting" was one manifestation of defensive sedentariness. Certainly Concordians' frequent invocations of the town's Revolutionary heritage was a kind of boosting, an attempt to associate themselves closely with their courageous, liberty-loving ancestors. But self-boosting was often needed to accompany identifications with the town's unique glories. Thoreau, who so highly cherished independence and bravery, felt uncomfortable about staying behind in the relatively sedate, sedentary community of Concord—especially when so many young would-be professionals, aspiring farmers, and business-men were leaving Concord for opportunities elsewhere. In such a situation, Thoreau found it necessary to "brag as lustily as Chanticleer in the morning" about his own independence, to boast that he was a frontiersman even while remaining in his native town. By claiming that he had "travelled much in Concord," he was not only trying to justify his own staying behind, but was also (perhaps unknowingly) supplying all those who remained behind with a justification for their choice, for their seeming lack of "manliness" and adventurousness.[88] Thoreau offered to those Concordians he could "wake up" an alter-native form of adventure, a kind of travelling which would be possible long after the frontier had closed.

Though the parents cannot determine whether the child shall be male or female, yet, methinks, it depends on them whether he shall be a worthy addition to the human family. — Thoreau, *Journal*, IV

The fathers and mothers of the town . . . don't want to have any prophets born into their families—damn them! — Thoreau, *Journal*, III

The Parents

Cynthia Dunbar Thoreau gave birth to David Henry (named after his father's brother) on July 12, 1817, in Concord, Massachusetts. John Thoreau, her husband, had been born in Boston—the son of an immigrant from the Isle of Jersey—on October 8, 1787, and first moved to Concord in 1800. After serving as a store-clerk in Concord and then in Salem, he became proprietor of his own store in Concord. His business did well until he entered into an unfortunate partnership with Isaac Hurd, a doctor's son. Following a period of conflict, dissolution of the partnership, and a court case concerning the dissolution (a case John Thoreau won),[1] he set off for Bangor, Maine, where he tried his hand selling to Indians and others. However, he came back to Concord; on May 11, 1812, he married Cynthia Dunbar. The War of 1812 provided him with a job as commissary at Fort Independence, for which job he was to receive a bounty of land.[2] After the war financial problems continued to plague him. By the time Henry[3] was born, John was manager of the Concord-based Jarvis store and was farming the Virginia Road land of his mother-in-law, Mrs. Minott. Harding informs us that John's health had deteriorated under the double strain and "he often found himself unable to walk the two miles into the village to the store."[4] Moreover, "Joseph Hurd, who had already exacted exorbitant fees in his years as executor of the Thoreau family estate, now demanded further compensation for the final settlement. Only a few weeks after Henry's birth, his father was forced to sign over his share in the family home in Boston that he had mortgaged two years before. It is said that in his proud honesty he even sold his gold wedding ring to satisfy his creditors." [5] When Henry was one year old, John moved the family to Chelmsford, where he maintained a grocery store and painted signs. Unable to keep his economic head above water in Chelmsford—apparently because he was too good-natured to collect from customers in debt to him[6]—he relocated the family in Boston, where he taught school for a time. The Thoreau family moved back to Concord for the last time in 1823.

In his journal, Thoreau gives an account—after his father's death—of John's early years. The impression given, whether intentional or not, is that of a restless, often harried small businessman, unable to establish roots or security for many years:

> Father first came to this town to live with his father about the end of the last century, when he was about twelve years old. (His father died in 1801.) Afterward he went into Lexington Academy (Parker's?) a short time, then into Deacon White's store as a clerk; then learned the dry-goods business in a store in Salem. (Aunt J. shows me a letter from him directly after his going there, dated 1807.) Was with a Hathaway. When about twenty-one, opened a store for himself on the corner where the town house stands of late years, a yellow building, now moved and altered into John Keyes's house. He did so well there that Isaac Hurd went into partnership with him, to his injury. They soon dissolved, but could not settle without going to law, when my father gained the case, bringing his books into court. Then, I think, he went to Bangor to set up with Billings, selling to Indians (among others); married; lived in Boston; writes thence to aunts with John on his knee; moved to Concord (where I was born), then to Chelmsford, to Boston, to Concord again, and here remained.[7]

In a letter to Ricketson after his father's death, Henry characterizes John as having had "pecuniary difficulties to contend with the greater part of his life." [8] One gets the sense that Henry did not perceive his father's early years as "successful"; in John's case, the "commercial spirit" had not brought fulfillment or stability.

By the time John had settled for good in Concord, he had four children to support: Helen (born on October 22, 1812—indicating that she had been conceived before her parents were married); John (born in 1815—the exact date not known); Henry; and Sophia (born on June 24, 1819). Undoubtedly, John must have felt heavy responsibilities to settle down and stay out of debt; obligated to his children and to a wife who must have been disturbed by his previous economic failures, he had little choice but to become as dependable a bread-winner as he possibly could be.

In 1823 John was finally able to gain some small measure of finan-cial stability by taking up pencil manufacturing. It must be noted, however, that John Thoreau did not actually *choose* what his life's work (pencil-making) was to be. His brother-in-law, the "undepend-able" bachelor Charles Dunbar, came upon a plumbago deposit during his travels in New England. He staked a claim and, "in one of the few practical moments of his life," he decided to start a pencil manufactur-ing business.[9] He entered upon a partnership with Cyrus Stow of Concord to mine the claim; however—in his undependable way—he had obtained rights to the land for only seven years rather than perma-nently. Harding hypothesizes that, in order to make as much of the seven years as possible, John was requested to return to Concord to help with the business. He moved his family into a house on Main Street and carried on his pencil-making in a shop at a separate loca-tion.[10] So it was that, even with respect to pencil manufacturing, John Thoreau had not taken the first initiative but had responded to an opportunity offered from his wife's side of the family; in this sense, his wife might be said to have been a major influence in determining the course of his life. Although John was able to maintain the business after Stow and Dunbar dropped out, it was by no means a great suc-cess. To be sure, John avoided bankruptcy, but it must have been a struggle; Harding indicates that "to supplement their income, they also manufactured stove polish, marbled paper, and sandpaper."[11] Making ends meet was the preoccupation of the 1820s and 1830s. It was not until 1838–39, when Henry apparently discovered a new technique for making pencils (with improved quality lead), that the father could begin to devote most of his time and energy to pencil-making.[12]

It certainly is true that we know little about John Thoreau's character. Edward Emerson calls him "a kindly, quiet man, not with-out humour, who, though a canny and not especially ambitious me-chanic, was intelligent and always tried to give good wares to his customers."[13] Unlike his wife, who took part in the controversies of village life, John Thoreau was, according to Sanborn, "a peaceful and rather silent man."[14] In another work Sanborn portrays him as a "cheer-ful but unobtrusive person, who was often said to have assumed deaf-ness a little more than needful, in order not to hear too much of his wife's rambles and resources of indignation, against this or that towns-man who had transgressed her strict rules of honesty and decorum."[15]

In *"Warrington" Pen-Portraits*, the father is contrasted with the mother —"one of the most graphic talkers imaginable"; John "was the most silent of men, particularly in the presence of his wife and gifted son. At the annual melon-party at his house, to which Mr. Robinson and his wife were invited, Mr. Robinson was very much struck by the silence among his guests, and nearly convulsed the friends with whom he was talking by quoting from Emerson, sotto voce, —'The silent organ loudest chants / The master's requiem.' " [16] In a piece for the *Inlander* (1893), Jones characterized him as "a very cautious and secretive man, methodical and deliberate in action."[17] Harding, who has investigated all known accounts of John, observes:

> John Thoreau took great pleasure in music and often played the flute in the parish choir as a young man. He liked to read, particularly the classics, and handed many good books on to his son. He was active in the Concord Fire Society.... His neighbors thought of him as "an amiable and most lovable gentleman, but far too honest and scarcely sufficiently energetic for this exacting yet not over scrupulous world of ours." His favorite occupation was to sit by the stove in his little shop and chat by the hour. Throughout his married life he lived quietly, peacefully, and contentedly in the shadow of his wife, who towered a full head above him.[18]

One wonders, however, if John's quietness—at least in his own home and in the presence of his wife—was also the quietness of desperation; indeed, John may well have been Henry's prototype of a man of "quiet desperation." Harding further characterizes John as "a quiet mousey sort of man . . . there is little evidence that he had much direct influence on his son. The two got along together well on the surface, but they had little understanding of each other's interests. Their relationship was based more on toleration than on enthusiasm." [19] Yet, that John *was* a "mousey sort of man" and that there *is* "little evidence" that he had great influence on Henry David is itself highly significant. This description suggests that by these "passive," "weak," or "submissive" qualities John might have had an enormous influence on his son. As we know, the father is a crucial model for the son's identity development—a potentially negative as well as positive model. Henry may have consciously rejected his father as model, while at the same time identifying with his virtues and dilemmas. Along with many children of his generation who perceived that their fathers were in some sense "failures," Henry needed—and sought—positive identity models throughout his early and middle years. In an age of identity crisis—for the nation and for sensitive individuals—his father could not provide him with a strong model of what a "man" should be or do (except for his scrupulous honesty, "kindness," relative unambitiousness, and apparent cheerfulness in the face of adversity). John may have provided his younger son with a blueprint for what to avoid in life: economic entanglements; living on the brink of bankruptcy—always wary of being in debt and of being betrayed by one's business partners; inability to control the circumstances of one's life; commitments that endangered one's autonomy and life-choices. Henry's own fears of commitment were motivated in part by his sense of what commitment had done to his father. By temperament John Thoreau was not cut out for the kinds of business manipulations in which he had become inextricably involved. Being a merchant, a storekeeper, a pencil manufacturer and proto-industrialist—submitting to the "commercial spirit," to what America was gradually becoming—could not, to young Henry's eyes, have appeared as a manly and independent way to live life. That his sister Helen had been born only five months after his father's marriage might well have suggested to Henry that marriage was also not a matter of free choice and was therefore to be avoided at almost any cost.

It is quite possible that Thoreau consciously saw his father as "emasculated" in a society that purported to value the manly independence and initiative of the frontiersman or farmer. Henry was in the position of many sons during an era when the paternally dominated home was coming more under the aegis of the mother. As farm and craft households declined in numbers, men were more likely to be removed from the everyday workings and decisions of the family. From the viewpoint of the child, the father—no longer continually "around" to assert his authority, and often too busy to tend to his offspring—might become "psychologically absent." Accordingly, the mother became a more dominant force in many homes; she presided over household activities, reared and educated the young, and set the tone of everyday life for her children. As the family moved from a producing to a consuming unit, she could have some say in household purchases, such as furnishings and appliances. To the child, the mother might appear to be a more significant figure than the father; with her continually present—physically and psychologically—the child's bond with her tended to be stronger and more intimate. The maternal quality of child-rearing and home life could either be reinforced or diminished, depending upon the personalities of the parents. An unusually "strong" woman, coupled with a relatively "weak" man could serve greatly to intensify the child's sense of maternal significance and domination.

In Thoreau's case, the sense of his father's emasculation and impotence was aggravated immeasurably by the characterological dominance of the mother and the "feminine" quality of the home.[20] Harding observes that Mrs. Thoreau "was a much more dynamic person and she dominated not only her meek spouse, but to a certain extent, the whole household." [21] Thus Henry might have learned relatively early from his father's submissive situation that women and domesticity, as well as business and commitment, were threatening and potentially emasculating.

A narration by George Frisbie Hoar of an event in his childhood may shed additional light on John's character:

> When I was a small boy a party of us went down to Walden woods, afterward so famous as the residence of Henry Thoreau. There was an old fellow named Tommy Wyman, who lived in a hut near the pond, who did not like the idea of having huckleberry-fields near him invaded by the boys. He told us that it was not safe for us to go there. He said there was an Indian doctor in the woods who caught small boys and cut out their livers to make medicine. We were terribly frightened, and all went home in a hurry.
>
> When we got near the town, we met old John Thoreau, with his son Henry, and I remember his amusement when I told him the story. He said, "If I meet him, I will run this key down his throat," producing a key from his pocket.[22]

This story suggests that John Thoreau—if the "he" of the story is indeed John rather than Henry[23] —was *not* just a "meek" and "mousey" man, that he was on occasion capable of speaking, if not acting, violently. While not too much should be made of this one incident (and Hoar, we must remember, said that "he" responded with "amusement"), there is some justification for believing that Henry's father may occasionally have spoken harshly to him—especially in those years when Henry began to act unconventionally and express unconventional aspirations. He must have been disturbed by his son's reluctance to help out in the family business or make the best economic use of his education. It can be hypothesized that Henry was consciously aware of his father's capacity for anger and, perhaps, unconsciously fearful of his potential for violence.[24] Indeed, silence—though it can suggest "meekness" or even stoicism—can also be a powerful form of aggression and can suggest suppressed rage, violence, or desperation. If John's son could perceive him as "harsh" or potentially violent, then he might have seen that there were other reasons (not related to his father's feelings toward *him*) why John could be angry. Perhaps Henry recognized that violence could be born out of frustration, out of a sense of entrapment and failure, that silence could be a form of protest against one's unsatisfactory life-situation and against those responsible for putting one in that situation. If Henry did have the perspicacity to recognize that John was frustrated, that he harbored dark angers and even violence under the surface, his feelings of compassion for his father, as well as his fear of John and of duplicating his fate, would have been greatly intensified.

Henry was ambivalent about his father. He hated John's submissiveness, resented his inability to provide him with a positive masculine model and to protect him from dependency upon his mother.[25] But Henry also loved "this amiable and most lovable gentleman," who was "far too honest and scarcely sufficiently energetic for this exacting yet not over scrupulous world of ours." Thoreau may well have identified with his father's values—values which could not assure "success" in an increasingly competitive, aggressive, business-industrial world. His identification with John and with his plight may have led Henry consciously to feel that it would be wrong to outdo him, that somehow he would hurt John by being more successful in the world than his honest and normally kind father. As Bruno Bettelheim observes, "To put the burden of surpassing one's parents on the relations between parent and child leads of necessity to unresolvable conflicts. If the youth succeeds, it emasculates the parent. As a result, youth cannot feel successful—partly out of guilt, and partly because he cannot be sure if it was he or his parent who wanted him to succeed." [26] Even before directly considering the role of the mother (or of oedipal conflict) it becomes possible to hypothesize that Thoreau was torn between, on the one hand, a desire to be "manly," independent, free from feminine, domestic, and village domination, in a position to challenge authority and surpass it, to be in some way "successful," and on the other hand, the fear and guilt accompanying manliness, ambition, and success, and a need to be nonaggressive and submissive, a need for "failure" which would allay guilt feelings. In short, one major influence John Thoreau had on his son was to plant deep in Henry's psyche the seeds of identity confusion.

Cynthia Dunbar, of Yankee and Scots heritage, had moved to Concord with mother and stepfather in 1798, where they lived on the Virginia Road farm. Cynthia's real father had died on June 22, 1787, the same year and shortly after she had been born. Asa Dunbar had been a 1767 graduate of Harvard College, where he had "headed a rebellion . . . which for a time threatened to paralyze President Holyoke's institution." [27] In leading this rebellion, Dunbar had become the "hero of his class." [28] Although he taught school for a short while, he also had been studying divinity and eventually settled down in Salem, Massachusetts as the colleague of Rev. Thomas Barnard. He married into the rich Tory family of Mary Jones (Weston, Mass.) on October 22, 1772. Because of the family's Tory connections, Asa found it necessary on more than one occasion to declare publicly his belief in the American cause.[29] Of his life thereafter, Sanborn tells us:

> His health was not good, and he had retired from his Salem pulpit, which he finally gave up in 1779.... He was studying law, and was an active Freemason in that year; and he came down to Lancaster from Keene in June, 1781, to give a fervid Masonic address.... He founded a sister lodge in Keene, which met at his house, and seems to have involved him in some debts. There he had law students, and was a social favorite, apparently, as his family were after his death.[30]

Before his death, he held the office of town clerk; he was buried, after a short illness, with "full Masonic honors." [31] Asa Dunbar's achievements are emphasized because they undoubtedly had an influence on Cynthia's conception of the ideal man. A daughter often is given to idealizing her father. Given the fact that Asa died before she came to know the "real" man, and that he was a man of accomplishment—Harvard graduate, campus hero, parson, active Freemason, lawyer, town clerk—it seems probable that he was imagined by his daughter to be even more formidable, courageous, successful than he actually was. In this case, there may also have been resentment on the daughter's part that her father "left" her before she got to know him—leaving her mother to play the role of both mother and father. For the first eleven years of her life, Cynthia saw her mother not as a loving, subordinate wife, but as the independent operator of a tavern in her home. Later, Cynthia would herself become the operator of a boardinghouse in her own home—while her husband was still very much alive. Finally, Mary Jones Dunbar married Captain Jonas Minott in 1798; she continued to live on the Minott's Concord farm until 1813—when her second husband died. There does not seem to be much biographical information on Minott; perhaps this should be taken as an indication that he was not the formidable masculine figure that Cynthia's real father—the "ideal" man of her imagination—had been.

In any event, Cynthia had married John Thoreau on May 11, 1812. Now, if the marriage was happy (as Harding and several other commentators claim it was), it was probably because their opposite natures complemented each other; John was certainly not made in the image of her own father. Unquestionably, people in early nineteenth-century Concord were reserved about discussing their marital difficulties; a proud woman such as Cynthia could not be expected readily to admit that her marriage was a "failure." It is appropriate to stress that Cynthia was pregnant with Helen before her marriage; could it be that the marriage was entered into unwillingly, at least from one partner's point of view? One would have to know more about the cultural meaning of premarital conception in those days. Did "respectable" people frown on such activities, or was it normal and accepted to engage in intercourse and conceive a child before marriage if both partners had definitely decided they were going to marry? Was the pregnancy an accident—forcing two people to marry who would have preferred, at least at that moment, to remain single? These questions cannot now be answered with complete certainty.[32] But the fact remains that, once Helen had been conceived, there was no turning back for Cynthia and John—none, that is, if John was an "honorable" man and Cynthia a "respectable" woman. One might speculate that Henry Thoreau also wondered whether there had been any coercion involved in the union of his parents. If Henry, whether justifiably or not, held sexual desire responsible for his parents' marriage (a marriage, he perceived, which had emasculated and entrapped his father, frustrated his mother), then it becomes more understandable why Henry was so distrustful of, and uncomfortable with, his own sexuality.

Cynthia was undoubtedly an extraordinary if—to those with a limited vision of women's roles—intimidating woman: she was vivacious, active, proud, assertive, activist, socially aggressive, status-seeking. Edward Emerson says,

> there is abundant and hearty testimony from many of her neighbors—to which I can add my own—to her great kindness, espe-

cially to young people, often shown with much delicacy; also to her thoughtfulness and her skill in making home pleasant, even on the smallest capital, by seasoning spare diet and humble furnishings by native good taste, and, more than all, by cheerfulness; for this good woman knew how to keep work and care in their proper places, and give life and love the precedence.[33]

One gets the feeling that it was she who held the family together when the going was rough. In spite of the family's "honest poverty" in those early years, Mrs. Thoreau struggled to give her home an atmosphere of gentility. Cynthia was perhaps an exaggerated example of how women were coming to see the home more as their domain. With the king having abdicated his castle, Mrs. Thoreau was the unchallenged queen; Annie Russell Marble quotes a friend of the Thoreau family as saying, "Well might a gifted woman exclaim, 'She looks like a queen,' when death at last had claimed the resolute spirit, and she lay silently receiving her friends for the last time." [34] In addition to presiding over her household, Cynthia also maintained a boardinghouse in her home, thus achieving a kind of economic independence from her husband.

Yet she was by no means only a presence in her own house. She was an exceedingly liberated woman for her day; had her culture been more accepting of liberated women, perhaps Cynthia ultimately would not have been as frustrated as she was. She would have been less dependent on the male figures in her life to determine her own status, and would therefore have made fewer demands on her husband and sons. As it was, Mrs. Thoreau made every attempt to establish her own identity by actively participating in village affairs and reform activities. She was a member of the Concord Female Charitable Society and the Bible Society as well as the founder of the Concord Women's Anti-Slavery Society. Her didactic bent, reformist activities, outspokenness, and sharp wit surely served as a model for Henry. Cynthia also "saw to it that the family took its part in the social life of the village and often entertained with parties and sociables for the young people of the church or the town." [35] She was avidly interested in nature, books, and intellectual issues; clearly she passed on her passionate interests to her younger son.

Mrs. Thoreau, however, was not all sweetness and light to those who knew her. Ellery Channing, who was Thoreau's friend from 1842 on, found it extremely uncomfortable to be in the same room with her; perhaps in her talk and demeanor, he felt an implicit judgment on his own unambitiousness and "irresponsibility." Of her, Channing says—

not without a hint of hostility: "I have heard many stories related by his [Henry's] mother about these early years; she enjoyed not only the usual feminine quality of speech, but thereto added the lavishness of age. Would they had been better told, or better remembered: for my memory is as poor as was her talk perennial." [36] Sanborn gives an illuminating account of a typical dinner-time conversation at the Thoreau home:

> Mrs. Thoreau . . . was, next to Madam Hoar, the mother of the Judge and the Senator, the most talkative person in Concord in my time—a very good talker, too, if there was time to listen. . . . Often have I sat at the family dinner-table engaged in talk with the son, as we sat on opposite sides of the board, facing each other, with the silent father between us at the head of the table, which, as the room was furnished, was the east end. Mrs. Thoreau, who helped to the puddings at the west end, catching some word in our conversation which interested her, would take up that theme and go on with it; often relating things to the credit of her son or other members of her family. Henry would sit silent and attentive, during the long interruption; then, as the last period closed, he would bow slightly to his mother, and resume our dialogue exactly where it had been stayed.[37]

Already recounted has been Sanborn's reference to Mrs. Thoreau's "rambles and resources of indignation against this or that townsman who had transgressed her strict rules of honesty and decorum." [38] William Robinson thought that Henry's mother "was one of the most graphic talkers imaginable, and held her listeners dumb." [39] Annie Russell Marble informs us that "her active, fluent, witty tongue, expressive of a brilliant mind, has been accounted as 'malicious liveliness.'" Marble goes on to say, "Perhaps too much emphasis has been laid upon her lively, assertive temper and her agile tongue. . . . Her conversation, however, was not limited to gossip or harangue, as has been covertly hinted." [40] In a personal reminiscence which appeared in the *Independent* of July 25, 1895, Irving Allen speaks of Cynthia's "command of the formidable female weapon of sarcastic rejoinder";[41] Edward Emerson indicates that she was "spirited, capable, and witty, with an edge to her wit on occasion." [42] Although it would be extremely unfair to characterize Cynthia Thoreau as only malicious, gossipy, indignant, sarcastic, there seems to be ample evidence to support the contention that she could be sharp and accusatory—intentionally or unintentionally cruel—around the house. Her husband

and children must have borne the brunt of her invective in their day-to-day encounters with Cynthia.

It is likely that Mrs. Thoreau felt frustrated in her desire for higher social status and greater prestige. Just as Marble characterizes Cynthia as "ambitious," [43] so Edward Emerson describes John Thoreau as "not especially ambitious." Harding observes that "there are many hints" that Cynthia "often wished her social position higher than it was. Her husband's quiet, easygoing ways did not bring her the status she sought." [44] It is quite possible that she often reminded John, explicitly or implicitly, that he was not helping her to fulfill her ambitions—indeed, that he did not fulfill her expectations of what a "real man" should be, that he could not live up to her own father. Marble says of John: "An unambitious man would not, from a limited income, have given his four children an education of marked liberality for those days." [45] John may well have seen in his children an opportunity to achieve success vicariously and justify his own life. One could argue alternatively that John was more anxious to have Henry join him in the family business than to have him "rise in the world." However, the evidence at hand suggests that Cynthia, much more than John, saw her children's achievement as potentially justifying her existence and mollifying her sense of frustration. A neighbor and friend of Edward Emerson, speaking of Mrs. Thoreau, told him that "for years the family had on ordinary days neither tea, coffee, sugar, nor other luxuries, that the girls might have the piano which their early musical taste showed they would want, and the education of all, especially the sending of the younger son to college, might be provided for; and yet her table was always attractive, and the food abundant and appetizing." [46]

Erik Erikson's discussion of the "common several outstanding traits" of mothers whose sons suffer from identity confusion seems directly applicable, in many respects, to Mrs. Thoreau:

> First, a pronounced status awareness of the climbing and pretentious or the "hold-on" variety. They would at almost any time be willing to overrule matters of honest feeling and intelligent judgment for the sake of a façade of wealth or status, propriety and "happiness"; in fact, they try to coerce their sensitive children into a pretense of a "natural" and "glad-to-be-proper" sociability. Secondly, they have the special quality of penetrating omnipresence; their ordinary voices as well as their softest sobs are sharp, plaintive, or fretful and cannot be escaped within a

considerable radius.... These mothers love, but they love desperately and intrusively. They are themselves so hungry for approval and recognition that they burden their young children with complicated complaints, especially about the fathers, almost pleading with them to justify their mothers' existence by their existence. They are highly jealous and highly sensitive to the jealousy of others. In our context it is especially important that the mother is intensely jealous of any sign that the child may identify primarily with the father or, worse, base his very identity on that of the father.[47]

Cynthia was status-seeking (though perhaps not to the extreme described by Erikson), possessed that quality of "penetrating omnipresence," and wished her children to justify her existence (as her husband could not).

It is my belief that Henry, above all the other children, was encouraged—consciously and unconsciously—to feel himself "special," "chosen"—indeed, a potentially "great man." In an 1851 journal entry, Thoreau suggests that as a youth he had euphoric experiences which gave him intimations of these possibilities:

This earth was the most glorious musical instrument, and I was audience to its strains. To have such sweet impressions made on us, such ecstasies begotten of the breezes! I can remember how I was astonished. I said to myself,—I said to others,—"There comes into my mind such an indescribable, infinite, all-absorbing, divine, heavenly pleasure, a sense of elevation and expansion, and [I] have had nought to do with it. I perceive that I am dealt with by superior powers. This is a pleasure, a joy, an existence which I have not procured myself. I speak as a witness on the stand, and tell what I have perceived." The morning and the evening were sweet to me, and I led a life aloof from society of men. I wondered if a mortal had ever known what I knew. I looked in books for some recognition of a kindred experience, but, strange to say, I found none. Indeed, I was slow to discover that other men had had this experience, for it had been possible to read books and to associate with men on other grounds. The maker of me was improving me.[48]

As Erikson indicates, such a sense of potential greatness coupled with a highly developed conscience creates "an obligation, beset with guilt, to surpass and to create at all cost." In turn, this sense of obligation "may prolong his identity confusion because he must find the one way

in which he (and he alone!) can re-enact the past and create a new
future in the right medium at the right moment on a sufficiently large
scale." [49] The man in whose image Mrs. Thoreau wished to shape
Henry was probably her own father—Henry's long-dead but much-
revered grandfather. Erikson describes with uncanny accuracy the
situation in which a "boy's male ideal is rarely attached to his father,
as lived with in daily life. It is usually an uncle or friend of the family,
if not his grandfather, as presented to him (often unconsciously) by
his mother." [50] In one interpretive swoop, Erikson suggests how three
generations—Henry's maternal grandfather, mother, father, and Henry
himself—may have been psychologically interrelated:

> The grandfather, a powerful and powerfully driven man—ac-
> cording to a once widely prevailing American pattern, another
> composite of fact and myth—sought new and challenging engi-
> neering tasks in widely separated regions. When the initial chal-
> lenge was met, he handed the task over to others, and moved
> on. . . . His sons could not keep pace with him and were left as
> respectable settlers by the wayside; only his daughter was and
> looked like him. Her very masculine identification, however, did
> not permit her to take a husband as strong as her powerful
> father. She married what seemed, in comparison, a weak but safe
> man and settled down. She does not know how she persistently
> belittles the sedentary father and decries the family's lack of
> mobility, geographical and social. Thus she establishes in the boy
> a conflict between the sedentary habits which she insists on, and
> the reckless habits she dares him to develop. At any rate, the
> early "oedipus" image, and the image of the overpoweringly
> bigger and greater father and possessor of the mother, who must
> be emulated or defeated, becomes associated with the myth of
> the grandfather. [51]

Without directly considering the oedipal question at this point, it may
be suggested that Henry was placed under the burden of measuring
up to his mother's ideal image of a man—an image that the father could
not emulate. Although his brother John was viewed by many Concordians as the more promising and certainly more popular brother, [52]
it was Henry who was chosen to attend Harvard—and thus follow in
the footsteps of Cynthia Thoreau's father. Marble indicates that Henry
himself was not overly excited about going to Harvard, that there were
"hints that this ambition was stronger on the part of his family than as

his own desire." [53] Channing informs us that Henry's "mechanical skill was early developed, —so much so that it was even thought to have had him bound as an apprentice to a cabinet-maker." [54] Yet the family (and Mrs. Thoreau, in particular) was anxious that Henry capitalize on those gifts which ultimately would provide him—and all the Thoreaus—with higher status and greater prestige. Harding indicates that, of John, Jr. and Henry, the latter was "unquestionably" the "more scholarly of the two." [55] It seems that Henry must have felt "chosen" —perhaps partly against his will—as soon as he perceived that he would become the family's, and especially his mother's, hope. [56] There was considerable financial sacrifice on the part of Henry's parents and siblings so that he could attend college. Edward Emerson observes:

> The comparatively small amount which it then cost to maintain a boy at Harvard . . . was enough seriously to strain the resources of the family. The mother had saved for the emergency, as has been said, the older sister helped, the aunts reinforced, and Henry helped by winning and keeping a scholarship and . . . by teaching school for periods during the College course. But, thinking over the sacrifices, I was told, by a friend of his mother's that he said that the result was not worth the outlay and sacrifice it had called for. [57]

Henry, then, was put in the unenviable position of "justifying" Cynthia Thoreau. The mother, in Thoreau's transitional era, was beginning to assert herself, but Cynthia's extreme assertiveness, coupled with John's passivity, was probably ahead of its time as the cultural norm. [58] Henry Thoreau experienced in an exaggerated way what other young men were beginning to experience—and would feel with greater force in future years—the dominance of the maternal figure and the "psychological absence" of the father. Perhaps this is one reason why Thoreau is now considered to have been ahead of his time. Erikson offers the insight that

> [in] the America of today, it is usually the mother whose all-pervasive presence and brutal decisiveness of judgment—although her means may be the sweetest—precipitate the child into a fatal struggle for his own identity: the child wants to be blessed by the one important parent not for what he does and accomplishes, but for what he *is*, and he often puts the parent to mortal tests. The parent, on the other hand, has selected this one child, because of an inner affinity paired with an insurmountable outer distance,

as the particular child who must *justify the parent.* Thus the parent asks only: What have you *accomplished?* and what have you done for *me?* [59]

Indeed, upon graduating from college, Henry would be involved in a fatal struggle for his identity. He would put his mother and father to "mortal tests." And he would be torn between the ambition to *do* what a "great man" does and the determination to *be* his own man—not his parents'. He would try to resolve the conflict by making his life's work an insistence on *being.* Yet, as Erikson indicates, any resolution to such a conflict does not come easily or quickly: "today doubt and delay are so obviously often due to the circumstance that young men and women find themselves involved in a doing into which they were forced by a compulsion to excel fast, before enough of a sense of being was secured to give to naked ambition a style of individuality or a compelling communal spirit." [60]

Carl Bode points out that "home" —though it remained "Home Sweet Home" in the popular fancy—was often not thought of as "a place to live in, but as a place to leave. It is assumed that the American, characteristically mobile, will go somewhere else and return home only in his thoughts." [61] In terms of child-rearing, mothers were often put in the ambivalent position of "rais[ing] sons and daughters who would be determined to ignore the call of the frontier—but who would go with equal determination once they were forced or chose to go." [62] On the one hand, then, children in such towns as Concord were prepared to "adjust" to the sedentary norms and values of the community, to love their families and hometowns; on the other, they were expected to be independent, to have the capacity to leave if opportunities seemed to be brighter elsewhere. In such a situation, there was always the danger that a mother could teach her son to love and depend upon her, the family, and the community too much, so that the son could not leave home when the time and opportunity came.

Mrs. Thoreau, it seems, pushed Henry toward autonomy and achievement while at the same time making him overly dependent on her. Isaac Hecker once said of her, "The lady of the house, Mrs. Thoreau, *is a woman.* The only fear I have about her is that she is too much like dear mother—she will take too much care of me." [63] Henry did indeed seem to need his mother's blessings.[64] It is clear that he was very much attached to his home and mother. Many villagers considered Henry to be "the overindulged son of Cynthia Dunbar Thoreau." Years later, he would still be referred to by Cynthia as "my Henry" or "my David Henry." [65] Priscilla Rice Edes told the following story on the front flyleaves of a copy of *Excursions:*

> Emerson was a lover of those woods and many hours they spent together. Once after a lecture by Thoreau someone remarked how much like Emerson he had spoken; his mother overhearing replied, "Yes, Mr. Emerson is a perfect counterpart of my 'David Henry'." She almost worshiped him.
>
> "David Henry" did not care whether he was decently clothed or not. The ladies of the charitable society proposed to make him some cotton shirts, but thot it best, first to ask his mother if it would be agreeable to him. Dear Mrs. Thoreau at the next meeting said, "I told my David Henry that you would like to make him some unbleached cotton shirts; he said, 'unbleached mother, unbleached. Yes, that strikes my ears pleasantly; I think they may make me some.' " [66]

Ellery Channing relates that before Henry graduated from college, he asked her what profession to choose. She answered (with what was probably a characteristic mixture of sweetness and hostility), " 'You can buckle on your knapsack, and roam abroad to seek your fortune.' " "The tears," says Channing, "came in his eyes and rolled down his cheeks, when his sister Helen, who was standing by, tenderly put her arm around him and kissed him, saying, 'No Henry, you shall not go: you shall stay at home and live with us.' " [67] When he was away from home in 1843 (at Staten Island), he was painfully homesick and wrote to his mother telling her so. Channing observes that from childhood, "Henry had quite a peculiar interest in the place of his birth,—Concord, the phrase *local associations*, or the delightful word *home*, do not explain his absorbing love for a town with few picturesque attractions beside its river." [68] Even during his experiment in self-sufficiency at Walden, "his mother and sisters made a special trip out to the pond every Saturday, carrying with them each time some delicacy of cookery which he gladly accepted. And it is equally true that he raided the family cookie jar on his frequent visits home. But any other behavior on his part would have hurt his mother's feelings—she prided herself on her culinary accomplishments and dearly loved to treat her son." [69]

I would contend that the young Thoreau came to be extremely ambivalent about his mother and their relationship. On the one hand, he loved her and greatly needed her maternal support and presence—especially without an "influential" father to balance out his dependencies or provide him with an identity model. She—and to a lesser extent, his sisters [70]—supplied a maternal presence that he needed and sought his entire life. He became highly dependent upon mother and home and never was able fully to break away, either in terms of separation by physical distance or by establishing a sexual relationship and household with another woman. In fact, women—by association with and transference from the mother—became lifelong objects of ambivalence for Henry. Thoreau not only depended upon his mother for acceptance, approval, and love; he also came to regard her as threatening, possessive, emasculating, limiting. He perceived that his father was "controlled" by women, and he could also see that he himself was dependent upon—and could not break away from—his mother. He must have been aware during adolescence that it was his mother who had wanted him to follow in her father's footsteps, that it was she who was setting the direction of his own life. She threatened to define his identity for him; he wanted to establish his own identity. Henry feared that women could control him—they could accept or reject him—and he often felt powerless to set his own terms. A woman like his mother could "pleasantly" tell him to "buckle up your knapsack" and thus reject him; his immediate response would be to cry and seek acceptance and comfort. In brief, his mother was an object of fear and hatred (feelings which he had difficulty facing) as well as love. In Thoreau's case, the ambivalence, the threats to the establishment of his own identity were so great that he had to respond intensely to them, by ultimately adopting a radical, rebellious life-style and radical views.[71] Indeed, Henry had to assert his self-sufficiency and independence all the more strongly because he felt so profoundly dependent. One of the main tasks of his life would be to establish his identity as "traveller in Concord": he could thereby be an adventurer without leaving Concord or his mother.

Childhood—from Eriksonian Perspectives

It should be apparent that thus far I have avoided a strictly Freudian frame of reference; it has seemed to me that one may well discuss Thoreau's personality—and some origins of his identity crisis—without direct reference to, or at least emphasis on, such matters as the oedipal complex, early childhood experience, or infantile sexuality. Erikson himself is profoundly influenced by Freud, and makes great use of Freud's discoveries in his own work. But Erikson makes it possible for us to—gives us a language to—discuss identity-formation without becoming entirely consumed by early childhood occurrences and wholly unconscious processes. Suggested in the previous discussion is that Thoreau could have been conscious, or to a degree conscious, of how his mother and father were influencing his own development, how their personalities and ambitions for him made the establishment of his own identity problematic. It is naive to think that in an "age of introversion" Thoreau could have been totally unaware of the parental influence and of his own mental processes.

What appears particularly striking to me is that a study of Thoreau's unconscious and childhood experience strongly reinforces the argument set forth previously in this chapter.[72] That is, young man Thoreau's identity problems were also seated in, and undeniably exacerbated by, conflicts rooted in the unconscious and early childhood. It remains for us now, with the help of Erikson's formulations (and his reformulations of Freudian psychology), to reconsider previously presented data, and introduce some new information, as it sheds light on Thoreau's early identity formation.

It is possible to assert that, partly because of his family's residential and economic instability during his early childhood, Thoreau was left with a heavy residue of what Erikson calls "basic mistrust." Henry's family did not settle permanently in Concord until 1823; during the first six years of his life they moved frequently. Channing says that "his was a moving family," and Sanborn gives an account of Thoreau's remarkable residential mobility: "He remembered a few incidents that occurred at the Minot farm, where he lived for a year; then, for a few months in a red house on the Lexington Road. . . . Then Henry's father, having been in debt to his stepmother's estate, and unable to pay, removed to Chelmsford. . . . When he returned to Concord in 1823, he lived with his sisters for some years in the house of his father on the square; but till 1826 in the brick house of the late Josiah Jones." [73] In his 1882 biography, Sanborn speaks of Thoreau's earliest memories of childhood and says that he "had a story for every house" he had lived in.[74] Furthermore, there is evidence that Thoreau's mother was not always "there" when he needed her in the first few years. Gozzi suggests that "during the period when the family lived in Chelmsford, while he was 1¼ to 3½ years old, his mother worked with his father in the store, trying to make the venture a success. Her working explains the Journal note (VIII, 64), 'Aunt Sarah [Thoreau] taught me to walk . . . when [I was] fourteen months old.' " [75] Although we do not have any direct data on breast-feeding (the mode of orality to which Erikson links the first life stage), it may be speculated that Henry frequently could not depend on his mother's breast when he desired it. These factors may help explain Thoreau's deep insecurities, and his tendencies to withdraw into himself [76] as an adolescent and adult.

Closely linked to "basic mistrust" was a fear of abandonment, a sense of loss and separation which plagued Henry throughout his life. He would devote considerable energy to seeking security and restitution for his losses. It can also be hypothesized that Thoreau sought in nature the security that his mother did not offer him in those early years. Returning to nature was like returning to the mother's breast; to withdraw to nature was, in some sense, to regress to early childhood, recoup his losses, and gain a sense that he was being cared for by his mother. Indeed, it might even be said that Thoreau's attachment to Walden was not only an attempt to return to the maternal breast but to withdraw to that most secure and peaceful of places, the womb. Thoreau communicates this womb-like sense of Walden in his journal:

> Twenty-three years since, when I was five years old, I was brought from Boston to this pond, away in the country,—which was then but another name for the extended world for me,—one of the most ancient scenes stamped on the tablets of my memory, the oriental Asiatic valley of my world, whence so many races and inventions have gone forth in recent times. That woodland vision for a long time made the drapery of my dreams. That sweet solitude my spirit seemed so early to require that I might have room to entertain my thronging guests, and that speaking silence that my ears might distinguish the significant sounds. Somehow or other it at once gave the preference to this recess among the pines, where almost sunshine and shadow were the only inhabitants that varied the scene, over that tumultuous and varied city, as if it had found its proper nursery.[77]

If, on the one hand, Mrs. Thoreau left her son with a legacy of mistrust, she most certainly also transmitted to Henry a sense of "basic trust" which depends on the *quality* of the relationship between mother and infant (not entirely related, for instance, to how much time she spent with her child). When she *is* present, the mother is deeply solicitous of the child's unique needs and gives him (or her) a solid sense that she (and the community of which she is a part) can be relied upon. Her own caring, trustworthiness, and approval constitute the foundation for the adult feeling that one is "all right" as one is, that the world can be trusted, and that somehow things will "work out." [78] The capacity for trust developed in the early years becomes a capacity for faith and hope. Erikson speaks of religion as an "institutional confirmation" and expression of faith; when religion loses its hold on people, alternative forms and objects of reverence must be discovered. Channing relates an anecdote about Henry at three which seems to indicate that even then he did not trust in a heaven which did not meet his own requirements. Thoreau was "told at three years that he must die, as well as the men in the catechism. He said he did not want to die, but was reconciled; yet, coming in from coasting, he said he 'did not want to die and go to heaven, because he could not carry his sled with him; for the boys said, as it was not shod with iron, it was not worth a cent.'" Channing concluded that this "answer prophesied the future man who never could, nor did, believe in a heaven to which he could not carry his views and principles, some of which, not shod with the vanity of this world, were pronounced worthless." [79] Given his sense of "basic mistrust" for many people and for organized religion, it became necessary for Thoreau to seek other forms of reverence. What remains extraordinary is that Thoreau, with such a well of mistrust from early childhood, was nevertheless endowed with deep resources of faith, hope, and acceptance by a mother who adored him, even if she was not always "there." Erikson tells us that the "shortest formulation of the identity gain of earliest childhood may well be: I am what hope I have and give." [80] Thoreau certainly carried with him into later life a capacity to live on hope and a remarkable ability to give hope to others; at the same time, he had to struggle with a deeply implanted distrust and a fear of vulnerability which occasionally threatened to overwhelm him. Indeed, the assertiveness of his hope may be partially attributed to the intensity of his mistrust. In an 1843 letter to Lucy Brown he would write, "What means the fact—which is so common— so universal—that some soul that has lost all hope for itself can inspire in another listening soul an infinite confidence in it, even while it is expressing its despair—?" [81]

Unfortunately we have precious few glimpses of Henry as a young child which would help us to understand his early psychosexual development. Surely he had many happy experiences as a boy, roving about in the world of nature. There was always a part of him that wanted to return to the innocent and carefree days of youth. He would later say in his journal on July 16, 1851: "I think that no experience which I have to-day comes up to, or is comparable with, the experiences of my boyhood. . . . Formerly, methought, nature developed as I developed, and grew up with me. My life was ecstasy. In youth, before I lost any of my senses, I can remember that I was all alive, and inhabited my body with inexpressible satisfaction; both its weariness and its refreshment were sweet to me."[82] Channing says, "He was reticent of biographical recollections, and had the habit not to dwell on the past. But he loved, I doubt not, to linger over the old familiar things of boyhood; and he has occasionally let fall some memory of the 'Milldam' when he was a boy, and of the pond behind it, now a meadow." [83] Yet Thoreau's early childhood was by no means entirely happy. He was afraid of thunderstorms and would usually run to his father for protection.[84] In a journal entry of January 7, 1856 Thoreau recalls several occurrences at Chelmsford which may be characterized as "traumatic." [85] He wrote "[I] swung on a gown (?) on the stairway" while at Chelmsford: "The gown (?) gave way; I fell and fainted, and it took two pails of water to bring me to, for I was remarkable for holding my breath in those cases." He speaks of having cut off a part of his toe and being "knocked over by a hen with chickens, etc., etc." He also remembers that, at the brick house in Concord, he was "kicked down by a passing ox." [86] Gozzi suggests that the child Thoreau, awake in his parents' bedroom, "many times witnessed—hearing more than he could see—his parents engaged in intercourse." [87]

There is evidence that Henry early became a serious and sober boy, insistent on his own independence, courage, and stoicism. He was known as "one who did not fear mud or water, nor paused to lift his followers over the ditch." Once, Channing relates, "when a follower was done up with headache and incapable of motion, hoping his associate would comfort him . . . , he said, 'There are people who are sick in that way every morning, and go about their affairs,' and then marched off about his." [88] About the age of ten, he "carried . . . his pet chickens to an innkeeper for sale in a basket, who thereupon told him '*to stop*,' and for convenience' sake he took them out one by one and wrung their several pretty necks before the poor boy's eyes, who did not budge." [89] Another story, related by Harding, indicates that Henry, when accused of stealing a knife from another boy, responded, " 'I did not take it.' Sure enough, the real thief was soon discovered, and Henry indicated that he had known all along who had taken it. When queried as to why he did not volunteer this information sooner, Henry answered only, 'I did not take it.' " [90] Channing characterizes young Thoreau as "a thoughtful, serious boy, in advance of his years,—wishing to have and do things his own way, and was ever fond of wood and field; honest, pure, and good; a treasure to his parents, and a fine example for less happily constituted younglings to follow. Thus, Mr. Samuel Hoar gave him the title of 'the judge' from his gravity." [91]

What can be made of such limited data? How could a boy, by the time he was ten, have acquired such a nickname as "the judge"? From a Freudian point of view it can be said, of course, that Thoreau developed a strong and demanding superego during the phallic stage. While I agree with this conclusion, I believe that it would be wise, before directly discussing the phallic stage and the oedipus complex, to consider how Erikson's "autonomy vs. shame, doubt" stage may illuminate these matters.

Erikson relates this stage of development to the anal (and sphincter) zone and to the retentive-eliminative modes. Of course we do not have evidence of toilet-training procedures in the Thoreau household. However, we may hypothesize that Mrs. Thoreau, dominating, ambitious, and impatient as she often was, may well have been strict with young Henry as he developed the capacity for "holding on" and "letting go," for a kind of proto-autonomy over his body and will. In fact, as mechanization and efficiency became more important in the early nineteenth century, this kind of strictness may have been growing more extant in the culture. Erikson notes that a "rigorous training"— which has as its ideal a "mechanically trained, faultlessly functioning, and always clean, punctual, and deodorized body"—can lead to the development of a "compulsive personality," who is "stingy, retentive, and meticulous in matters of affection, time, and money as well as in management of his bowels." [92] Without labeling Thoreau as an "anal-compulsive type" (for he was much, much more than any one "type"), it may be remarked that the child Henry—and the man—seem to have possessed many of the characteristics of "anality" and "compulsiveness" described by Erikson. Moreover, he characterizes this stage as being a "battle for autonomy," for as the infant "gets ready to stand on his feet more firmly," he "also learns to delineate his world as 'I' and 'you,' and 'me' and 'mine.' " [93] The battle between a strong-willed Mrs. Thoreau and young Henry may have taken the following form:

> If outer control by too rigid or too early training persists in robbing the child of his attempt gradually to control his bowels and other functions willingly and by his free choice, he will again be faced with a double rebellion and a double defeat. Powerless against his own anal instinctuality and sometimes afraid of his own bowel movements and powerless outside, he will be forced to seek satisfaction and control either by regression or by fake progression; that is, he will suck his thumb and become doubly

demanding; or he will become hostile and willful, often using
his feces...as aggressive ammunition; or he will pretend an
autonomy and an ability to do without anybody's help which
he has by no means really gained.[94]

Erikson concludes, then, that this stage "becomes decisive for the ratio
between loving good will and hateful self-insistence, between cooperation and willfulness, and between self-expression and compulsive self-
restraint or meek compliance. A sense of self-control without loss of
self-esteem is the ontogenetic source of a sense of *free will*. From an
unavoidable sense of loss of self-control and of parental overcontrol
comes a lasting propensity for *doubt* and *shame*." [95] One of the dangers
of the sense of shame—when a child is forced to "consider himself, his
body, his needs, and his wishes as evil and dirty" and continues "to believe in the infallibility of those who pass such judgment"—is that a
sensitive child may "turn all his urge to discriminate against himself
and thus develop a *precocious conscience*." [96] Of particular interest is
Erikson's observation that an adolescent of "precocious conscience . . .
goes through his identity crisis habitually ashamed, apologetic, and
afraid to be seen; or else, in an 'overcompensatory' manner, he evinces
a defiant kind of autonomy." [97]

There seems to be a kind of "defiant autonomy" expressed in
Henry's refusal to give information about the knife thief; he seemed to
revel in his ability to hold back information desired by others—as if
the information he withheld gave him greater control of the situation.
Henry had surely learned to hold back emotion—as when he witnessed,
without flinching, the killing of his pet chickens. It might also be hypothesized that his "remarkable" holding of breath indicates defiance,
an enjoyment of retentiveness, and a desire to assert his will. Perhaps
Thoreau's brand of stubborn autonomy in childhood and in later life
was in part an overcompensation for a "precocious conscience" and a
sense that only by militantly asserting his own will could he gain personal freedom.

Whatever the childhood roots of "defiant autonomy," it should be
recognized that Thoreau did manage to achieve a unique and memorable independence. As Erikson says, the "over-all contribution" of the
second life stage to "an eventual identity formation is the very courage
to be an independent individual who can choose and guide his own
future." [98] In fact, Thoreau's courage is especially impressive in light
of the shame and doubt that he must also have carried with him. Moreover, he would often feel the burden of shame as imposed by his par-

ents and neighbors in Concord who did not approve of his ways. It is to Thoreau's great credit that he struggled intensely against these feelings, that he fought to assert his autonomy; in doing so—and in writing about it—he helped to liberate others from fears of nonconformity in a rapidly evolving "other-directed" society.

Hoar's characterization of Henry as "the judge" suggests that the young boy did have a "precocious conscience"—attributable to developments in the "anal" (autonomy vs. shame, doubt) stage as well as in the subsequent "phallic" stage. Certainly, the boy Thoreau was a harsh judge not only of his peers (such as the "follower" in Channing's account), but of himself. Even at the age of ten, he may have felt capable of judging his parents. As Erikson observes,

> in a patriarchal era, a son with a precocious conscience and a deep sense of superior mission could, while still a child, feel spiritually equal to—nay responsible for—a father who, by his own desperate neediness, made it impossible for the boy to hate him. I would venture to suggest that certain kinds of greatness have as an early corollary a sense that a parent must be redeemed by the superior character of the child.[99]

"Judge" Thoreau would carry into adulthood a sense of deep obligation to be of superior and exemplary character.

Erikson characterizes the "phallic" stage (approaching the end of the third year) as being dominated by the "intrusive mode": "(1) the intrusion into space by vigorous locomotion; (2) the intrusion into the unknown by consuming curiosity; (3) the intrusion into other people's ears and minds by the aggressive voice; (4) the intrusion upon or into other bodies by physical attack; (5) and, often most frighteningly, the thought of the phallus intruding the female body." The central issue of this stage is "initiative vs. guilt." The child must emerge from the phallic stage "with a sense of initiative as basis for a realistic sense of ambition and purpose," yet he also emerges with a light or heavy burden of guilt. Erikson says that initiative is governed by conscience: "The child . . . now not only feels afraid of being found out, but he also hears the 'inner voice' of self-observation, self-guidance, and self-punishment, which divides him radically within himself: a new and powerful estrangement. This is the ontogenetic cornerstone of morality." It is during this stage that the infant becomes interested in, and excited about, sexuality. Boys "attach their first genital affection to the maternal adults who have otherwise given comfort to their bodies and . . . they develop their first sexual rivalry against the persons who are the sexual owners of those maternal persons." This then is the oedipal wish: to possess the mother and do away with the father. The "initiative" to achieve this secret fantasy is, however, accompanied by guilt and fear (of castration, of paternal retribution): "The child indulges in fantasies of being a giant or a tiger, but in his dreams he runs in terror for dear life." [100] That Thoreau experienced both the joyful, sensual fantasies and the insistent nightmares of doom during the phallic stage is strongly suggested by his account in the *Journal* of a recurring childhood dream:

> I can remember that when I was very young I used to have a dream night after night, over and over again, which might have been named Rough and Smooth. All existence, all satisfaction and dissatisfaction, all event was symbolized in this way. Now I seemed to be lying and tossing, perchance, on a horrible, a fatal rough surface, which must soon, indeed, put an end to my existence, though even in the dream I knew it to be the symbol merely of my misery; and then again, suddenly, I was lying on a delicious smooth surface, as of a summer sea, as of gossamer or down or softest plush, and life was such a luxury to live.[101]

Already noted has been Gozzi's contention that Thoreau as a child frequently overheard his parents' sexual activity. If this is so, such "traumatic" experiences could only have served to awaken and exacerbate forbidden sexual desires, as well as to implant deeply in his mind an association between his parents' sexuality and his own. In a situation such as Thoreau's in which the mother is strong and attractive, the father weak and submissive, the intensity of the oedipal wish may be greatly increased. It may seem, in the child's fantasy life, that the mother is actually accessible; the father is in the background and does not offer the constant threat of punishment, of castration, that a "strong" father does. Furthermore, the mother may adopt unconsciously and / or consciously a seductive, enticing stance toward her son, perhaps because her weak husband has not fulfilled her (sexually or otherwise), because she somehow seeks in her son what her husband has been unable to give her. She could live her life through the successes of her son. But the apparent success the son has in "replacing" the father can have terrifying psychic consequences. If it appears to the son that he may be, or has been, "victorious" in his oedipal wishes, he may feel enormous guilt.

In Thoreau's case the father was, if not actually absent—though he may have been at work a large part of the day—at least psychologically absent, in the background and overshadowed by the mother. So it may have seemed to Henry that he had enjoyed success in winning the mother away from the father. But I would contend that this success, this victory of "initiative," was accompanied by intense feelings of guilt brought on by replacement of the father. Also there may have been a deep-seated fear that he ultimately would be punished by the father for his success.[102] To the young Thoreau, it might have seemed, on some level, that he himself was the *cause* of his father's meekness and submission in the face of feminine control.

Furthermore, as has been indicated earlier, Henry found himself outdoing his father in the real world. He became his mother's hope for upward status mobility; he was a successful scholar and later a graduate of Harvard.[103] He was also adept at working with his hands. Henry's achievements no doubt highlighted his conscious sense of success compared with his father's relative failure, and he probably won great early favor from his mother for his accomplishments. Perhaps the most striking "replacement" of father by son took place with regard to John's pencil business. After Henry had graduated from Harvard, and after he had resigned from his teaching position in Concord, he found himself helping out in his father's pencil factory. The son discovered a new technique for making pencils (with an improved quality lead) and was in large part responsible for the increased success of his father's business: "As a result of the improvements, their pencil business was now extensive enough that a long series of sheds extending toward Sudbury Road was built on the back of the Parkman House. . . . as the pencil business increased, thanks to Thoreau's improvements, they were gradually able to drop the various sidelines and concentrate on the pencil business alone." [104] So Henry David had in effect replaced his father in his own business—took over his father's pencils, so to speak.

What previous biographers, including Gozzi, have failed to emphasize is that a *pattern* of challenging and surpassing the father (and other male figures) developed early in Thoreau's life and continued into his adolescent and adult years. Often he was put—or put himself—into a situation in which he might challenge or supersede fathers and father-figures; such situations could have reawakened the guilts and fears associated with the oedipal project. The more Thoreau challenged and achieved, the more intense became the feelings of guilt and the irrational fears of retribution. I suspect that Thoreau had to live with, and repress, these guilt feelings rising from the unconscious; also, as I have heretofore suggested, he may well have felt conscious guilt that he was outdoing the father whom he rejected as a positive identity model, but with whom he identified. Initiative or ambition was frequently associated with guilt in Thoreau's psyche. A powerful superego looked disapprovingly on the attempt to rise at the expense of another. Dreams of glory were accompanied by nightmares of destruction. The conflict between initiative and guilt became a profound source of identity confusion.

Thoreau's adolescent and adult rejection of material success can in part be traced back to the unconscious and conscious guilts he felt as a result of challenging authority. One way Thoreau could resolve his conflicts and mitigate his guilt was to forswear material success as a positive virtue. If he could somehow deny to himself that he had succeeded, or wanted to succeed in a conventional sense, he could reduce the intensity of his guilt and fear. Ambition would have to take unconventional forms in order to be psychologically acceptable. It was easier, in some respects, for Thoreau to renounce worldly success. With his gifts and ambivalences, it is no surprise that he eventually turned to writing as a profession; writing had rarely led to material security or success in America.[105]

It should be recognized that, while Thoreau had "defeated" his father and "won" his mother, it was in some sense the mother—dominant, controlling, limiting—who threatened ultimately to emerge victorious over both father and son. Kenneth Keniston, in discussing alienated adolescents who have won a Pyrrhic victory in the oedipal project, observes:

> What these young men most deeply long for is ... total fusion with a maternal presence.... But though in some psychological sense they believe they succeeded in vanquishing their fathers—reducing them into the weak, damaged, phony, and unemulable characters they now portray in their stories—they simultaneously lost the goal for which they strove. In place of the surrounding and comforting maternal presence, they won a mother who they now see, at best, as controlling and limiting, and at worst, as devouring and murderous. The intimacy they wanted with her was replaced by her stringent limitations on their initiative, by her possessiveness, by her efforts to make them unsexual, unaggressive, and conforming. And furthermore, by defeating their fathers, these youths lost the right of every boy to a father whom he can admire: instead they now see their fathers as psychologically

absent, not worthy of respect or emulation.... The real victors—
those who retain the capacity to affect, move, and change the
world around them—are women. Ironically, both father and son
end up in the same boat, controlled by the same women.[106]

It has already been suggested that Cynthia Thoreau was perceived on
some level by Henry as the kind of "controlling" mother described
above by Keniston. Henry loved and needed his mother. Indeed, he had
never resolved the oedipal conflict in childhood; he had never been
fully dissuaded from his wish to possess the mother and his fantasized
belief that he could do so. Thoreau's dependence upon his mother,
his close attachment to her, may in part be traced to his unresolved
oedipal complex. But he also feared emasculation at her hands. Only
by avoiding the identity which his mother wished to thrust upon him
(which included her design that he become a worldly success) could
he avoid domination and emasculation. Thus, he was motivated to invite failure not only by the guilt and fear associated with the defeat of
his father but by the fear of being defeated by Cynthia.

Henry's superego, his conscience (as defined by Freud and
Erikson) was demanding, punitive, and restrictive indeed;[107] the
"judge" judged himself most severely of all. It is probable that Thoreau's parents (and particularly his "moralistic" mother) were intent
on giving their son a strict upbringing. The culture itself, rooted in a
generally repressive Puritan heritage, demanded purity of motivation
and action. Together, family and culture told the child Thoreau what
was "wrong" and "bad," and he internalized these strict standards
with a vengeance. Because of the strength of his forbidden wishes,
fantasies, ambitions, and dreams of glory, his conscience had to be all
the more powerful and insistent. Out of his conscience's sense of the
impurity of initiative (including sexual initiative) came the need to
find purity in love and in work. Sexual desires were associated with
forbidden oedipal wishes, the fantasized fulfillment of which provoked
superego-imposed guilt. If women, by transference, suggested in some
ways his mother, then any sexual longings for them were somehow
"dirty" and punishable. "Success" with a woman, as well as worldly
success, could be identified with challenging and defeating the father,
with hostile feelings toward the parent one was supposed to love un-
conditionally.

While Thoreau has been identified as one of the most conscientious of men, it must be noted that, in one sense, his quest was an at-

tempt to escape from the stifling, restrictive, and guilt-inducing conscience imposed upon him by his parents and his culture. In an early poem he wrote:

> Conscience is instinct bred in the house,
> Feeling and Thinking propagate the sin
> By an unnatural breeding in and in.
> I say, Turn it out doors,
> Into the moors.
> I love a life whose plot is simple,
> And does not thicken with every pimple,
> A soul so sound no sickly conscience binds it.
> That makes the universe no worse than 't finds it.[108]

Although in some respects Henry always remained chained to the strict standards of "sinfulness" implanted in him by his parents and culture, he sought to liberate himself from the bondage of socially imposed conscience. In order to escape "instinct bred in the house" and turn conscience "out doors / Into the moors," Thoreau found it necessary to assert militantly that the source of true conscience was in each person's consciousness—a consciousness that was in harmony with nature and God, not with society.

The Elder Brother

I have yet to consider one "significant other" in Henry's immediate family circle—his elder brother (by two years), John, Jr. The relationship between the two brothers—Henry's ambivalence toward John and the sudden death of John in 1842—would prove more crucial to the development of Henry's identity than most biographers have suggested. Significantly, John has been described by one who knew him as "his father turned inside out." [109] While the father was silent (at least around the house), reserved, and cautious, John, Jr. was friendly, extroverted, cheerful. He was interested in intellectual matters but he was by no means a serious scholar like Henry. His great interest in birds was communicated to his younger brother; in fact, Henry learned a great deal of ornithology from his brother's notebooks.[110] Marble speaks of John's "thoughtful services to others": "For Emerson he procured a daguerreotype of little Waldo. . . . Again, Emerson refers to the little box-house for bluebirds on his barn, placed there by John Thoreau, where for fifteen years the annual visitants gladdened the Emerson household." [111] After a good education, he taught school in Taunton and Roxbury, finally joining his brother Henry as teacher and administrator at Concord Academy where they had both been students. By all accounts, he was a fine, popular teacher. His health was never particularly good. In an October, 1833 letter to George Stearns, he writes, "I had the nose *bleed* (ignoble complaint) on cattle-show day to such an extent that I fainted from loss of blood, and was not able to participate in the festivities of the day. I have since been rather weak, and have not taken much exercise." [112] Not only did he suffer from strength-sapping nosebleeds, but as Harding tells us, "there were times when what he called 'colic' confined him to the house all day. But tuberculosis was the real trouble."[113] In January 1842 he would die a sudden and terrible death by lockjaw.

There can be little doubt that the Thoreau brothers loved each other and enjoyed a close friendship. An 1837 letter from Henry to John, addressing his brother as a fellow Indian,[114] communicates warmth, humor, and care. It is quite suggestive that John is described as "his father turned inside out": I would hypothesize that, in some respects, John, Jr. was not only a friend but an alternative father for Henry—a "father-figure." He provided his younger brother with an identity model by being a male to whom Henry could look up and in whom he could believe. As Henry would later write in a memorial poem for John, "For then, as now, I trust, / I always lagg'd behind, / While thou wert ever first, / Cutting the wind." [115] John showed Henry that a boy—or man—did not *have* to be like his silent, secretive, and cautious father. John probably helped Henry to be more sociable than he otherwise would have been. The elder's sociability is strongly suggested in the 1833 letter to Stearns: "For my part I am exempt from all such temptations; as there is naught here save a few antiquated spinsters, or December virgins, if you will; and well may I sing, 'What's this dull town to me? no girls are here.' " [116] Furthermore, John acted as a "buffer" between Henry and his mother. As long as he followed in John's footsteps, Henry would not feel as strongly that he was being controlled or "emasculated" by his mother.

That John and Henry were comrades, that Henry looked up to John in some ways, should not rule out the possibility—indeed, the probability—that they were in some respects rivals. It seems likely that from the time Henry and John shared a trundle-bed under their parents' four-poster they were rivals (in an oedipal sense) for their mother's affection.[117] Henry recalls that when they lived in the "brick house" in Concord he had an altercation with his brother:

> Mother tells how, at the brick house, we each had a little garden a few feet square, and I came in one day, having found a potato sprouted which by her advice I had planted in the garden. Ere long John came in with a potato which he had found and had it planted in the garden—"Oh, mother, I have found a potato all sprouted. I mean to put it in my garden" etc. Even Helen is said to have found one. But I came crying that somebody had got my potato, etc., etc., but it was restored to me as the youngest and most original discoverer, if not inventor of the potato, and it grew in *my* garden, and finally its crop was dug by myself and yielded a dinner for the family.[118]

Surely this must not have been the only occasion of sibling rivalry or the only time that Henry "won" the battle.

The relationship among male siblings was changing as it became necessary for them to seek their fortunes in the world. Certainly, there had always been conscious and unconscious rivalries between brothers since Cain and Abel. But the shifting economic situation in Thoreau's time, the increasing emphasis on achieved rather than ascribed status, and the declining significance of age and birth order as determinants of parental preference and adult status, introduced new elements of competition.[119] Thus the younger son could challenge his older brother for parental and social approval and preference. Achievements of children could, in effect, become symbols of prestige for parents. It was no longer natural or assumed that the elder would take precedence over the younger and that the younger should assume a subordinate role. To the extent that some residue of the former tradition remained, it is likely that the younger brother would feel some ambivalence at the prospect of challenging or outdoing his elder.

It appears that there was reason for the conscious Henry to feel hostility toward John. In a culture which sanctioned competition between peers, even while extolling cooperation, it is not surprising to find that the two brothers were compared with each other by townspeople. John was the more popular and promising; in comparison, Henry was found wanting. In *"Warrington" Pen-Portraits*, we are informed that John was highly regarded: "Among his [William Robinson's] schoolmates were John and Henry D. Thoreau; 'David Henry,' as he was then called. Of the elder John, Mr. Robinson was very fond. He was a genial and pleasant youth, and much more popular with his schoolmates than his more celebrated brother. Mr. Robinson had a high opinion of his talents and said that he was then quite as promising as Henry D." [120] Whereas Henry is villified as having been an overindulged "mother's son" by Priscilla Rice Edes (on the front flyleaves of a copy of *Excursions*), John is described as "one of those saintly minded, clean young men that are seldom seen. He was a bright spot everywhere; the life of every gathering." [121] Raymond Adams contends that, "while the two were alive, John had eclipsed Henry. He was sociable, personable, popular. And young neighbors and their elders who had known John could not forget him in favor of Henry. Henry's later development did not impress them because John's earlier promise had impressed them so much." When John and Henry taught together, it was John who was generally thought to be the superior teacher. It can be argued that Henry, usually unable to express hostility toward his brother, instead became more resentful of the community which saw him as the "inferior" of the two brothers.

Erikson speaks of the school age child as needing to develop a sense of "industry," productiveness and mastery. The danger is that if one does not gradually gain competence, mastery, and social recognition, one may develop a sense of "inferiority." [122] That John was recognized by most Concordians as the more promising and popular of the two brothers suggests strongly that in some ways Henry did feel inferior to his brother. This inferiority might have become more intense and generalized as he grew older, and in such a situation, it is to be expected that Henry would be ambivalent toward his brother. He certainly loved John deeply, but he also could have felt threatened by him, felt hostile toward him. How could he live up to his brother's example? He did not have the charm, the extrovertedness, the social mastery of John; he could never be as popular as his brother. Therefore, though John did serve as a positive identity model for Henry, the younger brother may have come to feel, consciously and unconsciously, that he would have to develop other competencies to gain affection and acceptance. From Phoebe Wheeler's private infants' school [123] to the public grammar school (where "Thoreau was by no means a poor scholar" but where "many of his classmates considered him 'stupid' and 'unsympathetic' because he would not join their games" [124]) to Concord Academy, he developed intellectual and scholarly skills—though tempered by a certain "unambitiousness." If John was an extrovert, Henry would find things to do on his own. While John was no doubt cavorting with his classmates, Henry tried to develop his skills as a solitary woodsman and hunter. [125] He also became accomplished working with his hands and might have become a carpenter had he not showed more academic promise (in Latin, Greek, and math) than his brother. So it was that Henry was chosen to attend Harvard. While he might have felt inferior to his brother in terms of social popularity and recognition, he had at least won, through industry and innate talent, the recognition of his mother. Thus, while John was becoming a schoolteacher (and helping to support his brother's college education), Henry was going to the heady, prestigious Cambridge institution.[126]

It may be hypothesized that his "successes" over John evoked guilt feelings in Henry. John's frail health might well have heightened his feeling that he had somehow defeated his elder brother. Moreover, the very fact that he viewed his beloved brother and friend as a competitor, a rival (and a formidable one in many respects) probably caused Henry to experience deep guilt. Complicating and exacerbating the guilt was Henry's perception of John, Jr. as a father-figure; to feel hostile toward, compete with, and triumph over the brother was in some way to challenge the father. Undoubtedly Thoreau struggled to repress hostility toward his elder brother: when a person loves and worships a brother as Henry did John, it becomes too anxiety-provoking to face directly the negative feelings. But in the years following Thoreau's graduation from Harvard, events would occur that would bring these negative feelings painfully close to the surface—and thereby intensify his identity crisis.

Men are constantly dinging in my ears their fair theories and plausible solutions of the universe, but ever there is no help, and I return again to my shoreless, islandless ocean, and fathom unceasingly for a bottom that will hold an anchor, that it may not drag. — Thoreau, *Journal*, I

But whoso is heroic will always find crises to try his edge. Human virtue demands her champions and martyrs, and the trial of persecution always proceeds. — Emerson, "Heroism"

"A Parcel of Vain Strivings"

In early May of 1837, a week or two before Thoreau's graduation from Harvard, Mrs. Lucy Jackson Brown—Emerson's sister-in-law and a patron of Mrs. Thoreau's boardinghouse—was the recipient of a poem (wrapped around a bouquet of violets) written by Henry. The poem gave expression to a deep sense of identity confusion:

> I am a parcel of vain strivings tied
> By a chance bond together,
> Dangling this way and that, their links
> Were made so loose and wide,
> Methinks,
> For milder weather.[1]

Making use of the flower imagery which was then so prevalent,[2] Thoreau portrays himself as a "dangling man," loosely held together, a "bunch of violets without their roots," "a nosegay which Time clutched from out / Those fair Elysian fields." He suggests that no one truly understands his plight as he "blooms for a short hour unseen," that "the children will not know, / Till time has withered" his "tender buds," the "woe / With which they're rife." Having lived privately with these "woes" for so many years, "drinking my juices up," he feels—at the brink of graduation—the need to confide to a sympathetic older woman, other than his mother, that he has not achieved a sense of his own identity or "manhood." He is not ready to say with full certainty what his future "strivings" and ambitions will be, or the extent to which they will be "vain" or *in* vain. In the final two stanzas of the poem, Thoreau reveals that he is not without hope that the "milder weather" will come; his "stock," he says, will "by another year" bear "More fruits and fairer flowers." It is apparent that he has not lost the sense—nurtured in childhood—that he may some day bloom into "greatness"; the very fact that he writes a poem to express himself suggests that he sees himself as gifted and potentially creative.

The hopeful resolution is not altogether convincing, given the sense of personal disorganization and isolation dramatized in the earlier stanzas of the poem. Thoreau's growth as man or artist would by no means be completed "by another year"; the "graduate" was to go through an extended period of identity crisis. His identity was not entirely defined or fixed when he graduated; his personality was open to new influences, to events, and to change. Because he was still a "parcel of vain strivings" in 1837, he needed what Erikson calls a "psychosocial moratorium," a period "during which the young adult through free role experimentation may find a niche in some section of his society, a niche which is firmly defined and yet seems to be uniquely made for him." [3] A moratorium is a delay of adult commitments "granted to somebody who is not ready to meet an obligation or forced on somebody who should give himself time." In Thoreau's case, it would be necessary to insist upon, struggle for, such a period of delay (in effect, he had to create his own moratorium) because family and community were reluctant to grant him the time to find his "true" self. Thoreau's severe identity confusion, coupled with his family's and community's resistance to his search for unique selfhood, would make the period of delay, the prolonged adolescence much, much longer and more painful than he could have expected when he wrote "Sic Vita." As late as December 25, 1841, he would be saying, "I don't want to feel as if my life were a sojourn any longer. . . . It is time now that I begin to live." [4] As has been the case for many creative persons, the delay of adulthood would be "prolonged and intensified to a forceful and a fateful degree" for Thoreau; it would help to account for "very special human achievements and also for the very special weaknesses in such achievements." [5]

Although the undergraduate Thoreau had done well enough to gain some academic honors and prizes, he generally seemed intent on avoiding any remarkable successes in competition with his fellow students; as Erikson has observed, those persons beset by identity confusion often associate work with oedipal competitiveness and sibling rivalry and thus are subject to an increased sense of, and dislike of, competition.[6] An illness during the spring of 1836, which was probably an early bout with tuberculosis but which was not without the suggestion of a psychosomatic component related to a dislike of competitiveness and a fear of being *too* successful,[7] may have constituted one reason for the falling-off in his grades. However, a letter from President Josiah Quincy to Emerson[8] in June, 1837 states that Henry had "imbibed some notions concerning emulation and college rank, which had a natural tendency to diminish his zeal, if not his exertion. His instructors were impressed with the conviction that he was indifferent, even to a degree that was faulty." [9] A classmate, John Weiss, not only recalled Henry's "tranquil indifference to college honors" but his indifference to most of his fellow students; according to Weiss, he was "cold and unimpressible. The touch of his hand was moist and indifferent, as if he had taken up something when he saw your hand coming, and caught your grasp upon it. . . . He did not care for people; his classmates seemed very remote. This reverie hung always about him, and not so loosely as the odd garments which the pious household care furnished." [10] While Thoreau was not as unfriendly or indifferent as Weiss describes him,[11] it must be acknowledged that he was relatively uninvolved in college life and activities. He remained closely attached to Concord and went home as often as possible.[12]

In spite of his attachment to home and mother, his away-from-home experiences during the Harvard years had opened up to him a new world of possibilities. His exposure to great books, great writers, and Transcendentalism not only reinforced Henry's predisposition *not* to be successful in a commercial sense but also gave him intimations of other kinds of "greatness" he might attain. Thoreau's six-week stay in Canton, Massachusettes with Orestes Brownson in early 1836 (during which time he taught school and absorbed Brownson's brand of Transcendentalism) seems to have affected him profoundly. He would later write to Brownson that this period was "a new era in my life—the morning of a new *Lebenstag*." [13] It must have been a revelation to him to discover a "strong" male-figure (quite probably a father-figure) who rejected material success and who suggested alternative futures to those his parents had in mind for him. Emerson's *Nature* and "The American Scholar" (which Thoreau read soon after his graduation if he did not hear it at commencement) were highly influential statements of the richness of possibility for those of Thoreau's generation; they were calls to greatness and spiritual bravery. On the basis of Henry's essay on "The Literary Life," Sanborn argues that "up to this time [1835] no distinct tendency toward literature was noticeable in young Henry Thoreau."[14] It is not altogether clear when Thoreau actually began to consider writing as a possible vocation for himself; after all, as Marble notes, "At that time . . . an author or a naturalist had no sure entrance to public regard nor could he expect any adequate income."[15] Emerson himself was just beginning to make a career out of writing and lecturing. It seems likely that only after he came under the direct tutelage of Emerson in late 1837 and 1838 did it seem possible to Thoreau that he might be able to make writing (and lecturing) his *primary* profession, even if he had an earlier awareness of his literary potential. In any case, he had rejected a "blind and unmanly love of wealth" in his August 16, 1837 address on "The Commercial Spirit" and thus suggested that he was considering other alternatives. Given Thoreau's sense of his giftedness, specialness, and "chosen-ness," his sense of "might be," of "could be" must have been exceedingly strong.

Upon receiving his diploma, Henry had to "go out into the world." But for Thoreau this meant returning to Concord.[16] There was certainly a legitimate reason for coming back to Concord. Considering the depression economy in 1837, he had been fortunate enough to be offered the job of teacher in the Center School, and had quickly accepted. According to Marble, a college graduate in Thoreau's time "was expected to swell the ranks of clergy, physicians, lawyers, or, when other chances failed, to become a teacher."[17] In keeping with the family tradition[18] —therefore not surpassing the achievements of anyone else in the family—and following the example of his brother, Thoreau now became a teacher. That Henry did not aspire to one of the "higher" professions no doubt disappointed Mrs. Thoreau. But she had to agree that, given the economic situation, Henry had done well for himself, for the time being at least. Furthermore, she would have the luxury of having her prized son at home with her—even if she ambivalently wished that Henry was a Boston lawyer. To the Concord townspeople (whose opinions Mrs. Thoreau valued), Thoreau's acceptance of the teaching position must have seemed unimpeachably "well-adjusted."

But significantly, Thoreau almost immediately resigned from the seemingly enviable job he had so quickly accepted. There was little warning that he would resign. A letter dated September 7, 1837 from James Richardson, Jr. (who had been a classmate at Harvard) asks Henry to help find *him* a teaching post: "I hear that you are comfortably located, in your native town, as the guardian of its children.

...I heard from you, also, that Concord Academy, lately under the care of Mr. Phineas Allen of Northfield, is now vacant of a preceptor; should Mr. Hoar find it difficult to get a scholar—college-distinguished, perhaps he would take up with one, who, though in many respects a critical thinker, and a careful philosopher of language among other things, has never distinguished himself in his class as a regular attendant on college studies and rules. If so, could you do me the kindness to mention my name to him, as of one intending to make teaching his profession, at least for a part of his life." [19] How was Richardson to know that his "contact" Thoreau would be in no position to help arrange employment for other teachers? Channing relates the outward circumstances of Henry's September resignation:

> A fortnight sped glibly along, when a knowing deacon, one of the School Committee, walked in and told Mr. Thoreau that he must flog and use the ferule, or the school would spoil. So he did, —feruling six of his pupils after school, one of whom was the maidservant in his own house. But it did not suit well with his conscience, and he reported to the committee that he should no longer keep their school, if they interfered with his arrangements; and they could keep it. [20]

Thus did Thoreau, that very evening, throw the valued job back into the faces of his students (one of whom "all through life has cherished his grievance" against the punishment he received),[21] the townspeople, and his family. It seems to me that Thoreau must have in some way wanted to find a reason to resign at the first opportunity. Granted, the flogging issue was a very legitimate cause of contention, an early opportunity for sticking to principles. But Thoreau's behavior was *so* rash, so all-or-nothing, that one begins to wonder to what other issues Henry might have been responding.

It is not likely that Thoreau, upon returning to Concord after graduation, had intended to become a conventional success, or to embrace fully "adulthood" as defined by the community. With his sense of spiritual possibilities and his ambivalence about worldly success, Henry could only keep alive these possibilities by *not* succeeding in a conventional manner.[22] He was aware of the dangers of "success without identity" —that is, he feared he would be trapped by success and by social and family approval into an identity not of his own choosing or making. Having so readily accepted the offer to teach in the Center School, Thoreau realized with horror that he was becoming "fatally overcommitted to what he [was] not." [23] It was far preferable to remain uncommitted. Easy success could be a very tempting mistress; thus he had emphatically to resist the seduction.

Somewhat like Hamlet, returning from a cosmopolitan university to Elsinore, Thoreau returned from Harvard with the suspicion that there was "something rotten in Concord." [24] To a youth so recently inspired by a sense of what "might be," what "could be," and inwardly convinced of his potential for greatness, the scarcity of viable occupational and identity alternatives was undoubtedly distressing.[25] To be sure, Concord was offering more identity-choices than it had in the past, especially in terms of allegiance to secondary groups. But perhaps the most crucial identity-choice for a young man (and one of the few opportunities for a moratorium) was whether or not to *leave* Concord. For those idealistic young people like Thoreau who did not leave, the range of vocational (and other basic) identity-choices was severely limited. Staying in Concord, or returning to Concord after graduation from college, meant, for most, entering into a socially acceptable round of life. It meant becoming an "adult" member of the community; townspeople expected its young men to conform to their notions of what an "adult" should be. Concord had not institutionalized, or recognized the validity of, a prolonged adolescence, a moratorium— especially for one so fully trained for an adult role as Thoreau. Both community and family were pushing Thoreau to accept *their* version of adult identity. Resigning from the teaching post at the Center School was thus, in part, a declaration of moratorium, of Henry's determination not to be rushed.

It is apparent that Thoreau harbored hostility against authority, and particularly against the town authorities. While this response may have been partly conditioned by an unconscious fear and hatred of his father's "violence" (as rooted in the oedipal situation),[26] it was probably more strongly influenced by his sense (conscious as well as unconscious) that the father—and the town fathers—had "failed" —that they were weak, controlled, dependent, other-directed figures at the mercy of a "commercial spirit" antithetical to "free and manly lives" and at the mercy of women. These fathers had let him down by not providing him with heroic models for his own identity-definition. In his November 1837 "Indian" letter to John—one of the few positive male models he had—he portrays all men except himself (Tahatawan) as "squaws": "There is no seat for Tahatawan in the council-house." [27] In a lecture he would deliver before the Concord Lyceum the following April, he would characterize "society" (and undoubtedly his fellow townsmen) in exceedingly unflattering terms:

One goes to a cattle-show expecting to find men and women assembled, and behold only working oxen and neat cattle. He goes to a commencement thinking that there at least he may find the men of the country; but such, if there were any, are completely merged in the day, and have become so many walking commencements, so that he is fain to take himself out of sight and hearing of the orator, lest he lose his own identity in the nonentities around him.[28]

Now, upon his own commencement, these "nonentities" want him to submerge himself in the herd and "lose his own identity." He resents the fact that they refuse to grant him the moratorium he so desperately needs. To resign from the Center School was to avoid becoming one of these "working oxen."

But the act of resigning was also, I think, a manifestation of Henry's urgent desire for independence from the women (especially his mother) whom he *was* dependent upon and who threatened to control and dominate his life. In these respects, his mother was more to be feared and hated than his father, on both unconscious and conscious levels. In the "Indian" letter, Henry identifies women as the "enemy" —at least metaphorically:

Brother. I have been thinking how the Pale Faces have taken away our lands—and was a woman. You are fortunate to have pitched your wigwam nearer to the great salt lake, where the pale-Face can never plant corn.

Brother—I need not tell thee how we hunted on the lands of the Dundees—a great war-chief never forgets the bitter taunts of his enemies. Our young men called for strong water—they painted their faces and dug up the hatchet. But their enemies the Dundee were women—they hastened to cover their hatchets with wampum. Our braves are not many—our enemies took a few strings from the heap their fathers left them, and our hatchets were buried. —But not Tahatawan's—his heart is of rock when the Dundees sing—his hatchet cuts deep into the Dundee braves.[29]

Henry was rebelling against the town establishment (the town fathers and, indirectly, his own father), but he was also rebelling against his own dependence on mother and home, and against the emasculating ways in which his identity was being defined for him. After all, it was his mother who had decided that he would go to Harvard, follow in the footsteps of her father (not his), and raise the family's status. *Her* hatchet was "covered with wampum." Henry's success would be *her* success and would "justify" her; to Henry, failure might have seemed preferable to such success. Thoreau's rebelliousness was fed by his sense of how, on the one hand, he was being controlled and defined by the ambitions of his mother, and, on the other, of how he was unable to break away from her control and of how difficult it was for him to contemplate leaving Concord. Because he was so dependent upon her, he had to express his independence all the more dramatically. It is intriguing that Thoreau, upon hearing the request of the school committeeman, *did* ferrule his students—including, perhaps not so randomly, the Thoreau family's maid. Whom, other than those he was physically ferruling, did he really want to flog?

As if his resignation had not puzzled and disturbed his townsmen enough, it was soon thereafter that he began signing his name "Henry David Thoreau" rather than "David Henry." [30] Given his sense of the importance of language and naming, his name change must be considered a significant expression of his state of mind after resigning from the Center School. Though his family had, for the most part, called him "Henry David" since childhood, the fact that he would change his signature reveals how intensely the graduate felt the need to proclaim, at this juncture, that he was his own man—even though (and perhaps because) he was not convinced fully that he was. Many townspeople would never let Henry forget that his given name was "David Henry." Priscilla Rice Edes, on the front flyleaves of *Excursions*, refers to Thoreau as "David Henry" several times. She also has Mrs. Thoreau saying, "Yes, Mr. Emerson is a perfect counterpart of my David Henry" and "I told my David Henry that you would like to make him some unbleached cotton shirts." [31] If, as these quotes suggest, Mrs. Thoreau also preferred to call her son "David Henry" on occasion, there would be all the more reason for the son to insist that *he* was "Henry David." According to Mrs. Daniel Chester French, at least one Concord farmer said of Thoreau: "His name ain't no more Henry D. Thoreau than my name is Henry D. Thoreau. And everybody knows it, and he knows it. His name's Da-a-vid Henry and it ain't never been nothing but Da-a-vid Henry. And he knows that!" [32]

Harding suggests[33] that it was about this time that Cynthia told her son he could "buckle on [his] knapsack" and "go abroad to seek [his] fortune." When Henry began to cry, sister Helen comforted him by saying, "No Henry, you shall not go; you shall stay at home and live with us." [34] If Helen did indeed use "shall," one could say that Henry again was putting himself in a position to be "controlled."

He was being shamed and hurt by his mother—by the "bitter taunts" of the enemy—and had to turn to another woman for comfort. He was being made to feel by his mother that he had let her down, and that he should feel guilty. Certainly, his tearful outburst must have been humiliating for one who was so concerned with being "free and manly," a Stoic, a "Tahatawan." Here was a young man who could defy the town's, and his mother's, sense of propriety, but who shed tears at the prospects of venturing out on his own and leaving the "femininity" of his home. To make matters worse, his brother—to whom he was unfavorably compared by many townspeople—*was* teaching and had helped to put the "ungrateful" Henry through college.

Erikson observes that a creative man "must court sickness, failure, or insanity in order to test the alternative whether the established world will crush him, or whether he will disestablish a sector of this world's outworn fundaments and make a place for a new one." [35] This period would be a test of Thoreau's endurance and, to use his own word, "innocence"; he risked the possibility that he would not survive his moratorium, that he would "seek death or oblivion, or die in spirit." [36] Like an Indian running the gauntlet, Thoreau had to endure the censure of his community and the even more painful disapproval of his family. Moreover, his claims to autonomy were accompanied by a sense of shame and self-doubt, nurtured in childhood and intensified by his present situation. Helen Merrell Lynd has told us how disquieting and devastating, how all-encompassing, can be the experience of shame—characterized by feelings of failure, exposure, inferiority, anxiety, isolation, and censure from without and within.[37] To survive, Thoreau had to avoid being inundated by these feelings. Often there were times, however, when he felt the need to hide his face—even from himself. In the first entry in his journal (October 22, 1837), he says, "To be alone I find it necessary to escape the present, —I avoid myself. How could I be alone in the Roman emperor's chamber of mirrors?" [38]

Henry's fear of commitment to "success without identity" conflicted with his deeply implanted belief that he should be doing something constructive, that he was stagnating in indecisiveness. A letter of October 13, from Thoreau to his college roommate Henry Vose (then teaching school in upstate New York), is a mixture of envy for his friend's situation, irony, bitterness, and self-deprecation: "You don't know how much I envy you your comfortable settlement—almost sine-cure—in the region of Butternuts. How art thou pleased with the lay of the land and the look of the people? Do the rills tinkle and fume, and bubble and purl, and trickle and meander as thou expectedest, or are the natives less absorbed in the pursuit of gain than the good clever homespun and respectable people of New England?" Henry belittles teaching, but at the same time asks for Vose's help in finding him a job—probably the same sort of job he had rejected in Concord:

> I presume that by this time you have commenced pedagoguersing in good earnest. Methinks I see thee, perched on learning's little stool ... while round thee are ranged some half-dozen small specimens for humanity, thirsting for an idea.... The fact is, here I have been vegetating for the last three months. "The clock sends to bed at ten, and calls me again at eight." Indeed, I deem "conformity one of the best arts of life." Now should you hear of any situation in your neighborhood, or indeed any other, which you think would suit me, such as your own, for instance, you will much oblige me by dropping a line on the subject....[39]

Vose, in reply, sends "condolences" to Henry on his having "nothing to do" and tries to reassure his friend that he will be able to "find an ample fund of enjoyment in Concord, while waiting for a situation." He rightly concludes that Henry wrote to him "in a fit of ennui or the blues." [40] But it can be suggested that, during this period of "dangling," Henry was given to *frequent* fits of ennui and the blues.

Characteristically, Thoreau tried to keep a stiff upper lip in his relations with others—even if, in private, his lips occasionally trembled. Mustering his courage, he would say to himself that "All fear of the world or consequences is swallowed up in a manly anxiety to do Truth justice" (*J*, I: 28). Apparently at least some members of his family felt that his actions had to be defended in the face of community criticism. However, as he indicated in an October 27 letter to Helen who was then teaching in Taunton, he did not want to be apologized for:

> For a man to act himself, he must be perfectly free; otherwise, he is. in danger of losing all sense of responsibility or of self-respect. Now when such a state of things exists, that the sacred opinions one advances in argument are apologized for by his friends, before his face, lest his hearers receive a wrong impression of the man, —when such gross injustice is of frequent occurrence, where shall one look & not look in vain, for men, deeds, thoughts?

As well apologize for the grape that is sour, —or, the thunder, that it is noisy, or the lightning that it tarries not.[41]

Yet the same day that he writes this strong-willed letter, he sets down in his journal his sense of depression, of not being able to see his way clear: "So when thick vapors cloud the soul, it strives in vain to escape from its humble working-day valley, and pierce the dense fog which shuts out from view the blue peaks in its horizon, but must be content to scan its near and homely hills" (*J*, I: 6). In keeping with the imagery of fog, clouds, and vapors, Henry asks himself on November 18, "When a shadow flits across the landscape of the soul, where is the substance? Has it always its origin in sin? and is that sin in me?" (*J*, I: 12).

Even at this early stage of his development, Thoreau perceived nature as an escape from, or an alternative to, a community and family which disapproved of him, shamed him, did not understand him. Of the "taunts" of which he has been the target (and perhaps most particularly the taunts of his "queen-like" mother), he says to himself on November 13, "This shall be the test of my innocence—if I can hear a taunt, and look out on this friendly moon, pacing the heaven in queen-like majesty, with the accustomed yearning" (*J*, I: 9).[42] On November 21, he explains how he can gain perspective on his situation; if the soul is sometimes "fogged in," one "must needs climb a hill to know what a world he inhabits. In the midst of this Indian summer I am perched on the topmost rock of Nawshawtuct, a velvet wind blowing from the southwest. . . . Not a cloud is to be seen, but villages, villas, forests, mountains, one above the other, till they are swallowed up in the heavens" (*J*, I: 12–13). Henry quotes Goethe's description of a peaceful evening: " 'then feels one once more at home in the world, and not as an alien, —an exile. I am contented as though I had been born and brought up here, and now returned from a Greenland or whaling voyage' " (*J*, I: 9–10). Nature could provide a home for Thoreau when he felt alienated from his own home and community. Two days after the Goethe entry, he could say as he looked at the sunrise, "I am at home in the world" (*J*, I: 11).

During this phase of his moratorium, Thoreau's psyche hovered between a sense that if he was patient, he would find his way, and a feeling of impatience; he saw his prolonged adolescence as both a blessing and a curse.[43] On November 12, he says, "I yet lack discernment to distinguish the whole lesson of today; but it is not lost, —it will come to me at last. My desire is to know *what* I have lived, that I may know *how* to live henceforth" (*J*, I: 9). He could remark on December 16, "How indispensable to a correct study of Nature is a perception of her true meaning. The fact will one day flower into a truth. The season will mature and fructify what the understanding had cultivated" (*J*, I: 18). Just so, Thoreau could tell himself, the jumbled facts of his life would "one day" bloom into truths; his own "virgin mould" (*J*, I: 3) would before long yield mature fruit. When he speaks of the spring and of man, we know he is contemplating the eventual arrival of his own personal "spring":

> March fans it, April christens it, and May puts on its jacket and trousers. It never grows up, but Alexandrian-like 'drags its slow length along,' ever springing, bud following close upon leaf, and when winter comes it is not annihilated, but creeps on molelike under the snow, showing its face nevertheless occasionally by fuming springs and watercourses.
>
> So let it be with man, —let his own manhood be a more advanced and still advancing youth, bud following hard upon leaf. (*J*, I: 30–31)

During his "winter of discontent," Thoreau needed to believe that the seeds were germinating.

However, in a December 30 letter to Orestes Brownson, in which he talks of his days in Canton as "a dream that is dreamt" and asks Brownson if he knows of any job opportunities, Thoreau confesses that "the toothache occurs often enough to remind me that I must be out patching the roof occasionally, and not be always keeping up a blaze upon the hearth within, with my German and metaphysical cat-sticks." He could not be satisfied that the "hearth within" was warm; he felt under urgent pressure to earn a living: "say what you will, this frostbitten 'forked carrot' of a body must be clothed and fed after all."[44] The "influences" which had inspired him and which had led him into such a problematic life-situation might, he felt, let him down, leaving him confused and directionless: "It is hard to subject ourselves to an influence. It must steal upon us when we expect it not, and its work be all done ere we are aware of it. If we make advances, it is shy; if, when we feel its presence, we presume to pry into its free masonry, it vanishes and leaves us alone in our folly, —brimful but stagnant, —a full channel, it may be, but no inclination" (*J*, I: 28). By March 5, 1838, he is still not sure of his path—or whether there is *any* path which will bring him self-content. Of his writing he asks, "But what does all this scribbling amount to?" More generally, Thoreau poses one of the central questions of his life:

What may a man do and not be ashamed of it? He may not do nothing surely, for straightway he is dubbed Dolittle—aye! christens himself first—and reasonably, for he was the first to duck. But let him do something, or not rather something undone; or, if done, is it not badly done, or at most well done comparatively?

Such is man,—toiling, heaving, struggling ant-like to shoulder some stray unappropriated crumb and deposit it in his granary....
And is he doomed ever to run the same course? Can he not, wriggling, screwing, self-exhorting, self-constraining, wriggle or screw out something that shall live,—respected, intact, intelligible, not to be sneezed at? (*J*, I: 34)

That Thoreau was working reluctantly in his father's pencil factory at the time may help to explain the intensity of his questioning. If he did not work for his father, he was a "Dolittle" to others; if he *did* work for him, he was, in his own eyes, still a "Dolittle," an Apollo serving a King Admetus. It was probably during this period that Henry discovered how to make a better pencil; as previously suggested, this surpassing of the father in his own business might have sparked guilt feelings. Indeed, the very fact that Henry's father had been able to get him to work in the pencil factory may have led Henry to feel conscious and unconscious hostility toward him. To feel hostility toward a loved parent, to harbor the secret wish to dethrone the king, could lead the son to feel anxiety, fear, and guilt. With the emotionally uncomfortable, "incessant tinkering named 'hum of industry' " in his ears, could a "man do less than get up and shake himself?" (*J*, I: 35). Yet when the man *has* shaken himself, what could he *do* in such an awakened state? Even his writing could sometimes appear to Henry as "scribbling"—"stale, flat, and unprofitable" (*J*, I: 34).

Distressed by his situation, Thoreau had to do *something*. So it is not altogether surprising that, on March 17, 1838, he wrote a letter to his brother John (then teaching at Taunton) and suggested that they both "buckle up their knapsacks" and head for the west in search of teaching positions:

Suppose by the time you are released, we should start in company for the West and there either establish a school jointly, or procure ourselves separate situations. Suppose moreover you should get ready to start previous to leaving Taunton, to save time. Go *I* must at all events. Dr. Jarvis enumerated nearly a dozen schools which I could have—all such as would suit you equally well. I wish you would write soon about this. It is high season to start. The canals are now open, and travelling comparatively cheap. I think I can borrow the cash in this town. There's nothing like trying.[45]

In his earlier letters to John, he had indicated how much he missed him. John was one of the few men who was not a "squaw." Both brothers were interested in Indian lore; indeed, at the beginning of the March 17 letter, Thoreau acknowledged the receipt of a box of Indian relics John had sent from Taunton. With John at his side, Henry could feel himself a "brave," not dependent upon or controlled by his mother and sisters, not in bondage to a father who was himself emasculated. John, Jr. had "buckled on his knapsack" and established himself in a place elsewhere than Concord. He, at least, had escaped "domination." When Henry finally resolved, with much ambivalence, to buckle on *his* knapsack, it could only be if his elder brother accompanied him. As an important masculine model and even father-figure, John was in some way needed by Henry to approve his decision to leave Concord, home, and mother; he would give legitimacy and strength to his thrust for independence. Prudence Ward, then boarding at Mrs. Thoreau's, reported in a letter to her sister, Mrs. Edmund Sewall of Scituate, that John had accepted his brother's proposal: "Mrs. John Thoreau's children are soon to leave her; Helen and Sophia to keep school in Roxbury, and John and Henry to go West. They purpose instructing there, but have no fixed plan." [46] A week before, an apparently eager and hopeful Henry had identified implicitly with a persistent Indian: "The Indian must have possessed no small share of vital energy to have rubbed industriously stone upon stone for long months till at length he had rubbed out an axe or pestle, —as though he had said in the face of the constant flux of things, I will at length lead an enduring life" (*J*, I: 40). Probably in response to the prospects of his journey west with John, Henry writes a poem on "Friendship" for his journal of April 8: "Two sturdy oaks, I mean, which side by side / Withstand the winter's storm, / And spite of wind and tide, / Grow up the meadow's pride, / For both are strong" (*J*, I: 42). The previously referred to lecture on "Society" that Henry entered in his journal on March 14 and delivered April 11 at the Lyceum—in which he characterizes people as "working oxen" and "neat cattle" —may well have represented a sort of contemptuous and triumphant farewell gesture to Concord; it was his own personal declaration of independence from the community.

It is quite possible that, in spite of the preparations for the trip west, Thoreau was searching for some reason or excuse not to leave Concord.[47] A letter from Josiah Quincy provided Henry with a fine justification for not leaving immediately. Prudence Ward writes, "Today, April 13, Henry has had a letter from President Quincy, of Harvard, speaking of a school in Alexandria, Virginia, to be opened the 5th of May. He is willing to take it, and if accepted, this may alter or delay their journey." [48] Quincy wrote Thoreau that "the requisitions are, qualification and *a person who has had experience in school keeping.* Salary $600 a year, besides washing and Board; duties to be entered on ye 5th or 6th of May. If you choose to apply, I will write as soon as I am informed of it. State to me your experience in school keeping." [49] Thoreau *did* decide to apply for the job in Alexandria—which certainly did "alter or delay" the western journey of the brothers. Within the month, Henry had been rejected for the Virginia job, and John had procured a teaching position in Roxbury. By early May, the western enterprise had been abandoned, as evidenced in a Prudence Ward letter: "Henry has left us this morning, to try and obtain a school at the eastward (in Maine). John has taken one in West Roxbury. Helen is in another part of Roxbury, establishing herself in a boarding and day-school. Sophia will probably be wanted there as an assistant; so the family are disposed of." [50] But the family was not "disposed of" entirely: in the middle of May, Henry returned from Maine without a job. Upon returning he learned that Vose was resigning his position in New York. His application for that job, and another mentioned by David Greene Haskins, were both rejected. So it was that Henry, who spoke as if he were the most independent and adventurous of John Thoreau's children, remained in Concord, living in his father's—and even more emphatically his mother's—home.

The sequence of events reveals the ambivalence with which Henry contemplated leaving Concord. To be sure, if Quincy had not informed him about the Alexandria job, the Thoreau brothers may have headed west; John's influence on Henry, the strength he gave him, would probably have helped Henry overcome his ambivalence. But why did Henry decide to postpone the trip west? Was there still some deep, unavoidable reluctance on his part to leave Concord? After all, Quincy had emphasized in his letter that the school sought *"a person who has had experience in school keeping"*; Henry's experience amounted to six weeks in Canton and an abortive fortnight in Concord. It does not seem likely that with his limited experience (including a resignation) he would have had a particularly hopeful prospect of obtaining the Virginia position. Especially in view of the fact that Edward Jarvis—a Concord physician who had settled in Louisville[51] —had, in spite of the depression, "enumerated nearly a dozen schools which I could have," was it really worthwhile to apply to Alexandria and postpone the western trip? Thoreau may well have been upset by the offer from Quincy, just when he was on the verge of leaving.[52] He may also have feared that his decision to postpone the trip would alienate his brother. Two days after receiving Quincy's letter, a disturbed Thoreau wrote on April 15: "though we may audibly converse together, yet is there so vast a gulf of hollowness between that we are actually many days' journey from a veritable communication" (*J*, I: 43).

John had given up his Taunton post; perhaps he would have had no problems regaining his position. But if this was not the case, then Henry may have felt remorseful about encouraging John to leave Taunton while he applied for the Virginia job. When John secured the position in Roxbury, Henry probably felt relieved. "The Bluebirds," a poem entered into the *Journal* on April 26, may reflect that sense of relief. John was an ornithology buff and had put up a bluebird box on Emerson's barn; in the March 17 letter to his brother, in which he proposed the trip west, Henry had said, "The bluebirds made their appearance the 14th day of March—robins and pigeons have also been seen. Mr. E[merson] has put up the bluebird box in due form." [53] So the return of the bluebird in the final stanza of the poem may be an indication of Henry's happiness that he had not alienated John: "The bluebird had come from the distant South / To his box in the poplar tree, / And he opened wide his slender mouth / On purpose to sing to me" (*J*, I: 46).

It can be argued, on the basis of the evidence we have, that Thoreau, in all his job hunting (including his tour of central Maine), either intentionally or unintentionally invited failure. It is likely that even during this time of depression, Thoreau *could* have obtained a job someplace else if he really wanted it. Jarvis had told him of a number of excellent possibilities. The fact remains that Henry did not go west, even though he *knew* there were opportunities there. Without his brother's support and companionship, he definitely could not go. "Go *I* must," he had said in his March 17 letter to John, but he had not gone. Unable to leave Concord, dependent on home and mother but desperately seeking independence, Thoreau would have to find other modes of going, of travelling. A year had passed since he had given Mrs. Brown "A Parcel of Vain Strivings," but Henry was still waiting—with an increasing sense of urgency—for "milder weather," for his "stock" to bear "more fruits and fairer flowers."

There were, however, other reasons why Thoreau was reluctant to desert the Concord area: Ralph Waldo Emerson, Transcendentalism, and writing. Without taking into account these reasons, Thoreau's behavior in 1837–38—and his development as artist and person—could not fully be explained. Therefore, the next two sections will focus on these crucial influences.

In Search of a "Great Man"

The search after the great man is the dream of youth and the most serious occupation of manhood. — Ralph Waldo Emerson, Chapter One, *Representative Men*

A great person, though unconsciously, will constantly give you great opportunity to serve him, but a mean one will quite preclude all active benevolence. — Thoreau, *Journal*, I

During the period of job-hunting and working in the pencil factory—a period characterized by repudiation of "success without identity" and by "social and sexual starvation," Thoreau desperately sought to keep alive the flowers of his "garden"; he was a "nosegay which Time clutched from out / Those fair Elysian fields, / With weeds and broken stems, in haste." Erikson—also using floral imagery—describes this critical period in the lives of gifted men:

Potentially creative men ... build the personal fundament of their work during a self-decreed moratorium, during which they often starve themselves, socially, erotically, and, last but not least, nutritionally, in order to let the grosser weeds die out, and make way for the growth of their inner garden. Often, when the weeds are dead, so is the garden. At the decisive moment, however, some make contact with a nutrient specific for their gifts.[54]

Thoreau's gift was the ability to write, and he seemed to know it, perhaps (as Sanborn suggests) as early as 1835 when he was writing college essays. But what or who would be the "nutrient" specific to his gifts at the "decisive moment"? Who would help to nourish and cultivate the "inner garden," give direction to the "strivings," when he most needed it? In "Sic Vita," Thoreau recognizes the need:

> But now I see I was not plucked for naught,
>   And after in life's vase
>   Of glass set while I might survive,
>   But by a kind hand brought
>   Alive
>   To a strange place.

The "kind hand" who would transplant—indeed, transform—Thoreau turned out to be his fellow Concordian, popular lecturer, and Transcendental essayist, Ralph Waldo Emerson. By supplying the "nutrient," he became the cultivator of Henry's "inner garden." Had Emerson not come along at the "decisive moment," there is no telling how Thoreau might have developed, how he would have dealt with his identity confusion; quite possibly, the garden would have died with the weeds. In a journal entry of February 7, 1838, Thoreau (identifying with Zeno, the Stoic) may well have been describing the impact of Emerson (Xenophon) on his life, just when he needed to be saved from "success" and the shaming taunts of his townsmen and family:

> Zeno, the Stoic, stood in precisely the same relation to the world that I do now. He is, forsooth, bred a merchant—as how many still! —and can trade and barter, and perchance higgle, and moreover he can be shipwrecked and cast ashore at the Piraeus, like one of your Johns or Thomases.
>
> He strolls into a shop and is charmed by a book by Xenophon—and straightway he becomes a philosopher. The sun of a new life's day rises to him. . . . And still the fleshy Zeno sails on, shipwrecked, buffeted, tempest-tossed; but the true Zeno sails ever a placid sea." (J, I: 26–27)

While Thoreau, if not "bred a merchant" at least bred to adjust to the "commercial spirit," needed to repudiate "fleshly" success—and was therefore "shipwrecked, buffeted, tempest-tossed" in the human community—he also needed to feel that he was being true to something and someone, to a "philosophy" and a "philosopher." To use Erikson's words, Thoreau sought urgently an "ideology" to which he could be faithful and a "leader," a "great man" to whom he could be devoted.[55]

As circumstance would have it, Thoreau did not have to travel far in his search for a "great man"; he found him living in Concord. Undoubtedly, this proximity to a man of Emerson's stature must have excited—even awed—Thoreau. Perhaps it contributed to his sense that he was "chosen," that somehow "superior powers" had meant him to meet Emerson at this time. When their paths crossed, Emerson was already a prominent man of letters whose influence and notoriety were still on the rise.

He had moved to Concord with his new wife in 1835 after having resigned from his Unitarian pastorate in 1832 and after returning from a European journey during which he had met such literary figures as Carlyle, Coleridge, and Wordsworth. Firmly entrenched in Concord, in 1836 he published *Nature*, which was to become the Transcendental manifesto, and helped to organize the "Transcendental Club." Thus Thoreau's village became the "capital" of Transcendentalism and Emerson its foremost interpreter to the world. Such people as Margaret Fuller and Bronson Alcott befriended Emerson, and would-be Transcendentalists and intellectuals made pilgrimages to his abode.

In 1837, he delivered his stirring "American Scholar" address at Harvard. Yet Emerson was not content, at this stage of his career, to play it safe, to join the Harvard "establishment." Rather, he delivered a soul-searching and scathing address at the Harvard Divinity School, which caused an uproar. Such conservatives as Andrews Norton accused him of preaching and practicing "the latest form of infidelity"; others viewed Emerson as a hero, as a courageous radical, for articulating his dissatisfactions with formal religion and offering a fresh vision of the world as "mirror of the soul." In 1837 and 1838, then, Emerson was an influential and controversial figure. He was not only in a position to challenge the "establishment" but also to help young men of talent, moral earnestness, and energy gain some foothold in the literary and intellectual world.

It has not been determined precisely when Emerson and Thoreau met, but in the fall and winter of 1837–38, the two began to develop a close friendship.[56] Keeping in mind Thoreau's sense that his own father and the town authorities could not provide him with models for living, it is all the more plausible to say that Emerson, fourteen years his elder, became a "father-substitute." Previously, only his brother (and, perhaps, to a lesser extent Orestes Brownson) could play *that* role for Henry. Thus, somewhat like John, Jr., Emerson was Henry's father "turned inside out." In psychological terms, it can be claimed that Emerson became, through transference,[57] a father-figure for Thoreau.[58] That Emerson came, in part, to "stand for" his father would have crucial psychic consequences for Thoreau. Their relationship would not only be that of an older and younger man; it would take on the dense and dark undertones and tensions of a father-son bond. By the spring of 1841—with his elder brother ailing—Henry would seek psychological safety in Emerson's home (thereby escaping his own home), and even earlier he had found some measure of security in Waldo's influence. Yet that safety and security would be tenuous indeed; in so far as Emerson did become an ersatz father, Thoreau was confronted with many of the same problems he had with his own father. When Emerson "let him down" it was as if he were being let down by his father all over again; the resentment Henry felt was all the more intense because it was not directed at Emerson alone. Moving into Waldo's house, he would find *this* father, like his own, too often "psychologically absent"—either away on lecture trips or abdicating child-rearing and handyman roles. In this situation, the "mother" was "available," and Thoreau developed a relationship with Lidian Emerson which had romantic and oedipal overtones;[59] he became a rival of Waldo's for her affections. Moreover, Henry would eventually be put in the position of being Waldo's literary rival. Once again, he would find himself challenging, and trying to surpass, a father-figure.[60] Not only did his relationship with Emerson provoke conscious animosity (on both men's parts), but it stirred up coals of "infantile and juvenile wishes and fears, hopes and apprehensions."

It should not be overlooked that Emerson himself may have had deep psychological reasons for needing Henry at this time in his life. He had experienced great personal losses in the years preceding his friendship with Thoreau. He had, of course, lost his beloved first wife, Ellen Tucker, in February 1831; he never fully recovered from the untimely death of the woman he loved—the relationship with Lidian could never recapture the passion and tenderness of his one authentic romance. Moreover, four of Emerson's brothers had met with tragedy: Robert Bulkeley Emerson "was destined to live past middle age without developing mentally beyond the ability to pen a few childish, ink-blotted lines";[61] John Clarke (born in 1799) died of consumption while still a child; Edward Bliss (born in 1805), the "much admired lawyer and scholar who had from youth the leader's look,"[62] was stricken by consumption and died on October 1, 1834; Charles Chauncy (born in 1808), a young man of "immense promise"[63] and on the verge of marriage, died on May 9, 1835 of the "same lung disease that had taken his other brothers." Ralph Waldo was left desolate by these losses. Born in 1803, he had been the elder brother of Edward and Charles; now, only his own elder brother, William, had survived. After Charles' death, Emerson had asked, "When one has never had but little society—and *all that society* is taken away—what is there worth living for?" [64]

The "doctrine of compensation" developed partly out of a desperate need to compensate for these losses, to assuage grief and give meaning to life. Furthermore, Emerson's outliving of his brothers and his marriage to Lidian in the same year (1835) that Charles had died, may well have provoked guilt feelings. [65] In March of 1838, when Emerson and Thoreau were becoming close, and soon after his first mention of Henry in his journal, Emerson expressed his deep sense of guilt and regret:

Strange is it that I can go back to no part of youth[,] no past relation without shrinking & shrinking. Not Ellen, not Edward, not Charles. Infinite compunctions embitter each of those dear names & all who surrounded them. . . . I console myself with the thought that if Ellen, if Edward, if Charles could have read my entire heart they should have seen nothing but rectitude of purpose & generosity conquering the superficial coldness & prudence. But I ask now why [could] was not I made like all those beatified mates of mine *superficially* generous & noble as well as *internally* so. They never needed to shrink at any remembrance; & I—at so many sad passages that look at me now as if I had been blind & mad. Well O God I will try & learn, from this sad memory to be brave & circumspect & true henceforth & weave now a web that will not shrink. [66]

In the spring of 1837, when Emerson was about to learn (or had recently learned) of Thoreau, he worked on a notebook which would contain Charles' letters, journals, and other writings, with the hope of publishing some of them; he also looked into his own journal for material to be used for writing a memoir. [67] In that notebook, Emerson says of his brother:

The death of such a young man may create no gap in the public councils, nor strike a single pang through the public breast, but it is still a public loss. The time of preparation was just completed, the time for usefulness had just commenced. A whole life of action was before him, and he was thoroughly furnished unto every good work. Like his bosom friend and class-mate, Jackson, he has fallen at the very gate of an honorable and eminent career, and a thousand hopes are buried in his grave. [68]

It is not too bold to suggest that Thoreau helped to fill the void in Emerson's life left by the death—or mental incapacitation—of his brothers, especially Charles. Just as in religion Emerson was looking to gain reconciliation with his brothers and even deny that they had actually died ("They will have Christ for a lord & not for a brother," he says in March of 1838),[69] so did he seek in everyday life to replace his lost brothers with other persons. With Henry Thoreau, Emerson could play an "elder brother" or "fatherly" role; he could try to assuage his grief and accompanying guilt by seeing to it that the promise of his "younger brother" or "son" would be fulfilled, that Henry would not "fall at the very gate of an honorable and eminent career." By in effect adopting Henry, Emerson could resurrect his hopes for his brothers and feel that he was somehow making up for his transgressions. With Henry he would be *superficially* generous as well as internally so. Rusk says that Charles had suspected Waldo of "caressing ideas and hoarding them because of their appeal to the aesthetic sense rather than valuing them as aids in shaping conduct." [70] By cultivating Thoreau's garden, Emerson could use his ideas to shape conduct, thus answering to Charles' criticism. That Thoreau eventually failed (in Emerson's eyes) to live up to the promise and achievement he had envisioned for his younger brothers may help to explain why Emerson was so impatient and even bitter about his protegé in later years. In his eulogy for Thoreau, Emerson would complain, "I cannot help counting it a fault in him that he had no ambition. Wanting this, instead of engineering for all America, he was the captain of a huckleberry-party." [71]

By 1838 Emerson had become a "sponsor" for Thoreau's identity.[72] Young Thoreau had literary gifts and the potential for realizing them. But he was also at loose ends—he needed guidance and support. Emerson perceived his potential and encouraged—indeed, urged—Henry to apply himself and develop his gifts. Henry had written numerous required essays while he was in college;[73] probably more importantly, he also had begun writing verse by the time he left Harvard. Apparently, Emerson had seen some of Thoreau's early poetry, including "Sic Vita." He may have written that he was a "parcel of vain strivings," but the very fact that he wrote so eloquently of his feelings undoubtedly suggested that he had gifts. Emerson may well have perceived his younger, late adolescent self in this talented, idealistic "parcel." Having seen promise in the poems, as well as evidence of a kindred spirit, it is likely that he asked Henry if he could see more of his writing. Emerson himself told Sanborn:

My first intimacy with Henry began after his graduation in 1837. Mrs. Brown, Mrs. Emerson's sister from Plymouth, then boarded with Mrs. Thoreau and her children in the Parkman house, where the Library stands now, and saw the young people every day. She would bring me verses of Henry's, —the "Sic Vita," for instance, which he had thrown into Mrs. Brown's window, tied round a bunch of violets gathered in his walks, —and once a passage out of his Journal, which he had read to Sophia, who spoke of it to Mrs. Brown as resembling a passage in one of my Concord lectures.[74]

Indeed, it is generally believed that it was Emerson who "put Henry to work" on the journal. The "he" of Thoreau's first entry on October 22, 1837 was probably Waldo: " 'What are you doing now?' he asked. 'Do you keep a journal?' So I make my first entry to-day" (*J*, I: 3). After Thoreau began writing in his journal, Emerson was probably allowed enough glimpses into it to sharpen his sense of the young man's potential as a writer. Emerson gave Thoreau access to his well-stocked library, introduced him to admirers and followers who frequented his Lexington Road house, strongly encouraged him to write, and helped him to get published.

It is not difficult to imagine the exhilaration Henry must have felt—being taken under the wing of a prominent man of letters who knew many other great writers and who might be able to help his own writing career. Thoreau seemed to see in Emerson someone after whom he could pattern himself. James Russell Lowell, as early as 1838, observed, "I met Thoreau last night, and it is exquisitely amusing to see how he imitates Emerson's tone and manner. With my eyes shut, I shouldn't know them apart." [75] Because of the severity of his identity confusion, it is all the more understandable why Henry so readily adopted the "tone and manner" of his identity sponsor. However as the years passed and as Emerson's image grew more tarnished in Thoreau's eyes, he became increasingly irked at being considered an imitator.

On his side, Emerson took joy in having a "disciple," someone who seemed to live as the Transcendentalists—and especially as he himself—preached.[76] While Thoreau was plagued with inner doubts and turmoil during this period, it must be stressed that, viewed from the *outside* at least, he could be singularly impressive. The image that he presented to *others*—and that he no doubt wished to believe was not only an image but the truth—was that of an independent, courageous, stoic, honest, principled, intense, and sensitive young man. These character traits had been salient since childhood; it will be remembered that Channing described the young Thoreau as "a thoughtful, serious boy, in advance of his years—wishing to have and do things his own way, and was fond of wood and field; honest, pure, and good. . . . Thus Samuel Hoar gave him the title of 'the judge' from his gravity." Henry carried these qualities into his young manhood.

Yet this "judge" was not without a sparkling contentiousness, a love of good arguments, and a memorable sense of humor—simultaneously homespun and learned, witty, punning, exaggerating, satiric, and paradoxical. Had he not possessed this sense of humor—which was apparently passed from "sharp-tongued" and witty Cynthia to her son, and was partly rooted in the tradition of Yankee humor, but further developed by readings in classical, English, and continental literature —it is unlikely that either Emerson, his contemporaries, or future readers would have found him appealing. What Thoreau said of Carlyle's humor in "Thomas Carlyle and his Works" is directly applicable to his own situation:

> Of this indispensible pledge of sanity [humor], without some leaven of which the abstruse thinker may justly be suspected of mysticism, fanaticism, or insanity, there is a superabundance in Carlyle. Especially the transcendental philosophy needs the leaven of humor to render it light and digestible. . . . His humor is always subordinate to a serious purpose, though often the real charm for the reader is not so much in the essential progress and final upshot of the chapter as in this indirect side-light illustration of every hue.[77]

Though Thoreau says that "we could sometimes dispense with the humor . . . if it were replaced by this author's gravity," [78] it is clear that humor, however serious in intent, was indispensable to Thoreau's charm as friend, speaker, and writer.

In earlier sections on Thoreau's childhood, there was occasion to refer not only to his problems and unresolved dilemmas rooted in his childhood but also to his strengths: a capacity for hope and the ability to give hope to others; a "defiant autonomy" and courage which helped to liberate others from social pressures and fears of nonconformity; a belief in his potential for non-materialistic greatness and success; a strong sense of principles; competence in working with his hands, in academic and intellectual activities, and in writing. In seeking to explain why Emerson was so taken by Thoreau, it needs to be emphasized once again that Henry had strengths—what Erikson calls "virtues," [79] the "rudiments" of which are "developed in childhood" —as well as weaknesses. Erikson identifies these virtues as "Hope, Will, Purpose, and Competence." To be sure, Thoreau's virtues were by no means unalloyed with mistrust, shame and doubt, guilt, and fears of inferiority; indeed, it has been argued that his "ego-strengths" were in part a response to, and compensation for, his weaknesses. Even his memorable brand of humor may be understood partially as a means of self-defense, of parrying off or disarming those who might attack him, of expressing hostility and aggression. Perhaps Emerson, who knew so much about "compensation" and who had himself struggled to assert his virtues in the face of inadequacies, could feel a closer bond with Thoreau precisely because he suspected that his young friend's strengths had not been come by easily. It might be said that Thoreau, to his great credit, had the strength to develop strengths in the face of powerful psychological and social obstacles. That his strengths were born partly out of struggle with weaknesses should increase, rather than diminish, our admiration for his accomplishments. In any case, the point to be stressed here is that, whatever the *sources* of Thoreau's virtues, they *were* virtues to those who encountered the young man and who, like Emerson, were predisposed to value his strengths.

Erikson regards "fidelity" as the prime virtue of adolescence.[80] In addition to his other virtues, Emerson found in Thoreau a young man who seemed prepared to be loyal to him—who had in fact been loyal to his ideas and values even before he met him. Thoreau showed promise of being faithful both to Emerson and to his mentor's delineation of the "American Scholar."

In the first mention of Thoreau in his journal on February 11, 1838, Emerson revels in his discovery of the "American Scholar" incarnate:

> I delight much in my young friend, who seems to have as free & erect a mind as any I have ever met. He told as we walked this afternoon a good story about a boy who went to school with him, Wentworth, who resisted the school mistress' command that the children should bow to Dr. Heywood & other gentlemen as they went by, and when Dr. Heywood stood waiting & cleared his throat with a Hem! Wentworth said, "You need not hem, Doctor, I shan't bow." [81]

The story Henry told Waldo is itself significant. Thoreau like Wentworth had resisted the commands of a woman (his mother), of school authorities, and of the town elders; in Emerson, Thoreau found some-

one who could at least partially understand why *he* "refused to bow."
On February 17, 1838, Emerson writes, "My good Henry Thoreau
made this else solitary afternoon sunny with his simplicity & clear
perception. How comic is simplicity in this doubledealing quacking
world. Every thing that boy says makes merry with society though
nothing can be graver than his meaning. I told him he should write
out the history of his College life as Carlyle has his tutoring." [82] By
putting Henry in company with Carlyle, Emerson no doubt encouraged his disciple to see himself as possessing the seeds of greatness.
Perhaps he mentioned to Thoreau what he observed in his journal of
March 6, 1838: "Montaigne is spiced throughout with rebellion as
much as Alcott or my young Henry T." [83] Certainly such comparisons
could not help but ignite Henry's long-smoldering sense of his own
possibilities—and make him feel that his rebelliousness was part of a
great tradition. On the other hand, Thoreau could help Emerson to
see the concreteness of nature and the humble beauties of Concord. On
April 26, Emerson reports,

> Yesterday P.M. I went to the Cliff with Henry Thoreau. Warm,
> pleasant, misty weather which the great mountain amphitheater
> seemed to drink in with gladness. A crow's voice filled all the
> miles of air with sound. A bird's voice[,] even a piping frog en-
> livens a solitude & makes world enough for us. At night, I went
> out into the dark & saw a glimmering star & heard a frog &
> Nature seemed to say Well do not these suffice? Here is a new
> scene[,] a new experience. Ponder it, Emerson, & not like the
> foolish world hanker after thunders & multitudes & vast land-
> scapes[,] the sea or Niagara.[84]

Thoreau became a member of the Transcendental Hedge Club
(often meeting at Emerson's home) in late 1837. There he came into
contact with such luminaries as Reverend Frederick Henry Hedge,
Reverend George Ripley, Reverend Orestes Brownson, Reverend Jones
Very, Margaret Fuller, Elizabeth Peabody, Bronson Alcott, Reverend
Theodore Parker, Christopher Pearce Cranch, and Reverend John
Sullivan Dwight.[85] Henry had thus found a group of people who
could, to a greater or lesser extent, give support to his unconventional
views. Breathing in the heady and electric atmosphere of the Hedge
Club, Henry was refreshed and inspired.

In college Thoreau had written some excellent essays, but his
first published work was an obituary of Anna Jones, whom he had

interviewed on her deathbed in the Concord poorhouse. The obituary appeared in the *Yeoman's Gazette* on November 25, 1837.[86] His journal was growing by the day and would become an important sourcebook for all his writing efforts. He began, with Emerson's prodding, to submit material to *The Dial*, though much of his early work, which consisted mostly of poetry, was turned down by an unappreciative and demanding editor, Margaret Fuller.[87] In the spring of 1838, he gave his first lecture (on "Society") at the Concord Lyceum and became secretary of the Lyceum later that same year—after he had established himself as a teacher at the Concord Academy and thereby temporarily mollified his townsmen's opinions of him. In 1841 Waldo would offer Thoreau room and board in his own home in exchange for the performance of "odd jobs."

It is clear that Emerson offered "my young Henry T." a way to gain the independence he so desperately needed. By submitting himself to Emerson's tutelage and patronage, Thoreau could, to an extent, escape his dependence on his own household and gain a "new" father who would approve of him, believe in him, and put him to (personally meaningful) work. Emerson—and the Transcendental "ideology"[88] —provided Thoreau with the prospect of a new and integrated identity, a romantic self-concept which would help to resolve his ambivalences. Undoubtedly, Henry's relationship with Emerson, as well as the development of his writing aspirations, also help to explain why Thoreau did not want to be far from Concord. If the development of a liberating identity was linked to Emerson and Transcendentalism, then leaving his "identity sponsor" and the mecca of Transcendentalism might lead to the dissolution of that much-needed "self" he was building. Without having decided decisively about a career, and without being settled in an identity-defining job, in late 1837 and early 1838 it became imperative for Thoreau to cling tenaciously to the concept of self he was developing as writer and Transcendentalist. He could begin seriously to identify with Goethe, Zeno, Carlyle, Montaigne, Byron; while working at the craft of writing, he could think of himself as a potentially "great man." While his dreams of glory would be preserved, they would not be his mother's dreams. Thoreau's emerging sense of himself as a writer and Transcendentalist became one source of his ambivalence toward finding a teaching job. If he found and accepted a position far from Concord, particularly a demanding position, he might be cutting himself off from Emerson and any chances he might have to realize his true gifts. He would be cut off from the romantic-Transcendentalist identity which was giving him sustenance, shielding him from conflicts and feelings of inferiority, bolstering his confidence.

In Search of an Ideology

> What is popularly called Transcendentalism among us, is Idealism; Idealism as it appears in 1842. As thinkers, mankind have ever divided into two sects, Materialists and Idealists; the first class founding on experience, the second on consciousness; the first class beginning to think from the data of the senses, the second class perceive that the senses are not final, and say, The senses give us representations of things, but what are the things themselves, they cannot tell. The materialist insists on facts, on history, on the force of circumstances and the animal wants of man; the idealist on the power of Thought and Will, on inspiration, on miracle, on individual culture. — Ralph Waldo Emerson, "The Transcendentalist"

If Emerson was the "great man" in whom the young graduate Thoreau could believe, in whose image he could model himself, Transcendentalism (as articulated by that great man) was the philosophy to which he could be faithful. Unquestionably, the young Thoreau, unsure of his personal identity or of his place in the social and historical scheme of things, was in search of an "ideology," as Erikson uses the term:

> ...an unconscious tendency underlying religious and scientific as well as political thought; the tendency at a given time to make facts amenable to ideas, and ideas to facts, in order to create a world image convincing enough to support the collective and the individual sense of identity. Far from being arbitrary or consciously manageable (although it is as exploitable as all of man's unconscious strivings), the total perspective created by ideological simplification reveals its strength by the dominance it exerts on the seeming logic of historical events, and by its influence on the identity-formation of individuals (and thus on their "ego-strength").[89]

Erikson further explains,

> At the most it is a militant system with uniformed members and uniform goals; at the very least it is a "way of life," or what the Germans call a *Weltanschauung*, a world-view which is consonant with existing theory, available knowledge, and common sense, and yet is significantly more: an utopian outlook, a cosmic mood,

or a doctrinal logic, all shared as self-evident beyond any need for demonstration. What is to be relinquished as "old" may be the individual's previous life; this usually means the perspectives intrinsic to the life-style of the parents, who are thus discarded contrary to all traditional safeguards of filial devotion.[90]

It is in the late teens and early twenties, when the need for making choices and developing new loyalties is perceived as critical, that a person is most likely to seek for and adopt some form of ideology.[91] It is not surprising that Thoreau in his early twenties chose to identify himself with the "Weltanschauung," the "utopian outlook," the "cosmic mood" of an ideology—especially one which was so compatible with his psychological needs and predispositions.

Without going into a detailed background of the Transcendental movement—territory that has been well-covered in other studies[92] —it may be said that New England Transcendentalism did indeed grow out of a generation's need to "choose new devotions and discard old ones." The young were disenchanted with the religion of their elders; fed by German and English romanticism, as well as Oriental mysticism, they reacted against the "sensationalism" of Locke, the "rationalization" of religion, the "corpse-cold" quality of Unitarianism in New England. To Boston Unitarians, "moralism," "common sense," and "good behavior" had become more important than piety, inner holiness, intuition, inner richness. The spiritual sterility of the elders had to be rejected even if this meant relinquishing "all traditional safeguards of filial devotion." In 1838 Emerson would risk, and incur, the wrath of those who had ordained him. In the "Divinity School Address," he found his "parents" woefully wanting—and dared to tell them so. Speaking of Barzillai Frost he observes, with all the cruelty of a disillusioned youth:

> I once heard a preacher who sorely tempted me to say I would go to church no more. Men go, thought I, when they are wont to go, else had no soul entered the temple in the afternoon. A snow-storm was falling around us. The snowstorm was real, the preacher merely spectral, and the eye felt the sad contrast in looking at him, and then out behind him into the beautiful meteor of snow. He had lived in vain. He had no one word intimating that he had laughed or wept, was married or in love, had been commended, or cheated, or chagrined. If he had ever lived and acted, we were none the wiser for it.[93]

The Transcendentalists' criticism was not, however, limited to matters of religion. If the ideology had emerged out of a sense of the church's (and church elders') spiritual deficiencies, it had also been nurtured and strongly reinforced by a sense of what New England and America were becoming. The Transcendentalists rebelled not only against Locke's philosophical materialism, but against America's burgeoning materialism, commercialization, urbanization, and conformity. At a time when America was on the verge of "taking off," of making enormous strides "forward," the Transcendentalists vehemently questioned the value of such "progress." If America's coming of age would mean the sacrifice of conscience, individualism, harmony with nature, human dignity, piety, purity, then the Transcendentalists preferred to remain adolescents, uncommitted to the "adult" that America was becoming. While many of their countrymen were extolling the benefits of progress, the Transcendentalists advocated an extension of the moratorium, a further postponement of America's adulthood.

What Erikson says about ideologies in general seems directly applicable to the Transcendentalists:

> Youth . . . is sensitive to any suggestion that it may be hopelessly determined by what went before in life histories or in history. Psychosocially speaking, this would mean that irreversible childhood identifications would deprive an individual of an identity of his own; historically, that invested powers should prevent a group from realizing its composite historical identity. For these reasons, youth often rejects parents and authorities and wishes to belittle them as inconsequential; it is in search of individuals and movements who claim, or seem to claim, that they can predict what is irreversible, thus getting ahead of the future—which means, reversing it. This in turn accounts for the acceptance by youth of mythologies and ideologies predicting the course of the universe or the historical trend; for even intelligent and practical youth can be glad to have the larger framework settled, so that it can devote itself to the details which it can manage, once it knows (or is convincingly told) what they stand for and where it stands. Thus, "true" ideologies are verified by history—for a time; for, if they can inspire youth, youth will make the predicted history come more than true.[94]

The Transcendentalists, living in a time of transition, were faced with accepting a world not of their own choosing. As Emerson observed in "Self-Reliance," "Our housekeeping is mendicant, our arts, our occupations, our marriages, our religions, we have not chosen, but society has chosen for us." [95] Confronted with the prospect of a "hopelessly determined" future, they needed to believe that the future of their *parents'* making could or would be reversed. In the 1830s and 1840s the new order had not yet become so consolidated as to appear irrevocably entrenched. "Trade was one instrument," said Emerson in "The Young American," "but Trade is also but for a time, and must give way to somewhat broader and better, whose signs are already dawning in the sky." [96] The tentativeness of the emerging social order gave hope that the Transcendental ideology would eventually be "verified by history." Emerson expresses that hope eloquently in "The Transcendentalist":

> Amidst the downward tendency and proneness of things, when every voice is raised for a new road or another statute or a subscription of stock; for an improvement in dress, or in dentistry; for a new house or a larger business; for a political party or the division of an estate; will you not tolerate one or two solitary voices in the land, speaking for thoughts and principles not marketable or perishable? Soon these improvements and mechanical inventions will be superseded; these modes of living lost out of memory; the cities rotted, ruined by war, by new inventions, by new seats of trade, or the geologic changes; all gone, like the shells which sprinkle the sea-beach with a white colony to-day, forever renewed to be forever destroyed. But the thoughts which these few hermits strove to proclaim by silence as well as by speech, not only by what they did, but by what they forbore to do, shall abide in beauty and strength, to reorganize themselves in nature, to invest themselves anew in other, perhaps higher endowed and happier mixed clay than ours, in fuller union with the surrounding system.[97]

Inspired by the Transcendentalist vision, Thoreau could believe himself one of those "few hermits" whose "thoughts and principles" would one day become the ordering principles of society.

While there undoubtedly were theological, sociological, and historical reasons for the development of Transcendentalism, one must also look to the "character" [98] (personality and life history) of particular individuals to determine why they were attracted to the movement. Certain people embraced the ideology, not only because they agreed with its *publicly* stated principles, but also because it answered to their *private* needs. They were psychologically predisposed to accept Transcendentalism; the ideology helped them to deal with emotional conflicts and to justify their life-situations. Such was the case with Henry Thoreau.

As has been suggested previously, the "graduate" (and probably undergraduate) feared that his life was being determined by forces outside of himself, particularly family and community. Henry had to struggle to break away from home, mother, and father. He was only too aware of his dependencies, and only a radical sort of independence could give him self-respect and "manliness." Transcendentalism provided him with an ideology that emphasized manliness and self-reliance. He could ask, along with Emerson, "In looking at the class of counsel, and power, and wealth, and at the matronage of the land, amidst all the prudence and triviality, one asks, Where are they who represented genius, virtue, the invisible and heavenly world, to these?" [99] Just as Thoreau personally feared emasculation, so did Transcendentalism recognize the threat. "Society everywhere," warned Emerson in "Self-Reliance," "is in conspiracy against the manhood of every one of its members." [100] At a time when he needed to believe that his life was *not* "hopelessly determined" by a dominating mother and a father who was eager for him to help out in the family business, he could turn to the credo of his ideology: "You think me a child of my circumstances. I make my circumstances." [101]

Thoreau's independence could not take the form of material success. The prospects of conventional success evoked deep guilt feelings and anxiety. Such success was a surpassing of the father and a "giving in" to the controlling mother—a "success without identity." To succeed in a worldly sense was to awaken unconscious oedipal wishes, guilt, and fear as well as to put the conscious Henry in a position to outdo his father in the real world. Transcendentalism, stressing idealism over materialism, helped to justify on the level of societal critique what Thoreau felt on a much more private level.[102] There were opportunities for initiative without guilt in the Transcendental ideology; one could be a "great man," a "hero," without being wealthy. While Transcendentalism in some respects constituted a direct challenge to authority, it also allowed such people as Thoreau to *deny* that they were challenging their personal fathers. To yield to Nature (and to God in Nature), to become a "transparent eyeball," was to disavow any desire to defeat the father. To avoid participation in politics (as many Transcendentalists did) was to avoid any direct confrontation with the fathers; rather than challenging and perhaps defeating the fathers (and, by

transference, the personal father) in the public sphere, Thoreau preferred to withdraw, to become one of those "few hermits."

In a general sense, it may be suggested that Transcendentalism
provided such men as Thoreau with a partial escape from—indeed,
a transcendence of—guilt feelings. A remarkable passage from Emerson's "The Transcendentalist" illuminates how such an escape is
possible:

> In action he easily incurs the charge of anti-nomianism by his
> avowal that he, who has the Law-giver, may with safety not only
> neglect, but even contravene every written commandment. In
> the play of Othello, the expiring Desdemona absolves her hus-
> band of the murder, to her attendant Emilia. Afterward, when
> Emilia charges him with the crime, Othello exclaims,
> "You heard her say herself it was not I."
> Emilia replies,
> "The more angel she, and thou the blacker devil."
> Of this fine incident, Jacobi, the Transcendental moralist, makes
> use, with other parallel instances, in his reply to Fichte. Jacobi,
> refusing all measure of right and wrong except the determinations
> of the private spirit, remarks that there is no crime but has some-
> times been a virtue. "I," he says, "am that atheist, that godless
> person who, in opposition to an imaginary doctrine of calcula-
> tion, would lie as the lying Desdemona lied; would lie and de-
> ceive, as Pylades when he personated Orestes; would assassinate
> like Timoleon; would perjure myself like Epaminondas and
> John de Witt; I would resolve on suicide like Cato; I would
> commit sacrilege with David; yea, and pluck ears of corn on the
> Sabbath, for no other reason than that I was fainting for lack of
> food. For I have assurance in myself that in pardoning these faults
> according to the letter, man exerts the sovereign right which the
> majesty of his being confers on him; he sets the seal of his divine
> nature to the grace he accords.[103]

To a person like Thoreau, burdened with a guilty sense that he had
contemplated or committed "crimes," the Transcendental message
brought welcome relief: his crimes were pardonable. By insisting on
the legitimacy and inviolacy of each man's consciousness, Transcendentalism offered Thoreau absolution from the strict and restrictive
demands of his superego. Conscience, as rooted in a family and socially
defined morality, was supplanted by consciousness.[104] "True" con-

science, as redefined by Transcendentalism, was rooted in the divine nature of each person, not in the culturally imposed morality. In his journal Thoreau expresses his desire, destined to be frustrated all too often, to transcend morality and breathe in the fresh and guilt-free upper atmosphere:

> I never met a man who cast a free and healthy glance over life, but the best live in a sort of sabbath light, a Jewish gloom. The best thought is not only *without sombreness,* but even without morality.... The moral aspect of nature is a jaundice reflected from men.... Occasionally we rise above the necessity of virtue into an unchangeable morning light, in which we have not to choose in a dilemma between right and wrong, but simply to live right on, and breathe the circumambient air. (*J,* I: 265)

In another entry he says, "What offends me most in my compositions is the moral element in them. The repentant say never a brave word. Their resolves should be mumbled in silence. Strictly speaking, morality is not healthy. Those undeserved joys which come uncalled and make us more pleased than grateful are they that sing" (*J,* I: 316).

Transcendentalism was particularly appealing to a youth like Thoreau who feared adult commitments, who needed a period of moratorium. Built into the ideology itself was the belief that it was *not* an ideology (in the social and political sense of the word). As Emerson said, "You will see by this sketch that there is no such thing as a Transcendental *party;* that there is no pure Transcendentalist; that we know of none but prophets and heralds of such a philosophy."[105] Thus, it was possible for Thoreau to claim that he was not committed to a "party"—even as he embraced its principles. He could conform to an ideology which glorified nonconformity. In "Self-Reliance," Emerson describes the "healthiness" of "neutrality," the sadness of adulthood:

> The nonchalance of boys who are sure of a dinner, and would disdain as much as a lord to do or say aught to conciliate one, is the healthy attitude of human nature. A boy is in the parlor what the pit is in the playhouse; independent, irresponsible, looking out from his corner on such people and facts as pass by, he tries and sentences them on their merits, in the swift, summary way of boys, as good, bad, interesting, silly, eloquent, troublesome. He cumbers himself never about consequences, about interests: he gives an independent, genuine verdict. You must court

him; he does not court you. But the man is, as it were, clapped into jail by his consciousness. As soon as he has once acted or spoken with eclat, he is a committed person, watched by the sympathy or the hatred of hundreds, whose affections must now enter into his account. There is no Lethe for this. Ah, that he could pass again into his neutrality! Who can thus avoid all pledges, and having observed, observe again from the same un-affected, unbiassed, unbribable, unaffrighted innocence, must always be formidable. He would utter opinions on all passing affairs, which being seen to be not private, but necessary, would sink like darts into the ear of men, and put them in fear.[106]

Rather than become a "committed" person, as described by Emerson, Thoreau preferred to remain in a state of "neutrality"—committed to non-commitment.

Transcendentalism offered young Thoreau a kind of monasticism and ascetic discipline,[107] a period of purification and self-examination that the bustling outer world would not provide. Emerson may well have been thinking of his disciple when he spoke of the "many intelli-gent and religious persons [who] withdraw themselves from the com-mon labors and competitions of the market and the caucus, and betake to. a certain solitary and critical way of living, from which no solid fruit has yet appeared to justify their separation." [108] Although Tho-reau was well aware that "no solid fruit" had yet appeared, he knew that Transcendentalism at least acknowledged that such fruits usually did not ripen overnight. His ideology did not insist that he must dumbly succumb to an unwelcomed and identity-threatening adult-hood. Although waiting was often painful, it was far preferable to surrendering one's dreams. As Emerson put it:

New, we confess, and by no means happy, is our condition: if· you want the aid of our labor, we ourselves stand in greater want of labor. We are miserable with inaction. We perish of rest and rust: but we do not like your work.

'Then,' says the world, 'show me your own.'

'We have none.'

'What will you do, then?' cries the world.

'We will wait.'

'How long?'

'Until the Universe beckons and calls us to work.'

'But whilst you wait, you grow old and useless.'

'Be it so: I can sit in a corner and *perish* (as you call it), but I will not move until I have the highest command. If no call should come for years, for centuries, then I know that the want of the Universe is the attestation of faith by my abstinence. Your virtuous projects, so called, do not cheer me. I know that which shall come will cheer me. If I cannot work, at least I need not lie. All that is clearly due today is not to lie. In other places other men have encountered sharp trials, and have behaved themselves well. The martyrs were sawn asunder, or hung alive on meat hooks. Cannot we screw our courage to patience and truth, and without complaint, or even with good-humor, await our turn of action in the Infinite Counsels?' [109]

Thoreau's patience had been, and would be, sorely tried. Not only did he face the "sharp trials" of community and family censure ("For non-conformity the world whips you with its displeasure," Emerson said in "Self-Reliance"),[110] but he also had to face the distressing possibility that his creative garden could die with the weeds. Thoreau would learn that devotion to Transcendentalism was no easy accomplishment; it would require all the courage he could summon.

A Traveller in Concord

Unable—and probably unwilling—to find a teaching job outside of the Concord area, Thoreau sought to resolve his identity dilemma by founding, in mid-June of 1838, a private school in the family home (the Parkman House on Main Street).[111] Such a situation allowed Henry to stay only too close to home and mother while earning money, teaching, writing, and associating with Emerson and the Transcendentalists. He could be dependent and independent at the same time; while not making any final break with his family, he could still believe that he was evolving an identity of his own. Moreover, Thoreau could have his own way in designing educational strategy and tactics—no longer was he directly accountable to, or associated with, the community. In a poem of July 16 he had the strength to say, "In the busy streets, domains of trade, / Man is a surly porter, or a vain and hectoring bully, / Who can claim no nearer kindredship with me / Than brotherhood by law" (*J*, I: 51). To his "brother by blood," Henry wrote on July 8, "I am in school from 8 to 12 in the morning, and from 2 to 4 in the afternoon; after that I read a little Greek or English, or for variety, take a stroll in the fields. We have not had such a year for berries this long time—the earth is actually blue with them." [112] Not only was the earth rich—his life, he felt at this point, was rife with possibilities. On the same day that he wrote to John, he entered into his journal a poem on "Cliffs" which emphasized his peacefulness, his sense of perspective: "When deeper thoughts upswell, the jarring discord / Of harsh speech is hushed, and senses seem / As little as may be to share the ecstasy" (*J*, I: 52). Thoreau began to see that he might be able to attain "greatness" without having to leave Concord, that he could be a "hero" while staying at home, that he could in part establish his identity by identifying with a region, that he might still bear "fruits and fairer flowers": [113]

> What a hero one can be without moving a finger! The world is not a field worthy of us, nor can we be satisfied with the plains of Troy. A glorious strife seems waging within us, yet so noiselessly that we but just catch the sound of the clarion ringing of victory, born to us on the breeze. There are in each the seeds of a heroic ardor, which need only to be stirred in with the soil where they lie, by an inspired voice or pen, to bear fruit of a divine flavor. (*J*, I: 52)

This would be the first of many justifications for being a "traveller in Concord." He would not leave Concord again for any extended period of time until 1843.

Thoreau, however, did not always feel that he was winning the "glorious strife" during the summer and autumn of 1838. If he could "just catch the sound of the clarion ringing of victory," he could also hear the drums of defeat. First of all, he *was* still living in the family home, where he had arranged for his students to board; he was constantly reminded of his indebtedness to, and dependence on, his mother. For one who wished to be heroic, such reminders must have been painful indeed. In the second place, his private school venture was anything but an economic success. Harding suggests that his "difficulties with the Concord school committee" probably made Thoreau's job of attracting students all the more problematical.[114] On July 15, Henry, perhaps reflecting on his neighbors' cool and distrustful response to the new school, sought to defend himself by viewing his situation in cosmic perspective: "What though friends misinterpret your conduct, if it is right in sight of God and Nature. The wrong, if there be any, pertains only to the wrongdoer, nor is the integrity of your relations to the universe affected, but you may gather encouragement from their mistrust. If the friend withhold his favor, yet does greater float gratuitous on the zephyr" (*J*, I: 52). If his friends mistrusted him (and if from his earliest years he carried with him a residue of distrust), it was necessary, for emotional survival, that he learn to trust himself: "Whatever of past or present wisdom has published itself to the world, is palpable falsehood till it come and utter itself by my side" (*J*, I: 52).

Erikson speaks of one characteristic of "young great rebels" which we may note in Thoreau at this time:

> ... their inner split between the temptation to surrender and the need to dominate. A great young rebel is torn between on the one hand tendencies to give in and phantasies of defeat ... and the absolute need, on the other hand, to take the lead, not only over himself but over all the forces and people who impinge on him. In men of ideas, the second, the dictatorial trend, may manifest itself paradoxically at first in a seeming surrender to passivity which, in the long run, proves to have been an active attempt at liquidating passivity by becoming fully acquainted with it. Even at the time of his near downfall, he struggles for a position in which he can regain a sense of initiative by finding some rock-bottom to stand on, after which he can proceed with a total re-evaluation of the premises on which his society is founded.[115]

Thoreau often seemed to surrender to passivity, yet characteristically, he could usually experiment with passivity only by yielding himself to nature or the cosmos. At this point in his life, he could not surrender his will to people precisely because he had already surrendered so much; he was threatened by the depth of his passivity, especially with relation to his mother. Only in his relation to Emerson and to his brother (as well as, to a lesser extent, his father and older women) could Thoreau at all comfortably envision passivity. Nature was a much less threatening "master" (or, perhaps more accurately, "mistress") than other people. Moreover, he could *learn* from yielding to nature. As Erikson says, "Paradoxically, many a young man . . . becomes a great man in his own sphere only by learning that deep passivity which permits him to let the data of his competency speak to him." [116] As he became more deeply involved in nature, he would indeed be in a position to "let the data of his competency speak to him." He would have to surrender to nature in order to glean truth and beauty from it.

If Thoreau "gave in" or fantasized defeat, it was easier to surrender to the natural defeat of death. On August 10, he says, "Every pulse-beat is in exact time with the cricket's chant, and the tickings of the death-watch on the wall. Alternate with these if you can" (*J*, I: 53). By giving in to nature, by "becoming fully acquainted" with *that* kind of passivity, he could eventually gain strength and integrity. The journal entry of August 13 reflects this willingness to surrender to nature:

> If with closed ears and eyes I consult consciousness for a moment, immediately are all walls and barriers dissipated, earth rolls from under me, and I float, by the impetus derived from the earth and the system, a subjective, heavily laden thought, in the midst of an unknown and infinite sea, or else heave and swell like a vast ocean of thought, without rock or headland, where are all riddles solved, all straight lines making there their two ends to meet, eternity and space gambolling familiarly through my depths. I am from the beginning, knowing no end, no aim. No sun illumines me, for I dissolve all lesser lights in my own intenser and steadier light. I am a restful kernel in the magazine of the universe. (*J*, I: 53–54)

Dissolving himself in nature, Thoreau could see himself as eventually becoming the active force which would "dissolve all lesser lights in my own intenser and steadier light." In "The Thaw" (January 11, 1839) Thoreau dreamily reflects on passivity: "Fain would I stretch me by the highway-sidê, / To thaw and trickle with the melting snow, / That, mingled soul and body with the tide, / I too may through the pores of nature flow" (*J*, I: 71). Only in relation to nature was the prospect of losing one's identity not deeply threatening: "Drifting in a sultry day on the sluggish waters of the pond, I almost cease to live and begin to be. A boatman stretched on the deck of his craft and dallying with the noon would be as apt an emblem of eternity for me as the serpent with his tail in his mouth. I am never so prone to lose my identity. I am dissolved in the haze" (*J*, I: 75). It might be hypothesized that one reason Thoreau was drawn to Oriental writers was their celebration of passivity in relation to the cosmos. When he was tempted to "lose his identity" or escape himself, he could turn to Oriental philosophy and feel the beauty of being "dissolved in the haze." But even while he was experimenting with passivity and loss of identity, he struggled for a position in which to regain "a sense of initiative by finding some rock-bottom to stand on." On August 13, the same day he speaks of being a "restful kernel in the magazine of the universe," Henry reiterates, in the face of his identity confusion, his fierce desire to find a "rock bottom" of identity, of self-definition: "Men are constantly dinging in my ears their fair theories and plausible solutions of the universe, but ever there is no help, and I return again to my shore-less, islandless ocean, and fathom unceasingly for a bottom that will hold an anchor, that it may not drag" (*J*, I: 54).

Thoreau still had great difficulty finding a bottom that would hold an anchor. Having recently lost a tooth, he reflects that he is "no whole man, but a lame and halting piece of manhood" who has "felt cheap, and hardly dared hold up my head among men, ever since that accident happened." While he may have been indulging in some humor here, it is safe to say that he did *not* feel like a whole man. In late August or early September, the headmaster of Concord Academy resigned and Thoreau (whose school had only four or five students at the time), seeing an opportunity to remove at least his *job* from his parents' home, arranged to rent the building and take over "the name and good-will of the institution." [117] This must have seemed at least a minor victory of initative for Henry. On September 15, the same day that he announced the opening of Concord Academy in the *Yeoman's Gazette*, Thoreau rejoices in his journal:

> How unaccountable the flow of spirits in youth. You may throw sticks and dirt into the current, and it will only rise the higher. Dam it up you may, but dry it up you may not, for you cannot reach its source. If you stop up this avenue or that, anon it will come gurgling out where you least expected and wash away all fixtures. Youth grasps at happiness as an inalienable right. The tear does no sooner gush than glisten. Who shall say when the tear that sprung of sorrow first sparkled with joy? (*J*, I: 59)

This entry suggests that Thoreau, like many adolescents in the Sturm und Drang period, was given to frequent fluctuation of moods and that he himself was aware of the variability of his emotions. Years later, after describing in his journal the "Rough and Smooth" dream of his child-hood, he would say, "My waking experience *always* has been and is such an alternate Rough and Smooth. In other words it is Insanity and Sanity" (*J*, IX: 211). In the case of his Concord Academy "coup" we get the sense that he felt his spirits on the rebound, that he anticipated some "smooth sailing" ahead.

On September 23, Thoreau reflects (perhaps echoing the thoughts of his mentor Emerson), "If we will be quiet and ready enough, we shall find compensation in every disappointment" (*J*, I: 60). He would often invoke the doctrine of compensation when in danger of being overcome by disappointment. Certainly he must have wondered just how long he could remain "quiet and ready enough." If, in mid-September, he saw some hope that he could solve his economic and identity problems, his spirits must have been considerably dampened by the dearth of new students attracted to Concord Academy. On October 6, he wrote a letter to Reverend Andrew Bigelow in Taunton: "I learn from my brother and sister, who were recently employed as teachers in your vicinity, that you are at present in quest of some one to fill the vacancy in your high school, occasioned by Mr. Bellows' withdrawal. As my present school, which consists of a small number of well advanced pupils, is not sufficiently lucrative, I am advised to make application for the situation now vacant." [118] The "advice" must have been strongly worded, the situation bleak for Thoreau to consider leaving Concord. To remove himself from the town would be to weaken his developing association with Emerson and to make more problematical the task of self-definition. Thoreau was "saved," however, when he was not accepted for employment in Taunton. By December 7, he seems to recognize just how fleeting and variable is the sense of progress—including, no doubt, his own progress toward self-sufficiency and identity-formation: "We may believe it, but never do we live a quiet, free life, such as Adam's, but are enveloped in an invisible network of speculations. Our progress is only from one such speculation to another, and only at rare intervals do we perceive that it is no progress" (*J*, I: 61). The next day, probably feeling the renewed force of his own inner sense of giftedness and his alienation from the community, he implicitly identifies with Byron, the "wildest" and most "bohemian" of the major Romantic poets: "What was it to Lord Byron whether England owned or disowned him, whether he smelled sour and was skunk-cabbage to the English nostril. . . . Let not the oyster grieve that he has lost the race, he has gained as an oyster" (*J*, I: 62). Whether or not the oyster is visibly "winning," a pearl is slowly forming within. Thoreau would use the oyster-pearl image in the early 1840s, when there yet seemed to be such a discrepancy between internal possibility and visible achievements. Similarly, he would frequently make use of the imagery of hibernation to dramatize his personal situation. Just as an animal hibernates in the winter, so would Thoreau see his prolonged adolescence, his moratorium, as a kind of hibernation. In his December 15 poem, "Fair Haven," he writes, "Methinks the summer is still nigh, / And lurketh there below, / As that some meadow mouse doth lie / Snug underneath the snow" (*J*, I, 62). Like the oyster secretly secreting the pearl, the meadow mouse "snug underneath the snow" (and thus "invisible" to the world of men) maintains a summer heat and self-sufficiency even in the coldest winter. The oyster will one day yield a pearl; the meadow mouse will someday emerge from hibernation into a warm and welcoming summer. Thoreau came to rely more on such images the longer he waited.

At what must have been a discouraging time for young Henry, Concord Academy began to attract more students.[119] It is not altogether clear why the enrollment increased. It is likely that school enrollment was generally greater during the non-farming months. Perhaps his neighbors began to respect, grudgingly, Henry's teaching ability, educational strategy, and persistence; undoubtedly the support of such men as Samuel Hoar, Nathan Brooks, John Keyes and Emerson (all of whom had offered their names as referees for Henry's school) [120] contributed to the eventual respectability of the school. The relatively few journal entries during the fall and winter of 1838–39 may indicate how hard Henry was working on his teaching. Whatever the case, by January there were enough enrollees to call for the hiring of another teacher—John, Jr., who left his Roxbury teaching position to join his younger brother at Concord Academy. The enrollment of the school soon reached the maximum of twenty-five.[121] The school would continue until April of 1841, when John had to resign for reasons of poor health.

For Henry, this situation must have appeared the best of all possible worlds. Not only did he not have to give up anything (Emerson, Transcendentalism, his budding literary aspirations, Concord, his mother); he also had gained a masculine model, "father-substitute," buffer between him and his parents, and companion in his brother. With the coming of John there was a true January thaw in Henry's spirits. On January 20, 1839—probably after he had learned that John would be joining him—he reports in his journal: "The prospect of our river valley from Tahatawan Cliff appeared to me again in my dreams." He then inserts a poem: "Last night, as I lay gazing with shut eyes / Into the golden land of dreams, / I thought I gazed adown a quiet reach / Of land and water prospect, / Whose low beach / Was peopled with the now subsiding hum / Of happy industry whose work is done" (J, I: 71–72). The reference to Tahatawan harkens back to the letter Henry wrote to John in November of 1837, in which Henry identified with Tahatawan. In the letter, Tahatawan indicated he was a "brave" living in a land of talkative "squaws" and that he considered his brother to be a fellow brave and his talk "great medicine." Now, the two braves would be reunited, and Henry could be sure that he would not become a squaw, that he could be manly and independent, even if he continued to live in the "wigwam" dominated by his talkative mother. Working with his brother, he could see industry as "happy."

In the latter part of December 1838, Thoreau had entered an essay on "Sound and Silence" into his journal. In that unfinished essay, he extols silence (or, paradoxically, the "sounds of silence") as over against "noisiness":

> As the truest society approaches nearer to solitude, so the most excellent speech finally falls into silence. . . . where man is, there is Silence. . . . Silence is the universal refuge, the sequel of all dry discourses and all foolish acts, as balm to our every chagrin, as welcome after satiety as [after] disappointment. . . . These are garrulous and noisy eras, which no longer yield any sound; but for the Grecian, or *silent* and melodious, Era is ever sounding on the ears of men. (*J*, I: 64–68)

While Thoreau's discourses on silence may have been, as Paul suggests, partially a product of his reading of Sir Thomas Browne and Oriental scripture,[122] it is my contention that on a personal level Thoreau's emphasis on silence was a response to the constant (and occasionally harsh) talk of his mother—and other women living in the Parkman House. Even though Henry would become a great talker himself, he would no doubt have agreed with Emerson's journal entry of March 1838, "In conversation, women run on, as it is called. A great vice." [123] Talk, gossip, constant chatter were perceived by Thoreau as "squaw-like"; such sounds were a threat to manliness. On February 9, 1839, which was the same day that John announced in the *Yeoman's Gazette* the reopening of Concord Academy and his intent to teach alongside his brother, Henry wrote in his journal, "It takes a man to make a room silent" (*J*, I: 73). With the arrival of a "manly" model and companion such as John, Henry himself could be a man. While his father was unable to "make a room silent" when his wife was present, the two brothers together could assert their masculinity and independence.

On January 20, directly following the poem concerning his "Tahatawan Cliff" dream, Henry writes, "We two that planets erst had been / Are now a double star, / And in the heavens may be seen, / Where that we fixèd are" (*J*, I: 72). Harding sees this poem as the earliest indication that Thoreau was becoming interested in the opposite sex,[124] but given the time it was written and the entries that surround it, I would argue that Thoreau is talking of his relationship with his brother. Working and living together, John and Henry, long separated, would now become an inseparable "double star," "fixed" in Concord.

The "planet" image reappears again on February 10 in "The Peal of the Bells": "I am on the alert for some wonderful Thing / Which somewhere's a-taking place; / 'Tis perchance the salute which our planet doth ring / When it meeteth another in space" (*J*, I: 74). With the two planets about to meet in space, Thoreau was indeed anticipating "some wonderful Thing" with the reopening of Concord Academy. The spring term began on March 11, 1839. Less than a month later (April 4), Henry writes of the poet: "He is another Nature, —Nature's brother. Kindly offices do they perform for one another" (*J*, I: 75). That Thoreau could see himself, the budding poet, as "Nature's brother" suggests that his *own* brother was performing "kindly offices" for him.

Putting aside for the moment consideration of the school itself and subsequent developments in the Henry-John relationship, it may be said that John's joining Henry at Concord Academy—and the economic promise of the venture—served to "fix" Henry in Concord and solidify his image of himself as a "traveller in Concord." Given his deeply imbedded sense of potential greatness, and his contradictory needs to feel independent and yet stay close to home, it is understandable that Thoreau came to identify greatness and bravery with *physical* sedentariness. In December of 1839 he remarks in his journal, "Bravery deals not so much in resolute action, as in healthy and assured rest. Its palmy state is a staying at home" (*J*, I: 97). In the same month, he says directly, unquestionably thinking of his own situation, "The brave man stays at home" (*J*, I: 106). Thoreau understands that it is possible to go west, as so many other young men were doing, without leaving home: "Let us migrate interiorly without intermission, and pitch our tent each day nearer the western horizon" (*J*, I: 131). In effect, Henry could justify his sedentariness by redefining "travel": "The deepest and most original thinker," he says on August 13, 1840, "is the farthest travelled." [125] Seeking to find greatness and adventurousness in what was outwardly a tame life, Thoreau (in the "Lost Journal") muses,

> The biography of a man who has spent his days in a library, may be as interesting as the Peninsular campaigns. . . . If the cripple but tell me how like a man he turned in his seat, how he now looked out at a south window then a north, and finally looked into the fire, it will be as good as a tour on the continent or the prairies. . . . [My life] is as adventurous as Crusoe's—as full of novelty as Marco Polo's, as dignified as the Sultan's, as momentous as that of the reigning prince. (M, 181–82)

Because Thoreau was psychologically incapable of breaking away from home and mother, it became absolutely crucial to his self-concept that he be *radically* adventurous—in behavior and thought—while residing in Concord. In defending his way of life as independent, he supplied all those who did not travel west with a justification for, and glorification of, their sedentariness. When the frontier closed, Thoreau's concepts of "travelling" and "the West" would become even more pertinent; one could still be a pioneer, even if there was no physical frontier left to explore.

More generally, it should be noted here that "travelling in Concord" was only one of many paradoxes that Henry used to make sense out of and dramatize his own life-situation. If paradox is, in the literary sense, the uniting of seemingly contradictory elements, on the psychological level it is one way to resolve ambivalence. As already indicated, Henry was beset by deeply rooted psychological conflicts. While it is of course naive to think that Thoreau used paradox *only* because it helped him resolve personal dilemmas,[126] it would be equally naive to ignore the private origins of his predilection for paradox. In the early journals, Thoreau came to discover that paradox was not only an effective literary strategy, but also a felicitous way to deal with ambivalence and to define identity. Indeed, paradox came to be a governing personality mode for Thoreau. One can heartily agree with Krutch's contention that "to write without incongruity of things ordinarily thought of as incongruous *is* the phenomenon called Thoreau, whether one is thinking of a personality or of a body of literary work." [127] Erikson says that a man *is* his conflicts; surely this is especially true of Thoreau.

One example of Thoreau's use of paradox (aside from the just-discussed "traveller in Concord" stance) will suffice for the present. It has been argued that Henry was torn between "initiative" and "guilt," between his ambition to be a "great man" and his reluctance (born partially of guilt) to be great or successful in the conventional sense. Just after stating in a journal entry of June 26, "Truth is always paradoxical," he maintains, "He will get to the goal first who stands stillest" *(J*, I: 153). Thus, the "winner" is he who does not aggressively *try* to win, who does not desire to step over someone else in order to procure victory for himself. By asserting that one can be "first" (which implies the necessity of competing with others) *without* competing, by "standing still," one may be thereby great *and* guiltless. A day earlier, Thoreau had remarked, "Let me see no other conflict but with prosperity. If my path run before me level and smooth, it is all a mirage; in reality it is steep and arduous as a chamois pass. I will not let the years roll over me like a Juggernaut car" (*J*, I: 152). Yet Thoreau did want a kind of prosperity. Therefore, before resorting to paradox, he found it necessary to redefine "prosperity" (just as "travel" was redefined). On September 25 Thoreau says, "Prosperity is no field for heroism unless it endeavor to establish an independent and supernatural prosperity for itself" (M, 162). Such a redefinition of success made it possible for Henry to make direct use of paradox in the same entry: "Defeat is heaven's success. He cannot be said to succeed to whom the world shows any favor" (M, 162). Thoreau searched for a way to be a hero, a success, without provoking guilt feelings. Paradox provided him with a way to be psychologically comfortable with his ambition. Failure in the eyes of the world could be success to him.

There are many variations on this paradox in the early journal. The "great man" is seen as the "homeliest," the most seemingly inconsequential; the "bravest soldier" is seen as one who "yields." In the last analysis, however, the use of such paradoxes must be perceived not only in the light of Thoreau's deeply embedded ambivalences, but also in the context of what was happening in his life during the years 1839–1842—particularly his relationship with his brother, the Ellen Sewall romance, and John's subsequent death. The events of these years served both to prolong Thoreau's identity confusion *and* to shape his adult identity. His "travels in Concord" would be arduous journeys indeed.

Each hearty stroke we deal with these outward hands, slays an inward foe. — Thoreau, "Lost Journal" in *Consciousness in Concord*

We have nothing to fear from our foes; God keeps a standing army for that service; but we have no ally against our friends, those ruthless vandals whose kind intent is a subtler poison than the Colchian, a more fatal shaft than the Lydian. — Thoreau, *Journal*, I

My friend can only be, in any measure my foe, because he is fundamentally my friend. — Thoreau, *Journal*, I

It is the saddest thought of all, that what we are to others, that we are much more to ourselves, — avaricious, mean, irascible, affected, — we are the victims of these faults. If our pride offends our humble neighbors, much more does it offend ourselves, though our lives are never so private and solitary. — Thoreau, *Journal*, I

School Days

The Concord Academy situation probably provided Henry with some of his happiest moments.[1] He taught classics, science, and natural history, while his elder brother was the instructor in "the English branches" and mathematics.[2] John became the "preceptor" of the school—the chief administrator and headmaster.[3] Descriptions of the school tend to be idyllic. One student, Thomas Hosmer, remembered (as reported by Edward Emerson):

> after morning prayers, one or the other of the brothers often made a little address to their scholars, original and interesting, to put their minds in proper train for the day's work. Henry's talks especially remain with him: on the seasons, their cause, their advantages, their adaptation to needs of organic life; their beauty, which he brought actually into the school-room by his description; on design in the universe, strikingly illustrated for children's minds; on profanity, treated in a way, fresh, amusing, and sensible. At these times you could have heard a pin drop in the school-room.[4]

Horace Hosmer, another student, observed, "It was a peculiar school, there was never a boy flogged or threatened, yet I never saw so absolutely military discipline. How it was done I scarcely know. Even the incorrigible were brought into line." [5] Henry, then, was in a position to prove to the town that they had been wrong in employing corporal punishment—and wrong in rejecting him. Nor was the lack of corporal punishment the only innovation. "Recess" was extended from the usual ten minutes to a half-hour; the windows of the school were kept open for ventilation.[6] Sanborn speaks of the numerous field trips, such as "a weekly walk in the woods and pastures, or a sail or row on the river, or a swim in one of the ponds of the township, Walden or White or Bateman's Pond; and there was much instructive talk about the Indians who formerly lived or hunted there." [7] George Keyes, speaking of the school as "very pleasant indeed" told Edward Emerson that Henry and John even organized a survey of the Fair Haven Hill area in order to give the students practical experience in surveying.[8] The Thoreau brothers' school was, then, highly innovative, making use of progressive educational principles whenever possible.[9]

It may also be suggested that this teaching experience gave Thoreau his first genuine chance to be a "father," a model to those younger than he; while teaching he could feel more "adult," as he was caring for the up-and-coming generation. Furthermore, with his sociable brother as companion, he became involved in town social activities, participating in " 'all the parties, dances, and various schemes of entertainment which occupied the leisure hours of the young people of the village.' " [10] Henry, according to Sanborn, accompanied John to the Lyceum, Masonic balls, parties of the Concord Artillery, and other social gatherings where one could "pay attentions" to eligible young women.[11] Undoubtedly, the presence of his brother encouraged Henry to be more sociable and extroverted than he otherwise would have been.

While the two brothers seemed to get along exceedingly well with each other on the surface, and while the first months of their teaching together were relatively happy, I would argue that there was some covert rivalry and undercurrents of negative feeling between John and Henry. A remark by Horace Hosmer, and Edward Emerson's parenthetical explanation, strongly imply that the negative feelings were not entirely hidden: " 'Am satisfied that I misconstrued Henry's silence concerning John.' (The young Hosmer, at the time, felt that Thoreau did not care as much as he, who almost worshipped John.)" [12] Working together as they did, they assuredly put themselves in a position to be compared by their students and townspeople. Given the personable nature of John, it is to be expected that Henry often still got the short end of the comparison. Horace Hosmer observed: "In reading about Arnold of Rugby I have often thought that John Thoreau resembled him in conducting his school. To me that man seemed to make all things possible. Henry was not loved in the school. He had his scholars upstairs. I was with John only. John was the more human, loving; understood and thought of others. Henry thought more about himself. He was a conscientious teacher but rigid." Hosmer goes on to characterize Henry as having been in the "green-apple stage" while teaching at Concord Academy.[13] In general, the students tended to prefer John to Henry.[14] They would call Henry "Trainer Thoreau" because of the "militariness" of his demeanor,[15] and occasionally they would poke fun at him: "A picture of a booby in the current almanac resembled him so much that it was cut out and circulated among the pupils as a likeness."[16] If John was more popular among the students, he was also viewed as the more responsible and dependable of the Thoreau brothers—and the townspeople were therefore more willing to entrust their children to his care. Sanborn says, "in the village there was a prejudice, slight or strong, against a youth like Henry, just one-and-twenty, who had so much independence of thought and action. The number of pupils gained under John; for it was found that a boy learned more in a month at the Thoreau school than at the Town School under the Freemason's Lodge, where inattention, mischief, and whipping were in vogue."[17] Thus it seems likely that the community gave John more credit for the success of the school than Henry, who had, in fact, been the founder and who earlier had advocated (while teaching at the Center School) the principles now being implemented at Concord Academy. Many townspeople must have believed, with Horace Hosmer, that "John was the Architect and Henry only wrought out his plans."[18] Concord Academy apparently was often thought of as "John's school" by community members. In *"Warrington" Pen-Portraits*, Robinson says, "We find also in the paper [the *Yeoman's Gazette*], that, in the year 1839, John Thoreau (brother of Henry) kept the Concord Academy; and he 'was assisted by Henry D. Thoreau, the present instructor.'"[19] In a sense, then, John had taken over the school from Henry.

Such comparisons with his brother, in which he was seen by many as the inferior, must have been extremely painful for Henry. No matter how much he loved John, the situation forced him to see his brother as a rival. He had been overjoyed with the prospects of teaching with John, but he probably had not foreseen some of the unpleasant byproducts. Being unfavorably compared with John aroused feelings of inferiority. In spite of himself, it was only natural to feel some hostility toward his deeply loved and much-needed brother, as well as to members of the community who made unwelcome comparisons. Thoreau found it much easier to express hostility toward the community than toward his brother; it is unlikely that he acknowledged often or directly his hostile feelings toward John. Perhaps the "silence concerning John," noted by Hosmer, was Henry's way of expressing anger. Nor was it easy to acknowledge such feelings to himself; competitiveness and hostility, as directed to John, would provoke guilt and anxiety. If John was in any sense an "outer foe," then the threatening feelings were the "inward foe," to be combatted in any way possible.

On June 4, 1839, Thoreau writes, "The words of some men are thrown forcibly against you and adhere like burs" (*J*, I: 80). The suggestion is that either his townsmen or students (or both) were not entirely kind to him; it could be further speculated that some of the unkind words that "adhere like burs" involved an implied or stated comparison with his brother. Characteristically, Henry turned to nature and a cosmic perspective as a way of discarding the burs. In the same June 4 entry, Thoreau speaks of his attic's-eye view of the world:

> I sit here this fourth of June, looking out on men and nature from this that I call my perspective window, through which all things are seen in their true relations. This is my upper empire, bounded by four walls, viz., three of boards yellow-washed, facing north, west, and south, respectively, and the fourth of plaster, likewise yellow-washed, fronting the sunrise, —to say nothing of the purlieus and outlying provinces, unexplored as yet but by rats. (*J*, I: 80)

From such a perspective, Henry was able to transcend competitiveness, hostility, "peevishness," and guilt. On April 9 he says, citing the richness of nature: "There are the traits that conciliate man's moroseness, and make him civil to his fellows; every such pine root is a pledge of suavity. If he can discover absolute barrenness in any direction there will be some excuse for peevishness" (*J*, I: 77). Once again, on April 24, he attempts to put the unpleasant aspects of his situation in universal perspective: "Why should we concern ourselves with what has happened to us, and the unaccountable fickleness of events, and not rather [with] how we have happened to the universe, and it has demeaned itself in consequence?" (*J*, I: 77). Thoreau was not able, however, to drain off all his hostility (to the town or to his brother) by appealing to the cosmos. Though he might try to fight off his own "peevishness" and the unkind words of others by peaceful transcendence, he occasionally expressed his bitterness and contempt: "Some attain to such a degree of sang-froid and nonchalance as to be weavers of toilet cushions and manufacturers of pinheads, without once flinching or the slightest affection of the nerves, for the period of a natural life" (*J*, I: 76). When Thoreau needed to vent his spleen he was inclined to see civilized society (including those in his community who saw him as the "lesser brother" of John) as consisting almost exclusively of "weavers of toilet cushions and manufacturers of pinheads." Even if he was not the most sociable and lovable person, he could be a "great man"—without standing upon community-sanctioned "ceremony": "Cheap persons will stand upon ceremony, because there is no other ground; but to the great of the earth we need no introduction, nor do they need any to us" (*J*, I: 77–78).

One further possible source of rivalry—at least from Henry's point of view—should be mentioned here. Mrs. Joseph Ward and her daughter Prudence had been long-time boarders with the Thoreaus when Mrs. Ward's grandson, Edmund Sewall of Scituate, visited her in Concord in mid-June of 1839. Henry went sailing and hiking with him, and apparently took a great liking to the eleven-year-old boy.[20] Almost certainly referring to his new acquaintance, Thoreau wrote in his journal on June 22:

> I have within the last few days come into contact with a pure, uncompromising spirit, that is somewhere wandering in the atmosphere, but settles not positively anywhere. Some persons carry about them the air and conviction of virtue, though they themselves are unconscious of it, and are even backward to appreciate it in others. Such it is impossible not to love; still is their loveliness, as it were, independent of them, so that you seem not to lose it when they are absent, for when they are near it is like an invisible presence which attends you. (*J*, I: 80)

The subsequent journal entry is a poem, apparently written after Edmund had left Concord; the poem, "Sympathy" (*J*, I: 80–82), was later accepted for publication in the opening issue of *The Dial* in 1840. In "Sympathy," Thoreau praises the "gentle boy, / Whose features all were cast in Virtue's mould," and feverishly laments his loss: "Eternity may not the chance repeat, / But I must tread my single way alone, / In sad rememberance that we once did meet, / And know that bliss irrevocably gone." He speaks of the "gentle boy's" departure in elegaic, even tragic, terms and wonders, "Is't then too late the damage to repair?" The final verse arrives at a "Transcendental" (and, in terms of the poem itself, too easily gained) resolution: "If I but love that virtue which he is, / Though it be scented in the morning air, / Still shall we be truest acquaintances, / Nor mortals know a sympathy more rare."

That Thoreau was "infatuated" with young Edmund is clear from these journal entries; that he experienced a painful sense of loss upon the boy's departure is also evident (though the expressions of feelings may have been somewhat exaggerated for the sake of literary effect). Without delving here into the question of whether, or to what extent, his attachment to Edmund had "homoerotic" undercurrents,[21] it may be said that it was important to Thoreau to have the boy's friendship and affection. Thus, there may well be significance in Annie Russell Marble's remark (based on Sewall family explanations): "Henry was deeply interested in the boy but failed to win the cordial friendship given to the less reserved, and more sunny, John." [22] If this account is accepted, then we at least must entertain the notion that Henry was led to see himself as a rival of John's for Edmund's affection. To the extent that Henry "failed to win the cordial friendship" given to John, he must have felt some hostility toward his brother—and toward Edmund himself. Harding argues that Thoreau may have been a bit upset when Edmund returned to Concord as a student at the Thoreau school the next March because he suspected that the boy might somehow present an obstacle to his courtship of Edmund's sister Ellen.[23] He bases this conclusion on a journal entry (J, I: 129) of March 20, 1840: "We will have no vulgar Cupid for a go-between, to make us the playthings of each other, but rather cultivate an irreconcilable hatred instead of this."

It can further be suggested that, since both John and Henry were "in pursuit of Ellen" at this time, Henry's expression of "annoyance" may also have been directed—intentionally or unintentionally—at John, who was indeed "interfering" with his own courtship. *That* rivalry, in which Henry would find himself pitted against the brother he deeply loved, would be by far the most fateful and threatening of all.

Rivals for the Hand of a Maiden

Ellen Sewall, the seventeen-year-old sister of Edmund, visited Concord, the Wards, and the Thoreaus in late July 1839. A remarkably beautiful young woman,[24] she made a profound impression on Henry and John. According to Harding, Henry had met Ellen before, but "suddenly he saw her as though for the first time." [25] Perhaps she had just blossomed into cultivated young womanhood; perhaps Henry was himself a "late bloomer" in terms of perceiving women as potential romantic partners. On the same day as her arrival (July 20), Henry wrote a poem, "The Breeze's Invitation," into his journal: "Like two careless swifts let's sail, / Zephyrus shall think for me." That the poem is addressed to a woman is strongly suggested by Thoreau's reference to "king" and "queen": "Our green leaf shall be our screen, / Till the sun doth go to bed, / I the king and you the queen / Of that peaceful little green, / Without any subject's aid" (*J*, I: 86–87). Two days earlier—before Ellen's arrival—he entered "The Assabet" into his journal ("Up the pleasant stream let's row / For the livelong summer's day"); the poem was probably written with his brother in mind (and was, in effect, an early imagining of the Concord-Merrimack boat trip), but Henry later sent a copy to Ellen in Scituate. On July 25, Henry mused, "There is no remedy for love but to love more" (*J*, I: 88). Almost certainly, he must have had Ellen in mind.

There is a tendency among hard-headed, tough-minded critics to minimize the importance or even make fun of this love affair.[26] But I would submit that, for Henry, it was a serious matter. At the age of twenty-two, he was not only a late adolescent, but also a young adult needing to establish some form of intimacy. Though he might not have been particularly inclined toward the intimacies associated with women and marriage in 1839, surely someone like Ellen could begin to dissolve his disinclinations. We cannot know for certain whether she ever loved Henry or John, but she clearly did not dissuade them from pursuing her—at least in the early stages of their acquaintance. Even if Henry carried with him since childhood a deep ambivalence toward women and sexuality, and even if (as Gozzi argues) he had homoerotic tendencies, he was still in the *process* of developing an identity—including a sexual identity—and growing into what he hoped would be manhood and independence. He was not yet fixed in his self-conception. Moreover, when Henry met Ellen in mid-July of 1839, it was during a relatively confident and "social" time in his life: presumably, he was even in a position to support a wife. It would have been possible for Thoreau to envision marriage; he could still be a Transcendentalist (after all, even his "identity sponsor" was married), and he would be establishing once and for all his independence from the maternal home. Thoreau could be a very passionate, intense, romantic young man, who was capable of "giving all to love." On January 26, 1840, he wrote in his journal:

I would live henceforth with some gentle soul such a life as may be conceived, double for variety, single for harmony, —two, only that we might admire at our one-ness, —one, because indivisible. Such community to be a pledge of holy living. How could aught unworthy be admitted into our society? To listen with one ear to each summer sound, to behold with one eye each summer scene, our visual rays so to meet and mingle with the object as to be one bent and doubled; with two tongues to be wearied, and thought to spring ceaselessly from a double fountain. (*J*, I: 113–14)

Such an entry indicates that Thoreau was not dead-set against living with "some gentle soul"—almost certainly Ellen—or at the very least *considering* a romantic attachment.

Rather than present Henry as having been, in 1839, completely resistant to the possibilities of love and marriage, it is more accurate to portray him as ambivalent. To the extent that romantic involvement is a crucial determinant of identity, it may be said that Thoreau's feelings toward Ellen were closely tied to his as yet unresolved identity confusion. Though the prospect of involvement with Ellen may well have threatened Henry's developing concept of himself, it also offered him a much-needed way of "gradually clarifying" [27] his identity. It is my belief that Thoreau was not so ambivalent that he would not seriously consider marriage. And there seems little doubt—based on the data— that he did care deeply for Ellen and that she was a significant figure in his life. [28]

There was, however, another factor which enormously complicated Thoreau's feelings toward Ellen: his brother John had also fallen in love with her. This development (and John's subsequent illness and death) would prove to have even more far-reaching ramifications than the Henry-Ellen romance itself. Canby, who argues strenuously that there *was* a "Transcendental Triangle"—Henry, John, and Ellen—says, "It is a family tradition that he [Henry] did not know John was in love until after John's death in '42. This, I am sure is not true; but he may well have not known it before the 'aeon' in 1840." [29] It seems implausible to me, nevertheless, that Henry did not know, at least indirectly, of John's feelings in the summer and fall of 1839. To my knowledge, no one has yet realized the extent to which Henry's journal reveals his preoccupation with this rivalry and his ways of dealing with it, even in 1839. Nor has any biographer, as far as I know, suggested the far-reaching implications of the rivalry.

During Ellen's July visit, both John and Henry squired her around:

Many walks were taken, rows on the Concord River, hills climbed for views, woods explored. There is a legend that they carved their initials on a tree. There was endless talking too, evidently mostly by Henry with the others asking him questions. These expeditions were always accompanied by Ellen's Aunt Prudence who must have been young at the time and I fancy enjoyed her duty as chaperone.[30]

According to all accounts Ellen had a most happy stay in Concord and, writing to Aunt Prudence upon returning to Scituate, requested that she convey to the Thoreaus her "affectionate remembrance."[31] When John found out that she had left behind some Indian relics, "he forwarded them to her, enclosing a cleverly mounted insect as a joke, and a letter announcing that he and Henry were about to leave on a boating trip to New Hampshire, a vacation from their schoolkeeping duties."[32]

It is likely that, while they were making their trip on the Concord and Merrimack Rivers in a boat they had built in the spring of 1839, the two brothers were already rivals for the affections of Ellen Sewall. To what extent they acknowledged their rivalry to each other we can never know. There is one bit of evidence which suggests that a painful "crisis" occurred during the trip. On October 18, 1841—after Ellen had rejected both brothers but before John's death—Margaret Fuller (then editor of *The Dial*) wrote Henry, "The pencilled paper Mr. E[merson] put into my hands. I have taken the liberty to copy it. You expressed one day my own opinion that the moment such a crisis is passed we may speak of it. There is no need of artificial delicacy, of secrecy, it keeps its own secret; it cannot be made false. Thus you will not be sorry that I have seen the paper. Will you not send me some other records of the good week."[33] These remarks, which appeared as a postscript to a letter evaluating Thoreau's "Wachusett" poem and his general progress as a writer, indicate that Henry had already begun to work on his account of the "good week" on the rivers. Whether he then conceived his accounts as a potential book we do not know; certainly he did not know that the account would become a memorial for John. In any case, Fuller says that the crisis has passed: surely this *could* refer to the John-Henry rivalry for Ellen, which had ended by December of 1840. Moreover, it seems evident that the "crisis" was connected with the trip, because Fuller, after mentioning it, subsequently asks for "*other* records of the good week." Perhaps the week, tinged with fraternal competition, was not quite as "good" or idyllic as we have been led to believe.

Whether or not there was any unpleasantness between the brothers on the trip, there can be little doubt that Henry came to associate the "good week" not only with camaraderie and love the brothers had for each other, but also with the "delicate" combat in which they were engaged. On January 26, 1841, Thoreau speaks of a dream in his journal:

> I had a dream last night which had reference to an act in my life in which I had been most disinterested and true to my highest instinct but completely failed in realizing my hopes; and now, after so many months, in the stillness of sleep, complete justice was rendered me. It was a divine remuneration. In my waking hours I could not have conceived of such retribution; the presumption of desert would have damned the whole. But now I was permitted to be not so much a subject as a partner to that retribution. It was the award of a divine justice, which will at length be and is even now accomplished. (*J*, I: 177)

As will later be argued, this dream almost certainly refers to the Henry-John rivalry, to Henry's decision to yield to his brother, and to the agonizing sense that even yielding had not resolved the conflict. For present purposes, suffice it to say that Henry inserted a version of this dream into "Wednesday" of *A Week:*

> I dreamed this night of an event which had occurred long before. It was a difference with a Friend, which had not ceased to give me pain, though I had no cause to blame myself. But in my dream ideal justice was at length done me for his suspicions, and I received that compensation which I had never obtained in my waking hours. I was unspeakably soothed, and rejoiced, even after I awoke, because in dreams we never deceive ourselves, nor are deceived, and this seemed to have the authority of a final judgment.[34]

That Thoreau chose to include his January 26, 1841 dream (with reference to an "act in his life" many months ago) in his "Friendship" chapter of *A Week* strongly hints that the hostilities, however secret or subtle, had begun in the summer and early fall of 1839 and were experienced by Henry as he rowed on the placid river with his "Friend." Is it not possible that the "pencilled paper" passage, referring to a crisis during the "good week," may have contained a discussion of the troubled dream?

The association of the trip with Ellen and the fraternal rivalry is also suggested by their frequent juxtaposition in the *Journal*. It has already been mentioned that the July 25, 1839 entry is followed by an account of the first day of the excursion (August 31). On June 19, 1840, Thoreau describes how "the other day I rowed in my boat a free, even lovely young lady. . . . So might all our lives be picturesque if they were free enough, but mean relations and prejudices intervene to shut out the sky" (*J*, I: 144). The sentence which immediately follows this description of a boat ride with Ellen and "mean relations and prejudices" relates to the boat trip with John: "I shall not soon forget the sounds which lulled me when falling asleep on the banks of the Merrimack" (*J*, I: 144). While trying to confront the issue of whether to pursue Ellen (after John had been refused by her), Thoreau writes (on September 25, 1840), "Defeat is heaven's success. He cannot be said to succeed to whom the world shows any favor. . . . When we rise to the step above, we tread hardest on the step below" (M, 162). The next sentence is, "My friend must be my tent companion (M, 162). Surely this entry connects the issues of romantic competition and the Concord-Merrimack trip; John was literally Henry's "tent companion" on the trip, and Henry was anxious not to lose the friendship of such a companion.

Even if Henry did not know of John's feelings about Ellen during the trip, it is almost inconceivable that he did not become aware of the rivalry (or begin to anticipate it) upon return from the rivers. On September 13, the brothers rowed and sailed back into Concord; almost immediately John set out for Scituate. Harding reports,

> Aunt Prudence's suggestion that it was not quite proper to visit when Ellen's parents were away on a trip to Niagara Falls was quietly ignored. Ellen, however, was not in the least disturbed at his arrival. When one of her friends, Sarah Otis, called hinting that she would like to stay for a visit, Ellen put her off until after John had gone. George and Edmund, she thought, provided adequate chaperonage.[35]

So it was that Henry was left in Concord while his dearest friend and "tent companion" of the previous weeks went off to visit—and perhaps to court—an unchaperoned and all too available Ellen Sewall. Such a situation must have upset Henry immensely, especially since he himself knew "no remedy for love but to love more." On September 17,

Henry seems to be trying to tell himself that he should be patient, that it was right for him not to have hastily set out for Scituate as his brother had done, that he should not lose hope immediately and jump into a frightful fray. Once again he makes use of nature to confirm his own feelings: "Nature never makes haste; her systems revolve at an even pace. The bud swells imperceptively, without hurry or confusion, as though the short spring days were an eternity. All her operations seem separately, for the time, the single object for which all things tarry. Why, then, should man hasten as if anything less than an eternity were alotted for the least deed?" (J, I: 92). Yet Henry could not so easily assuage his fears or raise his spirits. A note from Ellen, which John brought home with him from Scituate, could not have helped or given him great hope: "I have enjoyed Mr. John's visit exceedingly though sorry father and Mother were not at home." [36] No doubt he identified with Aeschylus about whom he wrote on November 5, "Like every genius, he was a solitary liver and worker in his day" (J, I: 93). Thoreau however, could not find complete relief by thinking of himself as a proto-genius and "solitary liver." He regretted the turn of events which had led John and himself to be attracted to the same young woman. While admitting regret and sorrow, Thoreau tried not to give in to his feelings. On November 13, he tells himself, "Make the most of your regrets; never smother your sorrow but tend and cherish it till it come to have a separate and integral interest. To regret deeply is to live afresh." A day later, he resolves not to become overwhelmed by his depression: "There is nowhere any apology for despondency. Always there is life which, rightly lived, implies a divine satisfaction. I am soothed by the rain-drops on the door-sill; every globule that pitches thus confidently from the eaves to the ground is my life insurance" (J, I: 95).

I would hypothesize that the rivalry reawakened and aggravated Thoreau's ambivalences, fears, and guilt feelings. As has been argued, Henry probably harbored some hostility toward his brother, a hostility that was difficult to confront directly because he so much loved and respected his "elder." There was rivalry between the two during the oedipal period; during adolescence, Henry may well have viewed John as a competitor in terms of popularity, acceptance, and achievement. While teaching together, they had also, unavoidably, been compared to each other and thus put in a competitive situation. The townspeople usually compared Henry unfavorably with John. It was earlier suggested that Henry's surpassing (by going to Harvard) of his brother might have evoked guilt; if John can in any sense be seen as a father-surrogate for his brother, then the surpassing of him could have been linked (at least unconsciously) with the imagined defeat of his father. This would have intensified the guilt and anxiety experienced by Henry. But if there is any situation which seems to have established and aggravated a sense of competition between the two brothers, it was the romantic triangle. Thoreau undoubtedly was depressed about John's interest in Ellen, but he also felt rage: John might be responsible for his losing the only "available" woman he had ever remotely considered marrying. It is not altogether clear to what extent Henry was conscious of the anger he felt toward his brother, or to what extent he was able to repress his rage. But to the degree that he was conscious of it, he must have felt guilt. After all, John *was* his elder, a person to be looked up to and loved. What right had Henry to be angry at him? Shouldn't John "get first crack" at Ellen? However, even when he asked himself these questions, he could not rid himself completely of hostility which thus deepened the sense of guilt. He could not have felt such guilt if he had loved John less. On the one hand, Henry found himself in the position of having to yield to his brother, not only because it was the selfless (and perhaps more socially proper) thing to do, but also because of the inward guilt feelings which would be aroused if he did aggressively pursue Ellen. On the other hand, Henry could not completely resign himself to yielding. He continued to feel anger, aggression, and guilt as he entertained the hope that he might ultimately win Ellen, and that he might eventually defeat his brother. The dialectic between yielding and aggression is apparent in his writing during this perplexing period in his life.

It is no accident that in late 1839 Thoreau began to write frequently of bravery, war, and conflict in his journal. The issues and imagery of bravery and war allowed him to deal indirectly with the dilemmas of romance and fraternal rivalry.[37] To be sure, he did not make use of such issues and imagery *only* because of the disturbing rivalry. As Emerson said of him at his funeral, "There was somewhat military in his nature not to be subdued, always manly and able, but rarely tender, as if he did not feel himself except in opposition."[38] While there may be some implied criticism in Emerson's observation, he must be given some of the credit for encouraging Thoreau to think of himself as a brave soldier. In his essay on "Heroism," for instance, Emerson exclaims,

Our culture therefore must not omit the arming of the man. Let him hear in season that he is born into a state of war, and that the

commonwealth and his own well-being require that he should
not go dancing in the weeds of peace, but warned, self-collected
and neither defying nor dreading the thunder, let him take both
reputation and life in his hand, and with perfect urbanity dare the
gibbet and the mob by the absolute truth of his speech and the
rectitude of his behavior.

Towards all this external evil the man within the breast assumes
a warlike attitude, and affirms his ability to cope singlehanded
with the infinite army of soldiers. To this military attitude of the
soul we give the name of heroism.[39]

In "The Service," then, Thoreau was probably hoping to give Emerson
just what he wanted to hear about the "qualities of a recruit," of a
hero.[40] Moreover, Thoreau's "military nature" may partly be attributed
to his need to keep at a distance those many people by whom he felt
threatened. Erikson indicates that the counterpart to intimacy is "distantiation," the "lasting consequences" of which seem particularly helpful to understanding Thoreau's "military" disposition and imagery:
"the readiness to fortify one's territory of intimacy and solidarity and
to view all outsiders with a fanatic 'overvaluation of small differences'
between the familiar and the foreign." [41]

Whatever predilections Thoreau had for viewing experience in
military terms seem to have been exacerbated by the conflict with his
brother. It is entirely characteristic of this ambivalent man that he developed a paradoxical concept of bravery and heroism, a concept which
would allow him, whenever it was psychologically necessary, to equate
bravery with yielding, passivity, retreat, and defeat, thus justifying his
"disinterested" intention of letting John have a clear field in courting
Ellen and also subduing intense guilt feelings. On the other hand,
military imagery gave Thoreau an opportunity to express hostility and
aggressiveness, and to feel that he was "manly." Although he was not
fully conscious of what he was doing or why, neither was his attempt
to deal with the conflicts arising from the rivalry an entirely "unconscious" process.

Thoreau struggles in his journal to perceive himself as brave. On
December 2, 1839, he acknowledges his sense that life itself is a "battle"
in which each man must seek to retain his "honor"; his own competition with John may well have sharpened this sense of pervasive hostilities:

To be chafed and worried, and not as serene as Nature, does not
become one whose nature is as steadfast as she. We do all stand

in the front ranks of the battle every moment of our lives; where there is a brave man there is the thickest of the fight, there the post of honor.... Waterloo is not the only battle-ground: as many and fatal guns are pointed at my breast now as are contained in the English arsenals. (*J*, I: 96)

If this entry expresses Henry's willingness to see himself as involved in hostilities, the next recorded entries seek to define a special kind of bravery.

As if in preparation for such bravery, the next entry (not dated and therefore not necessarily belonging to the month of December), meditates poetically on the pleasures of passiveness, "Straightway dissolved, / Like to the morning mists—or rather like the subtler mists of noon— / Stretched I far up the neighboring mountain's sides" (*J*, I: 96–97). The December *Journal* mostly consists of a "Chapter on Bravery," which can be read partially in terms of the Henry-John rivalry. Thoreau begins,

Bravery deals not so much in resolute action, as in healthy and assured rest. Its palmy state is a staying at home and compelling alliance in all directions.

The brave man never heareth the din of war; he is trustful and unsuspecting, so observant of the least trait of good or beautiful that, if you turn toward him the dark side of anything, he will still see only the bright. (*J*, I: 97)

Here, Henry attempts to deny that he is competing with his brother or that he sees him as an enemy. Rather than "resolutely" pursuing Ellen, he will adopt the stance of "healthy and assured rest." Rather than going to Scituate, he will "stay at home." Instead of perceiving his brother as wittingly making him unhappy and despondent, he will be "trusting and unsuspecting," seeing only the "bright" side of John. Even more revealing is Thoreau's contention that

the coward was born one day too late, for he has never overtaken the present hour. He is the younger son of creation who now waiteth till the elder decease. He does not dwell on the earth as though he had a deed of land in his pocket.... He has only rented a few acres of time and space, and thinks that every accident portends the expiration of his lease. He is a non-proprietor, a serf, in his moral economy nomadic, having no fixed abode. When danger appears, he goes abroad and clings to straws. (*J*, I: 99)

One interpretation of this passage is that Thoreau sees the coward as the younger brother who waits for the elder brother to die so that he can come into the inheritance. Therefore, Henry, the younger brother, can only be brave by *not* waiting for (and wishing for) the death of his elder brother. He must not expect to take from John what is "rightfully" his (an opportunity to court Ellen). To be brave, the younger must stand on his own two feet, establish himself confidently in one place, and build a life independent of the elder brother. Only in this way could he become the elder son of *creation*—if not of John Thoreau, Sr.—who, as Thoreau says in "The Service," could step "buoyantly into his inheritance." [42] There may be an alternative interpretation of the passage. Is Thoreau in some sense advocating that the younger son should try to take over the inheritance of the elder while he is still living? Does this passage attempt to justify competition with the elder *before* his decease? [43] Whatever the interpretation, it must be admitted that the passage indicates a concern about the relations between younger and elder brothers.

Later in the same "Chapter on Bravery," Thoreau once again uses the imagery of "younger" and "older," this time in a biblical context: "When the world is declared under martial law, every Esau retakes his birthright, and what there is in him does not fail to appear" (*J*, I: 101). That Thoreau would invoke the story of Jacob and Esau suggests that fraternal rivalry—competition for the favor of one person—was a salient issue at this time in his life. Here, it seems that Henry (Jacob) approves of John's (Esau's) claim to his birthright (the right to pursue Ellen); after all, Thoreau has said earlier that the world *is* in a state of "martial law," where "all stand in the front ranks of the battle every moment of our lives." Unlike the biblical Jacob, Henry was unwilling to resort to trickery or deceit in order to claim what was rightfully Esau's—even if, deep down, he could not rid himself of envy for his brother's position, of a Cain-like rage toward John. Thoreau remarks that the brave soldier "may rally, charge, retreat in an orderly manner, but never flee nor flinch" (*J*, I: 101). Confronted by the possibility of competing with John, it was most "moral" to "retreat in an orderly manner." There were other kinds of bravery which Henry could lay claim to: "The bravest deed, which for the most part is left quite out of history, which alone wants the staleness of a deed done and the uncertainty of a deed doing, is the life of a great man" (*J*, I: 106). But the price of being a "great man" was high: it could not have been easy to live with the prospect of losing Ellen—especially of losing her to his brother. At some point during the autumn of 1839, he says sorrow-fully, "But alas! to be actually separated from that parcel of heaven we call our friend, with the suspicion that we shall no more meet in nature, is source enough for all the elegies that ever were written" (*J*, I: 108).

Henry was not fully resigned to being "separated from that parcel of heaven"; around Christmas time he got the opportunity to see Ellen again, when he accompanied John and Prudence on a trip to Scituate. After the visit had concluded, Ellen sent a letter to Prudence saying, "I have wished you and John and Henry here a thousand times this week." [44] It may be suggested that the sending of gifts was one way in which the Thoreau brothers covertly competed. Upon returning to Concord, Henry sent Ellen's father a volume of Jones Very's poems; John sent to Ellen some South American opals, books for Edmund, and an affectionate letter for George Sewall (Ellen's older brother). Henry soon thereafter countered by forwarding some of his poems to the young Scituate maiden. [45] The choice of Jones Very's poems as a gift seems strange because of the religiously conservative nature of Mr. Sewall. Could it be that Henry sent such a gift with the unconscious motivation of "scaring off" Ellen's father from the Thoreaus, therefore assuring that if he could not win Ellen, John could not win her either?

While at Scituate, close to the ocean, Thoreau began to write [46] "The Fisher's Son," which he finally entered into his journal on January 10. In the poem he confesses, "Oft as some ruling star my tide has swelled / The sea can scarcely brag more wrecks than I" (*J*, I: 113). He feared that any hopes he cherished toward Ellen would also be "wrecked." His sense of isolation—perhaps in contemplation of a life without Ellen—is poignantly expressed: "I have no fellow-laborer on the shore; / They scorn the strand who sail upon the sea; / Sometimes I think the ocean they've sailed o'er / Is deeper known upon the strand to me" (*J*, I: 111). He was no longer able to feel that even his brother was his "fellow laborer." But his moods ebbed and flowed like the tides. On January 19, he could say optimistically, "By a strong liking we prevail / Against the stoutest fort; / At length the fiercest heart will quail, / And our alliance court" (*J*, I: 113). A week later, Thoreau expresses his romantic aspirations in a passage previously alluded to: "I would live henceforth with some gentle soul such a life as may be conceived, double for variety, single for harmony." It is quite possible that the following passage, of February 11, 1840, also indicates Thoreau's reluctance to give up the battle, to end the hostilities: "It is never enough that our life is an easy one. We must live on the stretch;

not be satisfied with a tame and undisturbed round of weeks and days, but retire to our rest like soldiers on the eve of battle, looking forward with ardor to the strenuous sortie of the morrow" (*J*, I: 118).

Two lines from "A Freshet" communicate Thoreau's state of mind during these months of ambivalence, of teaching alongside the brother he loved and resented: "There is no fixture in the land, / But all unstable is as sand" (*J*, I: 122). The Ellen-John dilemma could only have complicated matters for Henry as he struggled to establish his identity. He must have felt often that he was getting nowhere as a suitor, as a teacher, as a poet. The continued waiting could lead to such melancholy reflections as appear in a poem of March 8:

> Two years and twenty now have flown;
> Their meanness time away has flung;
> These limbs to man's estate have grown,
> But cannot claim a manly tongue.
>
> Amidst such boundless wealth without
> I only still am poor within;
> The birds have sung their summer out,
> But still my spring does not begin....
>
> Shall I then wait the autumn wind,
> Compelled to seek a milder ray,
> And leave no empty nest behind,
> No wood still echoing to my lay? (*J*, I: 127–28)[47]

Now, almost three years after his graduation from Harvard, Henry was still frequently given to thinking of himself as a "parcel of vain strivings." Enthusiastically considering the "choice of parts" that a man may play, he remarks suggestively, "what a pity if the part of Hamlet be left out!" (*J*, I: 129). If Thoreau saw himself as having the potential to be many things, to play many parts, he also saw himself as a Hamlet, a divided and indecisive person whose resolution all too often was "sicklied o'er with the pale cast of thought." If on March 20 he could say that he would not have Edmund Sewall be a "vulgar Cupid for a go-between" in his pursuit of Ellen,[48] on April 8 he is ready to "withdraw into the garret": "The most positive life that history notices has been a constant retiring out of life, a wiping one's hands of it, seeing how mean it is, and having nothing to do with it" (*J*, I: 133). Withdrawal from this "mean" life (and from such "meanness" as sexual rivalry) could even go so far as dissolution. "The wisest solution,"

Henry says on April 20, "is no better than dissolution" (*J*, I: 134). Certainly such a solution made Henry less vulnerable.

The dialectic between aggressive pursuit and yielding is nowhere more clearly shown than in the journal entries at the time of Ellen's visit to Concord in June of 1840. On June 19, Henry writes blissfully of the boat ride he has taken with Ellen: "The other day I rowed in my boat a free, even lovely young lady, and, as I plied the oars, she sat in the stern, and there was nothing but she between me and the sky. So might all our lives be picturesque if they were free enough, but mean relations and prejudices intervene to shut out the sky . . ." (*J*, I: 144). The "mean relations" may refer to the rivalry, which has "intervened" and therefore made his relationship with Ellen less picturesque than it otherwise could have been. In any case, Thoreau seems both peaceful and passionate as he basks in the haze of that boat ride: "The faint bugle notes which I hear in the west seem to flash on the horizon like heat lightning. Cows low in the streets more friendly than ever, and the vote of the whip-poor-will, born over the fields, is the voice with which the woods and moonlight woo me" (*J*, I: 144). The next paragraph is a flashback to the Concord-Merrimack trip: "I shall not soon forget the sounds which lulled me when falling asleep on the banks of the Merrimack" (*J*, I: 144). By juxtaposition, Henry associates his feeling for Ellen with the trip, when he had shared with John both a tent and a boat—the very same boat Ellen shared with him the "other day." Thoreau concludes his writing on June 19 with one of his most aggressive images: "I should be contented if the night never ended, for in the darkness heroism will not be deferred, and I see fields where no hero has couched his lance" (*J*, I: 145). Surely this image of the hero couching his lance has sexual connotations. Taking into account its proximity to Thoreau's reflections on Ellen Sewall, it may represent his less than "pure" desire for Ellen and his sense that he may still entertain the possibility of aggressively pursuing this "lovely young lady."

However, the very next day, as if realizing the impurity of his intentions and the emotional necessity to leave the field open to his brother, Thoreau says,

> If we only see clearly enough how mean our lives are, they will be splendid enough. Let us remember not to strive upwards too long, but sometimes drop plumb down the other way, and wallow in meanness. From the deepest pit we may see the stars, if not the sun. Let us have presence of mind enough to sink when we can't swim. At any rate, a carcass had better lie on the bottom than

float an offense to all nostrils. It will not be falling, for we shall
ride wide of the earth's gravity as a star, and always be drawn
upward still, ... and so, by yielding to universal gravity, at length
become fixed stars. (*J*, I: 146)

Henry's initiative in pursuing Ellen is accompanied by guilt; therefore,
it is less threatening not to "strive upwards too long"; if one who
"falls" into the pit "wallows in meanness," one also may be drawn upward and become a "fixed star." "Yielding to universal gravity" (and
to his elder brother) is thus seen ultimately as a means of transcendence.
Almost immediately following in the journal of June 20, Thoreau reflects, "There are two ways to victory, —to strive bravely, or to yield.
How much pain the last will save we have not yet learned" (*J*, I: 147).
Henry appears to be aware of his dilemma: if he "strives bravely," he
will feel "mean" and guilty. If he yields, he will salve these feelings.
But will yielding be a "total victory," or will he experience other kinds
of pain (loss, anger, bitterness)? He has not yet learned the answer.
The next day, perhaps thinking again of the Concord-Merrimack trip,
he says, "I shall not soon forget my first night in a tent, —how the distant barking of dogs for so many still hours revealed to me the riches
of the night. Who would not be a dog and bay the moon?" (*J*, I: 147).
If he gives up Ellen, he most surely will be such a dog, baying at the
moon, bemoaning his loss. Because he is vulnerable to deep guilt feelings and fears of retribution if he does *not* yield, he prepares himself to
accept the loss—even if that means being "ruined": "I am content, I
fear, to be quite battered down and made a ruin of. I outgeneral myself
when I direct the enemy to my vulnerable points" (*J*, I: 151). For
solace Henry can turn to nature and invoke the virtues of waiting
("The landscape, by its patient resting there, teaches me that all good
remains with him that waiteth"—*J*, I: 152) and perseverance: "With
noble perseverance the dog bays the stars yonder. I too, like thee,
walk alone in the strange, familiar night, my voice, like thine, beating
against its friendly concave; and barking I hear only my own voice"
(*J*, I: 152).

After Ellen finished her June visit in Concord, John reciprocated
by visiting her in Scituate. As Harding suggests,[49] Henry's journal
entry of June 29 is probably an "envious" response to his brother's
situation and an expression of his estrangement from John: "Of all
phenomena, my own race are the most mysterious and undiscoverable.
For how many years have I striven to meet one, even on common
manly ground, and have not succeeded!" (*J*, I: 155). Though there

may be a trace of envy in this remark, Thoreau's writings in early and mid-July strongly suggest that he had more or less resigned himself to losing Ellen and that he was turning to other forms of identity-definition, other "inheritances" to compensate for his loss. If John had marched off to Scituate, Henry would begin marching to a different drummer. "A man's life," he says (in language and imagery which would be used again in *Walden*), "should be a stately march to a sweet but unheard music" (*J*, I: 156). Writing would be his salvation but he must not expect instant fame or wealth to accompany genius: "Let not the artist expect that his true work will stand in any prince's gallery." His life could have worth if he lived it heroically: "By earnest toil in the heat of the noon, let us get ready a rich western blaze against the evening of our lives" (*J*, I: 159). In spite of his loss, he must avoid "meanness," be "grateful for every hour," and "accept what it brings"; in such a way he—"the brave man"—will be able to "run through all extremes with impunity" (*J*, I: 162, 164). If he could overcome valiantly the tests and trials of experience, his life itself would become a work of art. "Not how is the idea expressed in stone or on canvas, is the question, but how far it has obtained form and expression in the life of the artist" (*J*, I: 167). To gain that true independence for which he was striving, he must learn "to accommodate one's self to all times, and take advantage of all occasions." Any loss could with heroism be translated into a gain.

In July, John made his final and most fateful trip to Scituate. Given the frequency of his visits to this town—which was not as "close" to Concord as it is today—it seems altogether likely that he had been courting Ellen. Henry must have at least suspected that John was not interested in her only as a friend. On the occasion of the July visit, it is quite possible that John acknowledged to his brother that he was going to propose to the "lovely young lady." [50] On July 10 Thoreau realizes that he could not change his brother's mind, even if he tried: "I am powerless to bend the character of another; he is like iron in my hands" (*J*, I: 166).

The journal entry of July 12, in which Henry identifies "my elder brother" with fate, necessity, and the east (Ellen lived east of Concord), indicates that he had "surrendered" to John and was girding himself to accept the inevitable by converting it to "the good":

What first suggested that necessity was grim, and made fate so fatal? The strongest is always the least violent. Necessity is a sort of Eastern cushion on which I recline. I contemplate its mild, in-

flexible countenance, as the haze in October days. When I am
vexed I only ask to be left alone with it. Leave me to my fate. It
is the bosom of time and the lap of eternity; since to be necessary
is to be needful, it is only another name for inflexibility of good.
How I welcome my grim fellow and aspire to be such necessity
as he! He is so flexible, and yields to me as the air to my body!
I leap and dance in his midst, and play with his beard till he
smiles. I greet thee, my elder brother, who with thy touch en-
noblest all things. Must it be so, then is it good. Thou commandest
even petty ills by thy countenance. (*J*, I: 168)

Using all his intellectual and emotional energies, Henry is able, for the
moment, to reconcile himself to his fate; by welcoming the "grim fellow" with open arms, he manages to make necessity yield to *him*. He
was prepared for the "worst," which he would then proceed to make
the best of all worlds.

What he might not have been prepared for was that Ellen, after
first accepting John's proposal, refused him. Harding, who has had
access to all existing documentation, gives the most specific account of
the proposal:

> When he and Ellen went for a stroll along the beach, Aunt Pru-
> dence went along as chaperone. But when Prudence decided to
> rest on some rocks, John took the opportunity to propose as
> soon as they got out of hearing. Ellen, in surprise, accepted, but
> hardly had she returned home when she began to feel that she
> had made a mistake. She realized, she said, that it was not John
> but Henry whom she preferred. When her mother learned of the
> engagement, she insisted Ellen break it immediately, for she was
> certain that the news would break Mr. Sewall's heart. He was an
> old-line conservative Unitarian and disapproved strongly of Emer-
> son and his associates. Both Thoreau boys were too Transcen-
> dentalist to please him as potential sons-in-law. John accepted
> her new decision regretfully and when he returned home, sent
> her a crystal as a memento of their friendship.[51]

Suddenly, it must have seemed to Thoreau that the field was open for
him again. On the same day (July 19) that John came back from his
sojourn in Scituate, Henry exclaims, "These two days that I have not
written in my Journal, set down in the calendar as the 17th and 18th of
July, have been really an aeon in which a Syrian empire might rise and
fall. How many Persias have been lost and won in the interim? Night is

spangled with fresh stars" (*J*, I: 170). If Harding's chronology is correct, then this entry is presumably a response to the just-obtained knowledge that John had been unsuccessful in his courtship of Ellen. If John's "empire" had fallen, Henry's was on the rise; just as the night was "spangled with fresh stars," so were there stars of hope sparkling on Henry's horizon. A week later Thoreau would again notice that the "stars come out gradually in troops from behind the hills and woods" (*J*, I: 170). It is probable that John indicated—either by directly telling his brother or "wearing his heart on his sleeve"—that he had lost Ellen. Whether John told him at the time why he had been turned down cannot be known with absolutely certainty. In *A Week*, Thoreau writes cryptically, "I heard that an engagement was entered into between a certain youth and a maiden, and then I heard that it was broken off, but I did not know the reason in either case." [52] He may well have imagined that Ellen had turned down John because she loved *him*.

During the next few months, Thoreau faced a painful dilemma. Should he resume his pursuit of Ellen—and even ask her to marry him—or, in deference to his brother, should he refrain from any active courtship? After all, in pursuing Ellen he would be trying to succeed where his brother had failed (and would perhaps alienate himself from John); if he actually won Ellen's hand, he would be hurting and defeating his beloved elder brother. Furthermore, it is my contention that Thoreau's sense that he might defeat his brother (and indeed, Henry may have felt that he had already been partially successful in winning Ellen away from John) made the "conscious" Henry uneasy and reawakened the deeply buried guilts and fears surrounding his imagined victory (or Pyrrhic victory) over his father and the winning of his mother. In challenging John and wishing to take away what was "rightfully" his, Henry was in some sense reliving the guilt-laden oedipal project. He was a Cain intent on murdering an Abel, a Jacob outmaneuvering an Esau, but he was also an Oedipus in position to kill his father. If he defeated the "outward foe" for Ellen's hand, he might be victimized by such "inward foes" as guilt and anxiety. Henry devoted much energy to dealing—at least indirectly—with this dilemma in his journal. For the most part, he sought to justify to himself further pursuit of Ellen, but he was not free from hesitation and compunction.

If neither he nor his brother tried to win Ellen, they would no longer be rivals; the "war" would be concluded. However, Thoreau found himself dissatisfied with a state of peace. On July 30 he observes, "it is not to us the eve of a ten years' war, but of a sixty years' idleness and defeat" (M, 136). Thus a "ten years' war" is preferable to "idleness and defeat." Peace makes swords rusty and men passive: "Our peace is proclaimed by the rust on our swords, and an inability to draw them from their scabbards —She does not so much work as to keep these swords bright and sharp" (M, 137). No longer is Thoreau predisposed to associate bravery with yielding: he feels it justifiable to attack, even if his enemy has withdrawn: "Sometimes I think I could find a foe to combat in the morning mist, and fall on its rear as it withdraws sluggishly to its daylight haunts" (M, 138). If he is to continue his rivalry for the hand of a maiden, let this war at least be infused with a sense of chivalry: "Nor let our warfare be a boorish and uncourteous one, but a higher courtesy attend its higher rivalry, though not to the slackening of its sterner duties and severer discipline" (M, 142). Certainly Thoreau has adhered to the code of chivalry by giving John the first opportunity to propose. Now it is only fair that his rival in the competition be honorable and give him a chance to win what he once called the "tournament of love." The call to arms, "the distant din of conflict," was heard clearly by Thoreau "in the deepest silence" (M, 146); surely, Henry *wanted* to hear the "sound of the clarion and trumpet" because he could then march to that "unheard music"—and into Ellen's arms.

Perhaps in contemplation of that hope's fulfillment, he rejoices on August 4: "A wave of happiness flows over us like sunshine over a field" (M, 148). Quite probably with Ellen in mind (who lived at an "oriental"—eastern—distance from Concord), Thoreau remarks, "Music is a flitting maiden, who now lives just through the trees younder, and now at an oriental distance" (M, 148). In the "eastern horizon," he imagines (on August 8) seeing an "oriental city" where "men lead a stately, civil life . . . as poetical as the pastoral" (M, 149). That Thoreau follows these romantic visions with a memory of the Concord-Merrimack trip ("For the livelong day there skirts the horizon the dark blue outline of Crotched Mountain" —M, 150) once again suggests how closely thoughts of Ellen were related to that brotherly excursion. Lured by the prospect of having a "poetical" life with this "gentle soul," Thoreau cannot be content simply to accept peace, if such peace means giving up his hopes. On August 12 he says, "A brave soul will make these peaceful times dangerous—and dangerous times peaceful" (M, 152). In a poem on war and chivalry, he is anxious to assert that he is not one of those "puny men, afraid of war's alarms" (M, 153). Quite significant is the fact that Thoreau begins to discuss Sir Walter Ralegh on August 19.[53] Ralegh was not one to shrink from rivalries or from approaching "forbidden" women, and Thoreau clearly wishes to identify himself with that aggressiveness—as a soldier, as a writer, and (in so far as pen and sword have phallic connotations) as a lover: "He wields his pen as one who sits at ease in his chair, and has a healthy and able body to back his wits, and not a torpid and diseased one to fetter them. In whichever hand is the pen, we are sure there is a sword in the other" (M, 158).

There is a possibly eloquent gap in the *Journal* between August 28 and September 21; this break may well be an indication that Henry was preoccupied with Ellen—and such preoccupations were seldom explicitly admitted in the *Journal*. If Thoreau, reticent in these matters, did write about his problems during this period, he made certain that no one else (including scholars) would read his ruminations.[54]

In early September Ellen had been sent off by her parents to Watertown, New York to protect her from the advances of the Thoreau brothers. Nevertheless, her Aunt Prudence continued to write to her from Concord about Henry and John.[55] By late September, Thoreau's reflections on Ellen and John were accompanied by a sense of dark foreboding. Just as the image of a "hero couching his lance" could give rise to feelings of guilt and anxiety, so did all images of himself as the aggressor, pursuing Ellen with sword in hand, beget misgivings.

On September 25, he enters a disturbing experience into his journal:

> As I sat on the cliff today the crows, as with one consent, began to assemble from all parts of the horizon—from river and pond and field, and wood, in such numbers as to darken the sky—as if a netting of black beads were stretched across it—after some tacking and wheeling the center of the immense cohort was poised just over my head. Their cawing was deafening, and when that ceased the winnowing of their wings was like the rising of a tempest in the forest. But their silence was more ominous than their din. —At length they departed as sullenly as they came. (M, 161–62)

Earlier Henry had written of the bluebird as the augury of spring, and John (the bird-lover and builder of a bluebird box for Emerson) had been associated with bluebirds. Here, another kind of bird—the black crow—seems to be delivering a personal and much less auspicious augury to Thoreau. In fact, it could be hypothesized that Henry saw the blackbirds as John—the dark side of John—incarnate; as he watched the birds, he could imagine John as silently, sullenly, and ominously disapproving of his desire to court Ellen. The "elder brother" had become a black and fearful necessity, threatening retribution. In the "Natural History of Massachusetts" (1842), Thoreau would associate the crow with the Indian—and thus, it can be suggested, with John:

> I have seen it suggested somewhere that the crow was brought to this country by the white man; but I shall as soon believe that the white man planted these pines and hemlocks. He is no spaniel to follow our steps; but rather flits about the clearings like the dusky spirit of the Indian, reminding me oftener of Philip and Powhatan, than of Winthrop and Smith. He is a relic of the dark ages. By just so slight, by just so lasting a tenure does superstition hold the world over; there is the rook in England, and the crow in New England.[56]

Immediately following Thoreau's description of the blackbird scene, he reflects, "Prosperity is no field for heroism unless it endeavor to establish an independent and supernatural prosperity for itself." Rather than trying to win what the elder brother still covets, it is less threatening to establish an independent prosperity, to come into one's own inheritance—not the brother's. Thoreau goes on to forswear "worldly" success (which would include the winning of Ellen); the only way to succeed is to lose by the world's standards: "Defeat is heaven's success. He cannot be said to succeed to whom the world shows any favor." There is something wrong in gaining a victory by defeating another person: "When we rise to the step above," he says, "we tread hardest on the step below" (M, 162). Increasing the likelihood that Thoreau is in part talking about John throughout this passage is the fact that his very next sentence is "My friend must be my tent companion." John had always been Henry's best tent companion (including their week on the rivers), and Henry is deeply concerned that his elder brother remain his friend. However, in order to maintain the friendship (and not incur the wrath of his friend) he must forswear designs on Ellen. The next day (September 26), Thoreau observes, "Every author writes in the faith that his book is to be the final resting place of the sojourning soul and sets up his fixtures therein as for a more than oriental permanence" (M, 162). Given the earlier connotations of "orient" (the east-Scituate-Ellen), it is entirely possible that Thoreau is telling himself here that, as an "author" he may be able to rise above his romantic aspirations ("oriental performance"), become once again a "fixed star" with his brother, and thereby find true peace of mind, a "resting place" for his confused, sojourning soul. His dream of reconciliation with the "fathers" (and, by transference, with such father-figures as John) is poignantly expressed on October 5: "At night we recline, and nestle, and infold ourselves in our being. Each night I go home to rest. Each night I am gathered to my fathers. The soul departs out of the body, and sleeps in God, a divine slumber" (M, 167). While he was "gathered up to [his] fathers" in a wish-fulfilling dream, Henry remained anxious about his relationship to male-figures (particularly his brother) during his wakeful hours.

The evidence reveals that, in spite of his fear, anxiety, guilt, and ambivalence, Thoreau finally did muster the resolve to pursue Ellen and probably even to propose to her. Many journal entries in October and early November suggest that he was steeling himself for that romantic quest. At the end of a poem on October 14 he reflects, "For the iron will be hot / And my wages will be got" (M, 175). Although the "maiden" of an October 17 entry is a "him," it could well refer to Ellen; alternatively, or perhaps additionally, it might refer to Henry's fervent wish to keep John as a friend:

> In the presence of my friend I am ashamed of my fingers and toes.
> I have no feature so fair as my love for him. There is a more than
> maiden modesty between us. I find myself more simple and sin-
> cere than in my most private moment to myself. I am literally
> true *with a witness*.
>
> We would sooner blot out the sun than disturb friendship.
> (M, 176)

The following day, Henry remarks cryptically, "Some questions which are put to me, are as if I should ask a bird what she will do when her nest is built, and her brood reared" (M, 176). One wonders if these questions, perhaps posed by John, concerned whether Henry was considering establishing a "nest" with Ellen. There was, in any case, some secret which Henry was guarding: "I cannot make a disclosure—you should see my secret. —Let me open my doors never so wide, still within and behind them, where it is unopened, does the sun rise and set—and day and night alternate. —No fruit will ripen on the common" (M, 176–77). Canby believes that this entry was part of a letter to Ellen, because "you" in the *Journal* usually indicates the draft for a letter or lecture.[57] It is, however, also possible that the "you" might be John, his parents, or anyone else who had reason to be concerned about his courtship activities. Henry, of course, would have been reluctant to divulge the "secret" that he was about to write a letter of proposal to Ellen. That Henry did have Ellen on his mind is evidenced by his entry of October 19: "My friend dwells in the distant horizon as rich as an eastern city there." His "friend" was in the "distant horizon" of Watertown at this point, but he still associated her with the "east" (Scituate). The entry of October 25 seems to represent Henry's final grappling with the possibility of yielding before he takes the plunge into proposal: "To yield bravely is infinitely harder than to resist bravely. In the one course our sin assists us to be brave, in the other our virtue is alone" (M, 178).

On October 26 the exiled Ellen wrote to Prudence from Watertown: "You are not the only person in Mrs. Thoreau's family whom such scenes call to mind. What delightful walks we had together in Concord last summer, to the cliffs, etc. Oh, those were happy times. . . . What great work is Henry engaged in now? . . . Will the school go on as usual this winter?" [58] This letter indicates that Ellen still thought affectionately of the Thoreaus, and by no means had forgotten Henry. If Prudence had communicated the contents of the letter to Henry, then perhaps he was further encouraged to write an ardent note to Ellen. Whether or not he knew of the letter, Thoreau apparently set out to compose a love letter. One of Ellen's daughters later said, "I have heard that it was a 'remarkable and beautiful' letter, but it was destroyed either by Ellen or her father." [59] Harding argues [60] that his entry of November 1 was probably part of the draft:

The day is won by the blushes of the dawn.
I thought that the sun of our love should have risen as noiselessly as the sun out of the sea, and we sailors have found ourselves steering between the tropics as if the broad day had lasted forever. You know how the sun comes up from the sea when you stand on the cliff, and doesn't startle you, but every thing, and you too are helping it. (M, 178)

It is possible to interpret this entry as partially an expression of regret that the course of their love had not run more smoothly, that both he and John had fallen in love with her, that the day *had* to be won with "blushes" and the sunrise was not as noiseless as it would have been had there been no rivalry. On November 3 and 4 there are indications that Henry was in the process of writing (if he had not already completed) a letter confessing his love. "The truth is only contained, never withheld," he confides one day, and the next he says, "We may have secrets though we do not keep them" (M, 179).

While waiting for a reply from Ellen—who would write back to him two days later [61]—Henry set down in his journal a poem:

I'm guided in the darkest night
By flashes of auroral light,
Which over-dart thy eastern home
And teach me not in vain to roam.
The steady light on t'other side
Pales the sunset, makes day abide,
And after sunrise stays the dawn,
Forerunner of a brighter morn.

There is no being here to me
But staying here to be,
When others laugh I am not glad,
When others cry I am not sad,
But be they grieved or be they merry
I'm supernumerary.
I am a miser without blame
Am conscience stricken without shame.
An idler am I without leisure,

A busy body without pleasure.
I did not think so bright a day
Would issue in so dark a night.
I did not think such sober play
Would leave me in so sad a plight,
And I should be most sorely spent
Where first I was most innocent.

I thought by loving all beside
To prove to you my love was wide,
And by the rites I soared above
To show you my peculiar love.[62]

The ominous tone of the poem suggests that Thoreau anticipated rejection, or that his hopefulness was tempered by grave doubts and ambivalence. Perhaps Henry realized, after he had written the proposal, that he had not rid himself of the "inward foes." When he speaks of his "sad plight," he may be referring either to the anticipated rejection or to his sense that he had alienated John by proposing to Ellen. His "innocent" love ("There is no remedy for love but to love more") had been complicated by a rivalry that had left him "sorely spent" and had transformed a potentially bright game into "sober play." "Conscience stricken" but "without shame," Henry had sought the hand of Ellen: but his conscience would give him no rest in his "shameless" pursuit.

The final stanza of the poem seems to express Thoreau's sense that he, the "idler without leisure," the "busy body without pleasure," has not been able to communicate adequately to Ellen the nature of his "peculiar love." By November 9, he was turning away from romance to further consideration of his identity as a "traveller in Concord"; he would "stay here to be": "The biography of a man who has spent his days in a library, may be as interesting as the Peninsular campaigns. . . . If the cripple but tell me how like a man he turned in his seat, how he now looked out at a south window then a north, and finally looked into the fire, it will be as good as a tour on the continent or the prairies" (M, 181–82). Preparing for the worst, "crippled" by his excursion into romance, Thoreau needed to assert the value of other pursuits.

The "worst" must have come soon thereafter, in the form of a letter to Henry.[63] When Ellen received Thoreau's ardent entreaties by mail, she consulted with Mr. Sewall before answering. On the way back to Scituate from Watertown, she wrote to Prudence Ward on November 18: [64]

> Last week Tuesday, the day I sent my last letter to you I received one from Father. He wished me to write immediately in a *"short, explicit* and *cold* manner to Mr. T."* He seemed very glad I was of the same opinion as himself with regard to the matter. I wrote to H.T. that evening. I never felt so badly at sending a letter in my life. I could not bear to think that both those friends whom I have enjoyed so much with would now no longer be able to have the free pleasant intercourse with us as formerly. My letter was very short indeed. But I hope it was the thing. It will not be best for either you or me to allude to this subject in our letters to each other. Your next letter may as well be to Mother perhaps, or Edmund. By that time the worst of this will be passed and we can write freely again. I do feel so sorry H. wrote to me. It was such a pity. Though I would rather have it so than to have him say the same things on the *beach* or anywhere else. If I had only been at home so that Father could have read the letter himself and have seen my answer, I should have liked it better. But it is all over now. We will say nothing of it till we meet. . . . Burn my last.[65]

Thoreau must have received this "short, explicit, and cold" letter by November 15; in his journal he expends much energy trying to transcend the pain: "Over and above a man's business there must be a level of undisturbed serenity, only the more serene as he is the more industrious—as within the reef encircling a coral isle, there is always an expanse of still water, where the depositions are going on which will finally raise it above the surface" (M, 184). But Henry would never forget Ellen. Not only did he continue to visit Ellen after her marriage to Reverend Joseph Osgood in 1844, but Sophia told her that shortly before Henry's death he had said, "I have always loved her." [66]

One legacy of the experience with Ellen was a deep sense of loss. Perhaps Ellen is the "turtle-dove" of the famous and mysterious passage on loss in *Walden*. Moreover, the affair confirmed Thoreau in his bachelorhood. [67] He felt an even greater ambivalence toward, and fear of, women; not only did he become even more wary of his dependence on women who could reject him, but he also grew more disgusted with his own romantic and sexual desires. The episode with Ellen was tinged with transferences from the oedipal past: just as he had competed with his father for the only "available" woman, so had he competed with his elder brother for a woman to whom they were both attracted. If John was a father-figure, then Ellen (and all possible mates) was in some sense a mother, and Thoreau's conscience told him it was forbidden to desire one's mother. Like Hamlet, he could say in the aftermath of this romantic experience, "Man delights not me—nor woman either" and "I say we will have no more marriage." [68] After this experience, he turned almost exclusively to such older women as Lucy Jackson Brown and Lidian Emerson for comfort, affection, and understanding. At least on a conscious level, these relationships were safer and purer, even if there was an underlying libidinal component to his feelings. His attachment to these women also allowed Thoreau to deny that he was deeply and "impurely" attached to his own mother. Thus, they were substitute mothers as well as substitute romantic objects.

The loss of Ellen was not ultimately as critical as the fact that he had competed with his brother for her affections. The most crucial legacy of this rivalry was an agonizing sense of guilt, remorse, and anxiety and the accompanying need—greatly intensified—for purification. We cannot know if John was deeply hurt by the rivalry and the rejection by Ellen; if he did communicate his hurt, directly or indirectly, to his younger brother, this would have exacerbated Henry's psychic suffering. Canby speculates that the younger brother's proposal "had once for all ended a relationship between Thoreaus and Sewalls which John may have felt with justice had a promise for the future. Ellen, though she had broken the engagement, was still corresponding with him, still keeping Concord in her heart." [69] Thus, John may have seen Henry's proposal as dashing any last hopes he may have had to be close to Ellen. The elder brother may have believed that she had turned him down primarily because her conservative father thought him to be a "Transcendentalist"; John may have felt that Henry was responsible for giving Mr. Sewall the impression that both Thoreau brothers were radically Transcendental. While John undoubtedly shared some of Henry's beliefs, he was by no means as radical as his brother. After all, Henry had said in a letter to his sister Helen on June 13, 1840, "That letter to John, for which you had an opportunity doubtless to substitute a more perfect communication, fell, as was natural, into the hands of his 'transcendental brother.' " [70] If alternatively, John had interpreted Ellen's refusal as an indication that she really loved Henry (as has been hinted by Koopman and Harding), then he would have had all the more reason to feel hostile toward his younger brother, even if he did not explicitly acknowledge it. Whatever the case, Henry had only to *imagine* that he had hurt his brother deeply and irreparably for him to feel guilty. He may have suspected that his proposal was an act of aggression against his brother, that on some deep level he was wracked with competitive rage and had secretly wished to hurt the brother he loved.

It is entirely possible that Henry's proposal to Ellen was made with a measure of depth ambivalence. Even if he avidly thought that he wanted to be accepted, and if he was hurt by the refusal, it is likely that in a way he was relieved by the rejection. If Henry had *expected* that he might be rejected even before proposing, it may well indicate that he wanted to be punished somehow in order to allay his guilt. The pain of the rejection itself could have been somewhat mitigated by the sense that he had not really triumphed over his brother. But the fact that he had asked her in the first place (and that Ellen had rejected and hurt his rival) left him with painful psychic scars which were never to be fully healed. Had John not died suddenly in January of 1842, the scars might have had a chance to heal; as it happened, John's death reopened and infected Henry's emotional wounds.

Aftermath

In the aftermath of his rivalry with John, Henry was plagued by a sense of guilt and sinfulness; confronted with these "inward foes," he urgently sought to purify himself and to create an identity which would bring him peace and satisfaction.[71] The journal entries became longer, as if Thoreau were trying to establish a compensatory intimacy with words and with himself, to sublimate his sexual desires.[72] How revealing it is that, on December 2, over two weeks after his last recorded journal entry, he yearningly reflects on the purifying qualities of water—and most especially of Walden:

> The lake is a mirror in the breast of nature, as if there were there nothing to be concealed. All the sins of the wood are washed out in it.... I love to consider the silent economy and tidiness of nature, how after all the filfth of the wood, and the accumulated impuritie[s] of the winter have been rinsed herein, this liquid transparency appears in the spring.... I should wither and dry up if it were not for lakes and rivers.... The thought of Walden in the woods yonder makes me supple jointed for the duties of the day. Sometimes I thirst for it. (M, 185–86)

It is as if such a baptism would allow him to return to a pre-oedipal (and pre-rivalry) past, to possess unambivalently an object of love. Two days later, Thoreau is still thinking of the pond: "The opposite shore of the pond seen through the haze of a September afternoon, as it lies stretched out in grey content, answers to some streak in me" (M, 187). In the coming years, Walden Pond would be associated more and more with the possibilities of self-purification and repentance.

More generally, Thoreau would seek purity in, and intimacy with, the natural world as an escape from the impurities of humanity and of himself; by turning to nature he could sublimate whatever seemed sinful. On December 10 he observes, "It is my own fault that he [the otter] must thus skulk across my premises by night. —Now I yearn toward him—and heaven to me consists in a complete communion with the otter nature" (M, 187).

However, even nature, from one point of view, was not pure enough to satisfy a Thoreau wracked with conflict and self-disgust. While in one respect Henry turned to nature for self-purification, he also discovered that he wished to rise above a nature which was itself "unclean." Using imagery reminiscent of Hamlet's disgusted discourses on grossness and corruption, Thoreau—perhaps contemplating his own death—says,

> How may a man most cleanly and gracefully depart out of nature? At present his birth and death are offensive and unclean things. Disease kills him, and his carcass smells to heaven. It offends the bodily sense, only so much as his life offended the moral sense. It is the odor of sin.

His carcass invites sun and moisture, and makes haste to burst forth into new and disgusting forms of life with which it already teemed. It was no better than carrion before but just animated enough to keep off the crows. The birds of prey which hover in the rear of an army are an intolerable satire on mankind, and may well make the soldier shudder. The mosquito sings our dirge—he is Charon come to ferry us over the styx—He preaches a biting homily to us. He says put away beef and pork—small beer and ale, and my trump shall die away and be no more heard. The intemperate cannot go nigh to any wood or marsh but he hears his requiem sung—all nature is up in arms against him. He who will dance must pay the fiddler. Gnats and mosquitoes are the original imps and demons....

May we not suffer our impurities gradually to evaporate in sun and wind, with the superfluous juices of the body, and so wither and dry up at last like a tree in the woods, which possesses a sort of embalmed life after death, and is as clean as the sapling or fresh buds of spring. (M, 188–89)

Thoreau's attitude toward nature was, then, paradoxical. The "poet-naturalist" would find himself saying in the "Higher Laws" chapter of *Walden*, "Nature is hard to overcome, but she must be overcome."

Journal entries of middle and late December show Thoreau once again struggling, with renewed force after the rivalry with his brother, to maintain his dreams of glory without provoking guilt, seeking to "rise" without "treading hardest on the step below." As formerly, paradox becomes the vehicle for dealing with ambivalence. On December 15, he says, "The most upright man is he that most entirely reclines—(the prone recline but partially). By his entire reliance is he made erect" (M, 191). The erect yet humble pine tree can be identified with "great men"—and Thoreau can identify himself with the pine:

Yonder pine stands like Caesar. I see Cromwell, and Jesus, and George Fox in the wood, with many savages beside.... So the forest is full of attitudes, which give it character. In its infinite postures I see my own erectness, or humbleness—or sneaking.... The fair proportions of a great man like those of a tree are but the balancing of his accidents[,] the vicissitudes are his sun[,] wind, and rain." (M, 192)

Gibbon had "very little greatness" because he was "ambitious and vain"

(M, 193), but George Washington was a "proper Puritan hero"; Thoreau finds "great" not only "his behavior in field and in council" but his "contented withdrawal to private life." Thinking of his own situation, Henry says admiringly of Washington, "He could advance and he could withdraw" (M, 196–97). In order to be "great," one need not be a celebrated and successful hero: "We want great peasants more than great heroes. . . . The great dwell in cottages on the moor, whose windows the sun visits from day to day with his ray, and of their greatness none knoweth but that there they dwell" (M, 200). On December 31 Thoreau reflects that "another man's sin never made me sad, it was my own"; as if in response to that sense of sin, he argues that "aspiration" must be accompanied by "respiration": "Every time he steps buoyantly up—he steps solidly down again, and stands the firmer on the ground for his independence upon it" (M, 202).

It was necessary for Thoreau to convince himself that there was something positive, some compensation, in every negative feeling or experience. If he was "fretful" and "despondent," he could claim that there was a "total disinterestedness and self-abandonment . . . that few attain to" in the experience of these feelings (M, 209). Positive action (including writing, since on January 13 he says, "Who keeps a journal is purveyor for the Gods") could prevent disturbing emotions from rising to the surface: "Each hearty stroke we deal with these outward hands, slays an inward foe" (M, 210). Convincing himself that "A true happiness never happened, but rather is proof against all haps," he is able to state, "I would not be a happy, that is, a lucky man, but rather a necessitated and doomed one" (M, 213). Happiness, he would say, is made of "gossamer and floating spider's webs" (M, 216). By elaborate effort he seeks to make something positive out of the uneasy sense that he is still a "parcel of vain strivings"—in love now as well as in vocation. The "dull prosaic evening" of delay, of moratorium, can also be perceived as the "wealthiest" of times:

> After so many years of study I have not learned my duty for one hour. I am stranded at each reflux of the tide—and I who sailed as buoyantly on the middle deep as a ship, am as helpless as a muscle on a rock. I cannot account to myself for the hour I live. Here time has given me a dull prosaic evening, not of kin to Vesper or Cynthia—a dead lapse—where time's stream seems settling into a pool—a stillness not as if nature's breath were held but expired. But let me know that such hours as this are the

wealthiest in time's gift — It is the insufficiency of the hour, which
if we but feel and understand, we shall reassert our independence
then. (M, 213)

Significantly, the "dead lapse" becomes exalted in its own right; because of the "insufficiency of the hour," delay is the most viable and
fruitful alternative. If he has not yet learned his duty, at least he is independent, not of kin to, or controlled by, Cynthia Thoreau.

Thoreau's capacity to find redeeming qualities in unpleasant experiences was almost limitless. Unquestionably referring to his broken
love affair with Ellen, he makes a classic statement of sublimation: "to
sigh under a cold cold moon for a love unrequited, is to put a slight
upon nature; the natural remedy would be to fall in love with the moon
and the night, and find our love requited" (M, 215). Thoreau literally
fulfilled his own prescription and fell in love with nature. The loss of
Ellen is certainly one major disappointment to which Henry refers in
his credo on compensation of the next day: "Disappointment will make
us conversant with the nobler part of our nature, it will chasten us, and
prepare us to meet accident on higher ground the next time —As
Hannibal taught the Romans the art of war. So is all misfortune only a
stepping-stone to fortune." Rather than viewing these "desultory moments" as worthless, Thoreau yearns to see them as "a step before me
on which I should set foot, and not stumbling blocks in the path. —To
extract its [misfortune's] whole good I must be disappointed with the
best fortune, and not be bribed by sunshine nor health" (M, 216).

There is evidence that Thoreau continued to be deeply troubled
about his relationship with John; indeed, it may be hypothesized that
the two brothers were not as close to each other as they had been in
the past, that their friendship had deteriorated since the rivalry for
Ellen. They continued to teach side by side and to live in the same
house: there was no way to avoid one another or forget that each had
inflicted hurt on the other. In a journal entry of January 21, Henry—
upset by his sense of alienation from his beloved brother—seeks to assure himself that the wrongs will be redressed, the wounds healed: "If
I have unintentionally injured the feelings of any—or prophaned their
sacred character, we shall be necessitated to know each other better
than before,—I have gained a glorious vantage ground then. And to the
other, the shaft which carried the wound, will bear its own remedy
with it, for we cannot be prophaned without the consciousness that we
have a holy fane for our asylum somewhere" (M, 217). As if the strains
of teaching and living alongside his brother (and being compared with

him) were too much, he remarks on January 24, "I almost shrink from the arduousness of meeting men erectly day by day" (*J*, I: 174). Considered the less responsible of the Thoreau brothers by the community, he wishes—at least figuratively—to give up the responsibilities of the school:

> Like overtasked schoolboys, all my members and nerves and sinews petition Thought for a recess, and my very thighbones itch to slip away from under me.... I exult in stark inanity, leering on nature and the soul. We think the gods reveal themselves only to sedate and musing gentlemen. But not so; the buffoon in the midst of his antics catches unobserved glimpses, which he treasures for the lonely hour. When I have been playing tomfool, I have been driven to exchange the old for a more liberal and catholic philosophy. (*J*, I: 175–76)

Though he may appear to be a buffoon or even a madman to townspeople, he acknowledges there is a method to his madness. The following day (January 25), Thoreau reveals his restlessness when he proclaims that he feels "the migratory instinct strong in me."

An extraordinary entry on January 26 suggests just how fully his anxieties concerning John had permeated his conscious and unconscious mind. He and his brother were to debate at the Lyceum with Alcott whether "forcible resistance is justifiable," [73] which was an issue that had consumed Thoreau's attention in his rivalry with John. On the day before the debate Thoreau described a haunting dream:

> I had a dream last night which had reference to an act in my life in which I had been most disinterested and true to my highest instinct but completely failed in realizing my hopes; and now, after so many months, in the stillness of sleep, complete justice was rendered me. It was a divine remuneration. In my waking hours I could not have conceived of such retribution; the presumption of desert would have damned the whole. But now I was permitted to be not so much a subject as a partner to that retribution. It was the award of divine justice, which will at length be and is even now accomplished. (*J*, I: 177)

Thoreau would later report that this dream (or a remarkably similar one) occurred on the Concord-Merrimack trip and concerned a "difference with a Friend, which had not ceased to give me pain"; in the dream, "ideal justice was at length done me for his suspicions, and I received the compensation which I had never obtained in my waking hours." [74] The "Friend" is unquestionably his brother. The "act" of "many months" ago in which he "had been most disinterested" refers to his decision to yield to John (rather than offer "forcible resistance") in the competition for Ellen. However John was unable to "win" her and Henry himself proposed to her. As previously argued, the younger brother's actions may have alienated John: not only had Henry pursued the woman he loved, but he also, by proposing, made sure that his elder brother would get no second chance.[75] Henry may have felt that he had "unintentionally injured" John's feelings, but John was nevertheless "suspicious" of his brother's motivations (or, at least, Henry *imagined* that his "Friend" was suspicious). Thoreau had completely failed in realizing his hopes—he had not, by his unselfishness, helped John to win Ellen; neither had he won her himself. In the process he had alienated his dearest friend, companion, and fellow "brave." One wonders what form the "complete justice," "divine remuneration," or "retribution" took in the dream. Whatever the case, Thoreau takes pains to deny that the "retribution" involved any hurt or violence to his brother: "In the compensation of the dream, there was no implied loss to any, but immeasurable advantage to all" (*J*, I: 177). If, in a previous dream, Thoreau had been "gathered to his fathers," in this wish-fulfilling dream he had been reconciled with John.

Yet it must be remembered that in his "waking hours" he had *not* received an emotionally satisfying, guilt-allaying "compensation." On January 28, Thoreau once again seems to be responding to that "difference with a Friend" alluded to in the dream:

> No innocence can quite stand up under suspicion, if it is conscious of being suspected. In the company of one who puts a wrong construction upon your actions, they are apt really to deserve a mean construction. While in that society I can never retrieve myself. Attribute to me a great motive, and I shall not fail to have one; but a mean one, and the fountain of virtue will be poisoned by the suspicion....

Advising his friend how he wishes to be treated he continues:

> I would meet men as the friends of all their virtue, and the foes of all their vice, for no man is the partner of his guilt. If you suspect me you will never see me, but all our intercourse will be the politest leave-taking; I shall constantly defer and apologize, and postpone myself in your presence. The self-defender is accursed in the sight of gods and men; he is a superfluous knight, who

serves no lady in the land.... As for apologies, I must be off with the dew and the frost, and leave mankind to repair the damage with their guaze screens and straw. (*J*, I: 178)

In this passage, Thoreau struggles to deny that he who sought to serve one particular lady from Scituate is the "partner of his guilt," but he is not able to convince himself of his innocence. If he wishes to be "off with the dew and frost" rather than make apologies, he ultimately realizes that the "guilty never escape, for a steed stands ever ready saddled and bridled at God's door, and the sinner surrenders at last" (*J*, I: 188).

On February 8, Henry explicitly acknowledges that he is a "partner of his guilt," that he is unable to escape his "vice":

In our holiest moment our devil with a leer stands close at hand. He is a very busy devil. It gains vice some respect, I must confess, thus to be reminded how indefatigable it is. It has at least the merit of industriousness. When I go forth with zeal to some good work, my devil is sure to get his robe tucked up the first and arrives there as soon as I with a look of sincere earnestness which puts to shame my best intent....

I was never so rapid in my virtue but my vice kept up with me.... Though I shut the door never so quick and tell it to stay at home like a good dog, it will out with me, for I shut in my own legs so, and it escapes in the meanwhile and is ready to back and reinforce me in most virtuous deeds....

Just as active as I become to virtue, just so active is my remaining vice. Every time we teach our virtue a new nobleness, we teach our vice a new cunning. When we sharpen the blade it will stab better as well as whittle. The scythe that cuts will cut our legs. We are double-edged blades, and every time we whet our virtue the return stroke straps our vice. And when we cut a clear descending blow, our vice on tother edge rips up the work. Where is the skillful swordsman that can draw his blade straight back out of the wound? (*J*, I: 207–8)

In a general sense, this passage illuminates the conflict-ridden nature of Thoreau's psyche. He must continually battle against the inner enemy; unable to destroy or hide from the devilish assaults of vice, he is beseiged with guilt. Only eternal vigilance can prevent vice from decisively winning the war and guilt from entirely ravishing the countryside and overwhelming consciousness. The concerns of the above pas-

sage may also be related to Thoreau's dream of January 26 and his dilemma with regard to John and Ellen. Even though he had intended to
be virtuous in his relations with brother and young woman, he recognized that he had caused hurt and heartbreak; he knew only too well
that his "disinterestedness" was accompanied by devilish feelings of
jealousy, combativeness, selfishness. He had hoped to remain true to his
"higher instinct," but he eventually wounded John with his "double-
edged blade." [76] John could not forget the wound—he remained "suspicious." Henry, to his dismay, could not allay his brother's—or his
own—doubts about his motivations; he could not "draw the blade
straight back out of the wound." When John accidently cut himself
with a razor blade the following year and died of lockjaw, Thoreau
sensed, in some shadowy corner of his mind, that it was he who had
wielded the fatal blade.

Living and teaching alongside John, Thoreau was daily reminded
that he was the partner of his guilt. He had affirmed, on February 2,
that there was nothing more important that the "good opinion of your
friend"; he came to realize that his most valued friend, who had for a
time been his "outward foe" for the hand of Ellen, had made his struggle with the "inward foes" all the more arduous. The battleground of
Thoreau's mind was bloody and dangerous. On February 13 he remarks
in his journal, "We have nothing to fear from our foes; God keeps a
standing army for that service; but we have no ally against our friends,
those ruthless vandals whose kind intent is a subtler poison than the
Colchian, a more fatal shaft than the Lydian" (J, I: 213–14). A "difference with a Friend" was far more painful than combat with an unambivalently hated foe. When one is at odds with a beloved friend one
must fight off the inward foes of guilt and anxiety. The poison is virulent
because it invades one's very bloodstream; the wound is all the more
damaging because it causes internal bleeding. Indeed, Henry's ill-health
during this period [77] may be partially attributed to the subtle poisons
and internal hemorrhaging caused by that "ruthless vandal," his dearest
friend. On January 19, Thoreau had said, "Sickness is civil war—We
have no external foes—even death will take place when I make peace
with my body—and set my seal to that treaty which transcendental
justice has so long required" (M, 215). With his resistance low, the
"civil war"—which often pits brother against brother—had escalated by
February 14 into a case of bronchitis. Although he says that "sickness
should not be allowed to extend further within us to preserve unin-
terrupted the continuity of serene hours," his inward foes are at his
heels. Thoreau recognizes that recuperation is a matter of escaping

guilt: "I shall never be poor while I can command a still hour in which to take leave of my sin" (*J*, I: 214). While sickness should not be *allowed* to "extend further than the body," it almost invariably *is* related to a sickness of soul in Thoreau's case. Nine days later he acknowledges the close linkage between body and soul. After arguing that "we do wrong to slight our sickness and feel so ready to desert our posts when we are harassed," he observes:

> There is a subtle elixir in society which makes it a fountain of health to the sick. We want no consolation which is not the overflow of our friend's health. We will have no condolence who are not dolent themselves. We would have our friend come and respire healthily before us; with the fragrance of many meadows and heaths in his breath, and we will inhabit his body while our own recruits.
>
> Nothing is so good medicine to sickness as to witness some nobleness in another which will advertise us of health. In sickness it is our faith that ails, and noble deeds reassure us. (*J*, I: 222)

The implication is that, to the extent that the "Friend" does *not* "respire healthily before us" (and John literally was of frail health), faith continues to ail and we remain sick. Earlier in this week of illness, he had raised the issue of that "difference with a Friend" which was ailing him: "Nothing will reconcile friends but love. They make a fatal mistake when they go about like foes to explain and treat with one another" (*J*, I: 218). As long as the friends remained even slightly unreconciled, the sickness could not be completely healed, the "civil war" would remain an uneasy stalemate. Thoreau's health would remain "precarious" in the coming months [78] as his faith continued to fail. After his brother's death, which made irreconcilable any differences with his friend, he would search desperately for a cure, for health.

As for these communities, I think I had rather keep bachelor's hall in hell than go to board in heaven. Do you think your virtue will be boarded with you? It will never live on the interest of your money, depend on it. The boarder has no home. — Thoreau, *Journal*, I

If Henry had been more than satisfied with his life situation when John and he had begun teaching together and living together under the parental roof, his satisfaction diminished greatly after the rivalry with his brother. It was no longer altogether pleasant to be in close proximity to John; in his presence, he could not escape thoughts of Ellen, the lingering sense that his brother was suspicious of him, his own hostility toward his much-loved brother, and his guilt. Disillusioned and dejected, he could no longer depend upon John—no matter how fervently he still loved him—to be his most significant companion and model, the "ordering principle" of his life. On January 28, 1841 Henry acknowledges that, in the "most momentous [circumstances], I have no ally but myself" (*J*, I: 180). Under the circumstances, it was necessary that he consider leaving the family household to avoid the painfulness of proximity. As he says on February 22, "Friends will be much apart; they will respect more each other's privacy than their communion, for therein is the fulfillment of our high aims and the conclusion of our arguments" (*J*, I: 220).

Perhaps the sense of having been let down by his brother accounts for his assertion on February 7 that the men in his life (his father as well as brother) have been inadequate: "I am not sure I should find out a really great person soon. He would be simple Thomas or Oliver for some centuries first.... A great man accepts the occasion the fates offer him" (*J*, I: 202-3). Thoreau sought to see himself as potentially that "great man"; yet he also needed to believe that there had been other such men. On the 12th he says,

Those great men who are unknown to their own generation are already famous in the society of the great who have gone before them. All wordly fame but subsides from their high estimate beyond the stars. We may still keep pace with those who have gone out of nature, for we run on as smooth ground as they.

The early and the latter saints are separated by no eternal interval.

The child may soon stand face to face with the best father. (*J*, I: 212–13)

The poignant implication is that he, the "child" who would be one of the "elect," has not yet met his "best father," that his own father and (by extension) elder brother have been lacking. Thoreau, however, did not wish to give up the hope that he would find his "best father" on this side of the grave. On February 7 he complains, "I would have men make a greater use of me," and the next day he indicates more specifically how he would wish to be "used": "I seek a man who will appeal to me when I am in fault. We will treat as gods settling the affairs of men. In his intercourse I shall be always a god to-day, who was a man yesterday. He will never confound me with my guilt, but let me be immaculate and hold up my skirts. Differences he will make haste to clear up, but leave agreements unsettled the while" (*J*, I: 206). John had "confounded" Henry with his guilt and could therefore not make the best "use" of him. His own father most assuredly would not treat him as a god. Cherishing the dream that Emerson will become his "best father," he muses—after discussing how he will put to use his journal—"As, when the master meets his pupil as a man, then first do we stand under the same heavens, and master and pupil alike go down the resistless ocean stream together" (*J*, I: 182). Then, on February 11 he adds, "I must serve a strong master, not a weak one. Help implies a sympathy of energy and effort, else no alleviation will avail" (*J*, I: 212). In the months to come, Emerson would give Thoreau ample opportunity to serve him—as a writer and as the handyman at his house. The journal of March 7 shows an admiring Henry perusing Emerson's "The Sphinx" and trying to glean lessons from his master's writing.

John had formerly served as a buffer between Henry and his mother; the elder brother's presence and companionship had allowed him to feel "manly" and independent. Together, the Thoreau brothers had been "braves"; they could not be turned into "squaws" by a talkative, dominating, emasculating mother. Now, with John no longer a wholly dependable comrade and with no apparent possibility of a marriage which would provide at least the outer trappings of independence, the mother was once again perceived by Henry to be a threatening force. Fears of dependence once more assumed prominence; it became necessary for Henry to assert vigorously his independence because he *did* feel so dependent. It is also likely that Cynthia Thoreau frequently reminded her son that he had not lived up to her wishes for him, thus making him all the more uncomfortable.[1] Knowing that he depended upon her for approval and affection, he also knew that she could induce in him feelings of guilt and shame. Henry's mother, then, was one of those whose "subtle poisons" could damage him.

Of course Thoreau could deny his dependence on home and mother by turning to an older woman, such as Lucy Jackson Brown. As early as January 4, 1841, he had written of her [2] in his journal, "I know a woman who is true to me and as incessant with her mild rebuke as the blue sky" (M, 207). But it was even more crucial to assert his independence from all women. On February 4 he speaks of a "cowardly yielding to young etiquette" and of giving up one's seat to a woman:

> When presumptuous womanhood demands to surrender my position, I bide my time, —though it be with misgiving, —and yield to no mortal shove, but expect a divine impulse. Produce your warrant, and I will retire; for not now can I give you a clear seat, but must leave part of my manhood behind and wander a diminished man, who will not have length and breadth enough to fill any seat at all. (*J*, I: 193–94)

Probably the most promising way to assert independence while remaining dependent, as well as to distance himself from John, was to escape the household but to stay in Concord. Additionally, such a solution would allow him to develop his identity as writer without constant distractions and to continue his close relationship with his mentor, Emerson. Indeed, during this period Thoreau frequently reflects on his identity as writer in his journal; on one occasion he refers to the riches which his journal will hold "after months or years" and on another he comments, "Nothing goes by luck in composition" (*J*, I: 225).

There is much evidence that Henry gave considerable thought to establishing his own home in the early part of 1841. Harding tells us that he thought of purchasing an old farm or renting land and building a cabin; such locations as the orchard side of Fair Haven Hill, the Cliff, the Weird Dell, and Baker Farm came under scrutiny as possible homes. On February 10 Thoreau reached the point of asking a farmer whether he could rent some land. The farmer agreed, but Henry had second thoughts about becoming tied down to a parcel of land.[3] As he would warn himself on March 27, "I must not lose any of my freedom by being a farmer and landholder. Most who enter on any profession are doomed men" (*J*, I: 241–42). In a letter to his mother on February 22, George Ward (the younger brother of Prudence) wrote, "Henry will have to take care that he don't hurt himself seasoning—a very common occurrence. When he gets settled on his farm—I should like to look in upon him." [4] Regardless of the dangers of "seasoning," Thoreau yearned, albeit ambivalently, to take leave of the triviality and meanness of home life; on February 19, he says, "When I contemplate a hard and bare life in the woods, I find my last consolation in its untriviality. Shipwreck is less distressing because the breakers do not trifle with us" (*J*, I: 217). The prospect of launching his own ship, "cutting away" from the dock, filled him with hope and reawakened dreams of glory: "My future deeds bestir themselves in me and move grandly towards a consummation, as ships go down the Thames. A steady onward motion I feel in me, as still as that, or like some vast, snowy cloud, whose shadow first is seen across the fields. It is the material of all things loose and set afloat that makes my sea" (*J*, I: 225).

It is probable that Thoreau was further prodded to leave the Parkman House by an invitation from George Ripley to join the Brook Farm community.[5] He proclaimed himself far too independent to live in such a place: on April 9 he would boast that "true reform can be undertaken any morning before unbarring our doors. It calls no convention. I can do two thirds the reform of the world myself" (*J*, I: 247). But the establishment of Brook Farm must have been perceived by Henry as a challenge to him to give up conventional living arrangements. In response to the invitation, Thoreau writes in his journal on March 3,

> As for these communities, I think I had rather keep bachelor's hall in hell than go to board in heaven. Do you think your virtue will be boarded with you? It will never live on the interest of your money, depend upon it. The boarder has no home. In heaven I hope to bake my own bread and clean my own linen. The tomb is the only boarding-house in which a hundred are served at once. In the catacomb we may dwell together and prop one another without loss." (*J*, I: 227)

The unkind allusions to "boarding-houses" reveal that, while Thoreau was not anxious to live in a cooperative utopian community, he was most anxious to escape his mother's home—which was, in fact, a boardinghouse. He is painfully conscious that he must strike out on his own in an entry of March 13: "How alone must our life be lived! We dwell on the seashore, and none between us and the sea. Men are my merry companions, my fellow-pilgrims, who beguile the way but leave me at the first turn in the road, for none are travelling *one* road so far as myself." He continues, in the same passage, "Parents and relations but entertain the youth; they cannot stand between him and his destiny" (*J*, I: 239). Though young Thoreau was aware that "almost in proportion to the sincerity and earnestness of the life will be the sadness of the record" (*J*, I: 239), he maintained his determination to break away. We get the sense that his home life was becoming more and more unpleasant the longer he deferred leaving it. On March 19 he notes with obvious distaste for his own household: "No true and brave person will be content to live on such a footing with his fellow and himself as the laws of every household now require. The house is the very haunt and lair of our vice. I am impatient to withdraw myself from under its roof as an unclean spot. There is no circulation there; it is full of stagnant and mephitic vapors" (*J*, I: 240). Contaminated by his relations with family members, seeking purity and independence, he could gain some relief by retiring to his chamber (*J*, I: 240–41), but for the most part such retirement could not stem the rising feelings of stagnation, as admitted to on March 30: "I find my life growing slovenly when it does not exercise a constant supervision over itself. Its duds accumulate" (*J*, I: 242).

The fact remained, however, that for all his protests Thoreau had not yet moved out. External circumstances and internal ambivalence combined to make it difficult for Henry to break away. If there was one single event which spurred him to leave, it was the closing of the Thoreau school on April 1 because of John's ill-health. Harding says,

> John had never been in hearty health. As early as 1833 he had suffered from nosebleeds so violent that he fainted. There were times when what he called "colic" confined him to the house all day. But tuberculosis was the real trouble. Frail and thin—he weighed only 117 pounds—he could stand the strain of teaching no longer. Since Henry did not care to carry on by himself, the doors of the school were closed and John left immediately on a tour of New Hampshire.[6]

So it was that less than six months after the traumatic Henry-John-Ellen affair, John became so ill that he had to give up teaching. As previously suggested, one possible source of guilt Henry had felt in relation to his brother even before the Ellen affair was John's frailty (a frailty that was psychologically mirrored in the "meekness" of Thoreau's father). When Henry felt hostile toward John and when he had "defeated" John in some respects, he might have fantasized that he was the *cause* of his brother's weakness—just as he might have imagined earlier that he was the cause of his father's meekness and submissiveness. These fantasies could have exacerbated Henry's guilt feelings. When John could no longer "stand the strain of teaching," so soon after the rejection by Ellen and the "difference with a Friend," Henry may well have imagined that he was responsible for the falling-off in his brother's health. Feelings of remorse—perhaps deeply hidden—ensued. Henry "did not care" to teach without his revered brother. John's illness gave Henry a relatively graceful way to bow out of teaching and concentrate on his writing. Perhaps Henry secretly feared that the community would not find the school acceptable without John as headmaster.[7] But he also may have been influenced to stop teaching by guilt feelings which told him he should not continue or succeed in this activity while the brother he had injured could no longer teach. In any case, it seems probable that Thoreau *could* have continued to teach successfully in the school, that he could have hired another teacher to take John's place at least temporarily. Had the school not closed, it is possible that Henry's educational career would have assumed more importance in his later life.

With his brother's illness and the sudden demise of the Thoreau school, Henry was faced with many of the same problems he had for a time solved when the school had opened. Once again, he had to confront squarely the problem of making a living. To be sure, he could still work in his father's pencil factory, but he did not want to be tied down to that enterprise, an Apollo bound to serve an Admetus. He had a higher destiny to fulfill. Furthermore, with John absent (or, upon returning from New Hampshire, still weak and unable to work), Thoreau was literally without a male figure in the house who could insulate him from his mother's rebukes (however kind in intent), her reminders that he was not living up to her expectations, her attempts to "control" his life. The "femininity" of the house was all the more apparent without John there. Add to this mixture the guilt that he felt as a result of his brother's illness and the accompanying need for purity, and we have ample reason to suspect that Henry thought it absolutely imperative to get out from under the family roof at this time.

Thoreau was so desperate that he, the erstwhile "traveller in

Concord," applied for an opening at the Perkins' Institute for the Blind in Boston; not surprisingly, he was turned down. Still acutely sensitive to the dangers of "success without identity," Henry refrained from applying to any other schools. On the day of the school's closing, he acknowledged in a poem that the sun was hidden behind the clouds, but that "foul weather shall not change my mind, / But in the shade I will believe what in the sun I loved" (*J*, I: 243). On April 5, he speaks of "this long series of desultory mornings" (with no teaching to keep him occupied and self-supporting) and of his need for a pure, "clean" life in a home of his own making: "I only ask a clean seat. I will build my lodge on the southern slope of some hill, and take there the life the gods send me. Will it not be employment enough to accept gratefully all that is yielded me between sun and sun? Even the fox digs his own burrow. If my jacket and trousers, my boots and shoes, are fit to worship God in, they will do" (*J*, I: 244). Two days later, while apparently thinking of buying the Hollowell farm, Thoreau struggles to make sense out of his prolonged adolescence:

> My life will wait for nobody, but is being matured still irresistibly while I go about the streets and chaffer with this man and that to secure it a living. It will cut its own channel, like the mountain stream, which by the longest ridges and by level prairies is not kept from the sea finally. So flows a man's life, and will reach the sea water, if not by an earthly channel, yet in dew and rain, overleaping all barriers, with rainbows to announce its victory. It can wind as cunningly and unerringly as water that seeks its level, and shall I complain if the gods make it meander? This staying to buy me a farm is as if the Mississippi should stop to chaffer with a clamshell. (*J*, I: 244–45)

Although he had serious reservations about committing himself to the buying of a farm, and asked himself, "What have I to do with plows? I cut another furrow than you see," Thoreau was on the verge of becoming a landowner. Once more, a woman would stand in the way of his independence. Harding indicates,

> [He] decided to purchase the Hollowell Place, just across Hubbard's Bridge on the Sudbury River, about two miles southwest of Concord village. Its real attractions, he thought, were that the nearest neighbor was a half a mile away and that its owner had permitted the house and barns to become dilapidated and the fields to grow up to birches. He feared that if he did not buy it soon,

the owner might "improve" it by cutting down the trees and getting out the rocks that filled the fields. They quickly came to terms and Thoreau was making a wheelbarrow to move his possessions when the owner returned and asked to buy the farm back since his wife had changed her mind, and offered Thoreau ten dollars for his trouble. Thoreau refused the ten dollars, but with some regret returned the property and began looking elsewhere.[8]

By so narrow a margin did Thoreau avoid becoming a farmer. In spite of the urgent need to break away from home, he was wary of the pitfalls and responsibilities of landholding. Somehow, even farming was too tame, too much of a threat to his identity as Transcendentalist and writer. On April 10, he observes, "I don't know but we should make life all too tame if we had our own way," and on the next day he adds, "A greater baldness my life seeks, as the crest of some bare hill, which towns and cities do not afford. I want a directer relation with the sun" (*J*, I: 248). As long as he continued to remain in Concord, and stay dependent on his mother, almost any living situation would appear too tame. There was something distasteful to him about the farms he had seen; he seemed discouraged and depressed after touring the countryside and bickering for land:

> I have been inspecting my neighbors' farms to-day and chaffering with the landholders, and I must confess I am startled to find everywhere the old system of things so grim and assured. Whereever I go the farms are run out, and there they lie, and the youth must buy old land and bring it to. Everywhere the relentless opponents of reform are a few old maids and bachelors, who sit round the kitchen fire, listening to the singing of the teakettle and munching cheese-rinds. (*J*, I: 249–50)

On April 18 he says with a hint of irritation, "My necessities of late have compelled me to study Nature as she is related to the farmer, —as she simply satisfies a want of the body" (*J*, I: 250). Thoreau, on the other hand, was impatient to get on with the cultivation of his spirit and writing gifts—tasks not entirely compatible with tilling the soil. Thus, on the same day he attempts to assure himself that, regardless of the obstacles, the seemingly never-ending delay, the "necessities," he would eventually come into his own: "our life is only a retired valley where we rest our packs awhile. Between us and our end there is room for any delay. It is not a short and easy southern way, but we must go over snow-capped mountains to reach the sun" (*J*, I: 250).

It is around this time, when Thoreau was trudging over "snow-capped mountains," that Emerson provided him with a halfway house, a glimpse of the sun, by offering him one year's room and board with his family in exchange for "what labor he chooses to do around the house." By April 26 Henry reported that he was "at R.W.E.'s." Such an arrangement allowed Henry to escape the vexations of his own house, to gain some measure of independence while avoiding final commitment to adult identity and responsibility, to be close to his "master," and to live at the heart and hearth of Transcendentalism. For the time being, Emerson could be the sympathetic father and "identity sponsor" he could not find at the Parkman House. Waldo was one man he would not mind serving; yet in the process of serving him, he also would be furthering his own lofty aspirations. Henry would have time to read widely in Emerson's well-stocked library (which contained, among other works, a collection of Oriental writings); he would also have much free time in which to write. He could develop his identity as lecturer, writer, and Transcendentalist in earnest, without the immediate worry of supporting himself financially. On his side, Emerson also believed he was benefitting from the arrangement. Rusk informs us that Waldo had been stirred by economic and social reforms such as Brook Farm. Even if he was not inclined to join that community, he still wished to experiment with some form of cooperative living. He thought to invite the needy Alcotts to live with him for a year of "labor and plain-living," but the plan did not come to fruition. Taking in Henry Thoreau as a boarder at least partially satisfied Emerson's need to experiment.[9] Moreover, the high priest of Transcendentalism did not show the same aptness working with his hands as he did working with words. Having recently lost Alexander McCaffery who had done chores around the house in exchange for board and education,[10] Emerson found Thoreau well-suited to take his place. His young friend could also be counted on to be the "man of the house," to care for his children and keep his wife Lidian company when he was away on lecture tours. Waldo valued Henry as a friend who could show him the beauties and mysteries of nature; as early as "Woodnotes" (1840), he had described Thoreau as a "forest seer." With Henry boarding in his home, Emerson would have the chance to encourage and to oversee his budding writing career at close range. He was anxious that Thoreau's promise be fulfilled and not only because he could be the "American Scholar" and artist that Emerson had prophesied. As has already been explained, Emerson hoped that his career could somehow compensate for the truncated careers and lives of Waldo's brothers and relieve his guilt feelings associated with their untimely deaths. Sherman Paul characterizes this first stay with Emerson as Henry's "most productive period as a poet." [11]

Thoreau must have been relieved and thankful when Emerson gave him the opportunity to move in. There is every indication that he repaid his benefactor's kindness in full during the remaining months of 1841; he did handyman's work in and around the house, became closely atttached to Emerson's wife and children (especially five-year-old Waldo), and maintained a warm friendship with Emerson. [12] But Henry knew that his stay at Emerson's was only a way-station on his trip to the sun, an interlude which would allow him to recover from the emotional traumas of the previous two years and to crystallize the sense of identity he had been evolving before the courtship of Ellen and the rivalry with John. In short, the period at Emerson's was to be the final stage of his "moratorium." He hoped to emerge from his stay at "R.W.E.'s" with a firm sense of identity, commitment, and destiny. He would not merely become "another Emerson": he would be prepared to be his own man.

As if to emphasize to himself that Emerson's house was not his ultimate home, he says on the day before he moves in, "There is all civilized life in the woods. The wildest scenes have an air of domesticity and homeliness, and when the flicker's cackle is heard in the clearings, the musing hunter is reminded that civilization has imported nothing into them" (J, I: 252). In the back of his mind was a wildness not to be found in the large, pleasant house on Lexington Street; even at Emerson's there was danger of becoming a "squaw"—especially for one who deep-down was so dependent. On April 26, the day of his arrival, he reasserts (as he feels anew his dependencies) his determination to be a "brave," to avoid entrapment in any house. Nature is the only "woman" he can trust:

> The charm of the Indian to me is that he stands free and uncon-
> strained in Nature, is her inhabitant and not her guest, and wears
> her easily and gracefully. But the civilized man has the habits of
> the house. His house is a prison, in which he finds himself op-
> pressed and confined, not sheltered and protected. He walks as
> if he sustained the roof; he carries his arms as if the walls would
> fall in and crush him, and his feet remember the cellar beneath.
> His muscles are never relaxed. It is rare that he overcomes the
> house, and learns to sit at home in it, and roof and floor and
> walls support themselves, as the sky and trees and earth. (J, I: 253)

Less than a week later, we find Thoreau once more girding himself against becoming too enamoured of his life at Emerson's. Such a "life in gardens and parlors is unpalatable" to him because it "wants rudeness and necessity to give it relish" (*J*, I: 256). He had said, on April 26, that it was a "great art to saunter": he had to learn to master that art, to avoid the quicksand of "civilization," if he was ever to reach the Holy Land of his dreams.

It was important to Thoreau that he conceive of himself as ever looking and moving westward. This self-conception allowed him to feel "wild" and independent even while living in the relatively tame environment of Emerson's and within walking distance of his mother. On May 2 he entered a poem, "Wachusett," into his journal. No longer protected from dependence by his relationship with John, he perceives Mount Wachusett as an alternative brother to whom he can literally look up and in whose presence he can feel brave and free. The mountain is apostrophied as "thou western pioneer/Who know'st not shame nor fear," who "Standest alone without society." If he has not been an absolutely worthy brother to John (and vice versa), then perhaps the mountain can provide satisfaction: "Upholding heaven, holding down earth, / Thy pastime from thy birth, / Not steadied by the one, nor leaning on the other; / May I approve myself thy worthy brother!" (*J*, I: 256–57). On May 9, he identifies himself with the pine which "stands in the woods like an Indian, —untamed, with a fantastic wildness about it" and whose needles "All to the west incline" (*J*, I: 258–59). Like the pine, Thoreau could be physically sedentary but still incline to the west. The final day of May, he further develops his sense that he can travel west while remaining in Concord: "It is a wide theatre the gods have given us, and our actions must befit it. More sea and land, mountain and valley here is, —a further West, a freshness and wildness in reserve when all the land shall be cleared" (*J*, I: 262). In a letter to Lucy Jackson Brown on July 21 he playfully counsels her to "go dwell in the West" so that he can fancy her "at evening dwelling far away behind the serene curtain of the West, —the home of fair weather."[13] But Thoreau himself had no intention of leaving his hometown; he was, in fact, pondering the creation of a poem to be entitled "Concord." "For argument," he says on September 4, "I should have the River, the Woods, the Ponds, the Hills, the Fields, the Swamps and Meadows, the Streets and Buildings, and the Villagers. Then Morning, Noon, and Evening, Spring, Summer, Autumn, and Winter, Night, Indian Summer, and the Mountains in the Horizon" (*J*, I: 282). Having committed himself to Concord, he needed to reassure himself that he could be an adventurer there; indeed, by writing about Concord, by subsuming the town in his writing, he could, like adventurers of old, conquer it.

The period at Emerson's was on the surface relatively placid and sociable. But a firmer conception of future directions was taking root in Thoreau's psyche; his "true character," he insisted, underlay all his words and actions, "as the granite underlies the other strata" (*J*, I: 257). He was aboil with the conviction that he could attain "greatness" if he but stuck to his course, however fraught with impediments. On May 6, he tells himself, "I shall not mistake the direction of my life; if I but know the high land and the main, —I shall know how to run. If a ridge intervene, I have but to seek, or make, a gap to the sea" (*J*, I: 258). Whenever he evaluated the extent of his development by societal criteria, he became impatient and self-accusatory. Therefore, he struggled not to judge the speed and quality of his own progress by the standards of the "bustling" and "hasty" era in which he lived, an era, he was learning, which could be cruel to sensitive and gifted souls: "Methinks history will have to be tried by new tests to show what centuries were rapid and what slow. Corn grows in the night" (*J*, I: 263). Although his progress might be considered slow by the "daylight" criteria of contemporary society, he assured himself that he was growing, that an abundant harvest was to be anticipated. Although the times were not "ripe" for the "Laws of Menu"—(*J*, I: 264) which he had been reading in Emerson's library—nor for his own kind of giftedness, he was ripening nonetheless by his own standards. "Truth," he says, "is such by reference to the heart of man within, not to any standard without. There is no creed so false but faith can make it true" (*J*, I: 276). Even in "midsummer"—before harvest—his thought "rustles . . . as if ripe for the fall," and he is able to "anticipate the russet hues and the dry scent of autumn, as the feverish man dreams of balm and sage" (*J*, I: 280). To protect himself from either self-condemnation or his community's, he found it necessary to "make my own time" (*J*, I: 294).

Thoreau, then, counseled himself to remain patient, to "keep the faith" that he would reach the sun, make it to the sea. The moratorium could be prolonged, final commitment postponed, as long as the *expectation* of eventual triumph was maintained. Given the long-standing and deeply-embedded *fear* of commitment to any one course of identity, it is not surprising that he was often tempted to make the moratorium an *end in itself*. Sometimes he speaks with such delight and reverence of the postponement that we suspect that he preferred

it to full commitment: "Some hours seem not to be occasion for anything, unless for great resolves to draw breath and repose in, so religiously do we postpone all action therein. We do not straight go
about to execute our thrilling purpose, but shut our doors behind us,
and saunter with prepared mind, as if the half were already done"
(*J*, I: 285). Preparation for fulfillment was thus fulfilling in itself.
There is much indication that Henry took great joy in being a "man
in reserve": the moment before committing one's forces to battle was
the most precious.[14] Indian summer was in some ways more enticing
than either the ripeness of fall or the abundance of true summer. On
September 8, he wrote to Lucy Brown: "It is nothing but Indian
Summer here at present. I mean that any weather seems reserved
expressly for our late purposes whenever we happen to be fulfilling
them. I do not know what right I have to so much happiness, but
rather hold it in reserve till the time of my desert." [15] Holding the
"happiness in reserve" is itself obviously a source of great happiness.
To Thoreau, a "man in reserve" was far preferable to one who had
unwisely dissipated his resources:

> If in any strait I see a man fluttered and his ballast gone, then I
> lose all hope of him, he is undone; but if he reposes still, though he
> do nothing else worthy of him, if he is still a man in reserve,
> then is there everything else worthy of him. The age may well
> go to pine itself that it cannot put to use this gift of the gods.
> He lives on, still unconcerned, not needing to be used. The great-
> est occasion will be the slowest to come. (*J*, I: 297–98)

Even by his own timetable, however, and in spite of his fears of
commitment, Thoreau was becoming impatient to live on his own
terms, to fulfill his mission rather than just dream of it. "The great
person," he said on May 31, "never wants an opportunity to be great,
but makes occasion for all about him" (*J*, I: 262). Though his very
desire for "greatness" had been a critical source of his identity-con-
fusion and had been in part responsible for the prolonged moratorium,
Henry was now anxious to seize the opportunity for greatness. The
thought of establishing his own home where he could get down to
writing—marginal to "civilization" but still in Concord—once again
took strong hold on his imagination. On July 21, he confesses to
Lucy Brown,

> I grow savager and savager every day, as if fed on raw meat,
> and my tameness is only the repose of untameableness. I dream

of looking abroad summer and winter, with free gaze, from some mountain-side, while my eyes revolve in an Egyptian slime of health, —I to be nature looking into nature with such easy sympathy as the blue-eyed grass in the meadow looks in the face of the sky. From some such recess I would put forth sublime thoughts daily, as the plant puts forth leaves.[16]

By the fall, Thoreau began to feel wary about his indebtedness to Emerson, father, and all others who had helped to support him. Contemplating the prospect of living on "some mountainside," he wished to feel under obligation to no one but "god":

> There is but one obligation, and that is the obligation to obey the highest dictate. None can lay me under another which will supersede this. The gods have given me these years without any incumbrance; society has no mortgage on them. If any man assist me in the way of the world, let him derive satisfaction from the deed itself, for I think I never shall have dissolved my prior obligations to God.... The truly beneficent never relapses into a creditor; his great kindness is still extended to me and is never done.... If any have been kind to me, what more do they want? I cannot make them richer than they are. (*J*, I: 279–80)

On September 8, he reiterates his determination not to be held to any obligation or service not consonant with his own destiny. Writing to Lucy Brown that he is "unfit for any practical purpose. . . . as gossamer for ship-timber," he indicates that while he may be a "pencil-maker tomorrow" and thus "can sympathize with God Apollo, who served King Admetus for a while on earth," he will "hold the nobler part at least out of the service." [17] Not only do these remarks reveal his sense that his father (and other male figures) had made him feel like an Apollo serving an Admetus; they also reveal the depth of Thoreau's resolution not to become like his father—who was himself answerable to creditors and to the "queenly" Mrs. Thoreau on many occasions. On October 18, Margaret Fuller wrote to him, "Let me know whether you go to the lonely hut." [18] Surely, he was seriously asking himself that question.

At some point during the fall of 1841, he wrote to Isaiah Williams, a former Concord teacher who had gone to Buffalo to study law, that he was "living with Mr. Emerson in very dangerous prosperity." [19] Prosperity meant danger to Thoreau partly because it threatened "success without identity." When Williams—who had lamented leaving

Concord, Emerson, and Transcendentalism in earlier letters—reported to Henry that "Time's devastating hand is beginning already to obliterate the traces of my youthful feelings—and I am becoming more & more contented with my present situation and feel less and less a desire inexorable to return and be a child once more," [20] Henry's sense of prosperity's dangers was fully aroused. He would not allow the "shades of the prison-house" to blot out *his* intimations of immortality.

By December, Thoreau's impatience to find his own home and to define his identity had reached its zenith. The falling snow gave him encouragement that he could find purity in "these degenerate days of men" (*J*, I: 293). On December 13 we find him reflecting that his only "repose" can be "in entire and healthy activity" (*J*, I: 293), such activity as he had envisioned for himself in his forest hideaway. He yearned, he said, for the "unexplored secrecy of the wood that charm[s] us and make[s] us children again" (*J*, I: 299). Then on December 24, he reveals the concrete plan he has in mind: "I want to go soon and live away by the pond, where I shall hear only the wind whispering among the reeds. It will be success if I shall have left myself behind. But my friends ask what I will do when I get there. Will it not be employment enough to watch the progress of the seasons? (*J*, I: 299). The following day he explicitly acknowledges his desire to end his prolonged moratorium: "I don't want to feel as if my life were a sojourn any longer. That philosophy cannot be true which so paints it. It is time now that I begin to live" (*J*, I: 299).

According to Harding, Thoreau was probably thinking of Sandy Pond in Lincoln, where he had spent six weeks in the summer of 1837 along with Charles Stearns Wheeler in his hut. However, Thoreau was unable to get permission from the Flints to build such a hut on their land. [21] It must not be discounted as a possibility that he was considering Walden Pond—certainly *the* pond in his previous writings —as a possible site even at this early date. In any case, had Thoreau established himself in a hut by the shores of *some* pond as early as 1842, he would have begun to live on his own terms much sooner than he actually did. While remaining uncommitted to the responsibilities of "civilized" adulthood and to work which is "too often threatening the pericarp of the heart as well as the head" (*J*, I: 300), he could have committed himself to his writing and to a "manly" and independent identity. He would have been escaping mother, father, Emerson, the community, while still within walking distance of them. Grieved at the thought of any "unmanly submissions" (*J*, I: 303), he could have felt free and "wild," while at the same time remaining dependent. Thoreau

would have had the opportunity to be "great" without surpassing
father and brother and thus provoking guilt; as he recognized on
December 29, "greatness" could be "homely": "All true greatness
runs as level a course, and is as unaspiring, as the plow in the furrow.
It wears the homeliest dress and speaks the homeliest language. . . . The
good have not to travel far" (*J*, I: 301). Going away to the pond
would allow Thoreau to "respire and aspire all at once," to cleanse
and purify himself. "I can see nothing so proper and holy," he says on
the 29th of December, "as unrelaxed play and frolic in this bower God
has built for us. The suspicion of sin never comes to this thought"
(*J*, I: 302). If society was "sick" and "diseased," as he observed on the
last day of the old year, then he could find health of body and spirit
in his private and holy bower. But Thoreau was not to fulfill his resolution for the New Year and a new life. The sudden, painful death of his
brother would serve to upset his precarious equilibrium and to set back
his progress toward a satisfying identity, even as it ultimately shaped
and solidified his identity. His life would *continue* to be a sojourn far
longer than he imagined; the moratorium would be further extended,
the adolescence agonizingly prolonged. It would be years before he
would make good on his resolution to "live away by the pond." In
the meantime, Thoreau would remain homeless.

A man can attend but one funeral in the course of his life, can behold but one corpse. — Thoreau, *Cape Cod*

I feel as if years had been crowded into the last month. — Thoreau, *Journal*, I

Where is my heart gone? They say men cannot part with it and live. — Thoreau, *Journal*, I

The Event

Henry Thoreau began the New Year with some measure of hope and resolution. Living at Emerson's, he was thinking of moving to a home of his own. As late as January 3 he remarked in his journal, "Why should not Nature revel sometimes, and genially relax and make herself familiar at my board? I would have my house a bower fit to entertain her. It is a feast of such innocence as might have snowed down" (*J*, I: 311–12). But in the very first month of the year, an event occurred which would, for a time, dissipate his resolution, shake his emotions, reaggravate and prolong his identity crisis. The event would postpone his great achievements but also make them more possible; it would help transform him into the intense and needful man who did go to Walden and into the creative artist who would write *Walden*. Although biographers [1] have dutifully noted the event and suggested its influence on Henry, they have for the most part been content to let the matter drop after brief consideration. The deep and lasting significance of the event has yet to be recognized or emphasized strongly enough.

It will be remembered that there had been a falling out (however slight or dimly acknowledged) between the Thoreau brothers within the previous year. No longer did Henry teach or live alongside the brother he deeply, but ambivalently, loved.[2] No longer could his brother be depended upon to act as a buffer between him and his parents. Then in the first week of 1842, John and Henry were brought together again under the most tragic of circumstances. On January 1, John—26 years old—who at least had grown no worse in health since he had been forced to give up teaching [3]—cut his ring finger while stropping his razor blade. A letter to William S. Robinson in *"Warring-ton" Pen-Portraits* contains the most vivid and accurate account of the accident and John's subsequent death on January 11:

> I cannot close this hasty note without referring to the sudden death of our friend Thoreau, whom you knew and loved so well. The cause seems very simple. He was stropping his razor on Satur-day afternoon, and cut off a little piece of the end of his finger, next to the little one, on his left hand. It was very slight, —just the skin deep enough to draw blood. He replaced the skin, and immediately put on a rag without letting it bleed. He paid no more attention to it for two or three days, when he found that the skin had adhered to the finger slightly on one end, but the other part had mortified. In the evening he went to Dr. Bartlett, who dressed the finger; and, with no apprehension of further difficulty, he went home. On his way he had strange sensations, acute pain in various parts of his body; and he was hardly able to get home. The next morning (Saturday) he complained of stiffness of the jaws; and at night he was seized with violent spasms, and lockjaw set in. On being told that he must die a speedy and painful death, he was unmoved. "Is there no hope?" he said. "None," replied the doctor. Then, although his friends were almost distracted around him, he was calm, saying, "The cup that my father gives me, shall I not drink it?" He bade his friends all good-by; and twice he mentioned your name. Not long before he died, in the interval of his suffering, he thought he had written something, and said, "I will carry it down to Robinson; he will like to read it." He died Tuesday, at two o'clock, P.M., with as much cheerfulness and composure of mind as if only going a short journey.[4]

In "Brother Where Dost Thou Dwell" (1843), Henry would write of his brother's last days: "Is thy brow clear again / As in thy youthful years? / And was that ugly pain / The summit of thy fears? / Yet wast thou cheery still, / They could not quench thy fire, / Thou dids't abide their will, / And then retire."[5]

While John was dying in such an agonizing manner, Henry was his attentive and devoted nurse;[6] at the moment of death, he was hold-ing his elder brother in his arms.[7]

The letter to Robinson contains no specific information about Henry's reaction to John's death. But two letters—only recently dis-covered[8]—from Lidian Emerson to Lucy Jackson Brown shed considerable light on his response. The only discrepancy with the "War-rington" description of the event itself is the indication that John cut his thumb rather than his ring finger. Lidian begins on January 11 by informing Lucy of

> the strange sad news that John Thoreau has this afternoon left this world. He died of lockjaw occasioned by a slight cut on his thumb. Henry mentioned on Sunday morning that he had been home helping the family who were all ailing; and that John was disabled from his usual work by having cut his finger. In the evening Mr. Brooks came for him to go home again, and said they were alarmed by symptoms of the lockjaw in John. Monday John was given over by the physicians, and to-day he died, retaining his senses and some power of speech to the last. He said from the first he knew he should die, but was perfectly quiet and trustful, saying that God had always been good to him and he could trust Him now. His words and behavior throughout were what Mr. Emerson calls manly, even *great*.[9]

Lidian then goes on to speak of Henry's behavior:

> Henry has been here this evening and seen Mr. Emerson but no one else. He says John took leave of all the family on Monday with perfect calmness and more than resignation. It is a beautiful fate that has been granted him and I think he was worthy of it. At first it seemed not beautiful but terrible. Since I have heard particulars and recollected all the good I have heard of him. I feel as if a pure spirit had been translated. Henry has just been here. (it is now Wednesday noon) I love him for the feeling he showed and the effort he made to be cheerful. He did not give way in the least but his whole demeanour was that of one struggling with sickness of heart. He came to take his clothes, and says he does not know when he shall return to us. We are wholly indebted to John for Waldo's picture. Henry and myself carried him to a sitting but did not succeed in keeping him in the right attitude, —and still enough. But John by his faculty of interesting children succeeded in keeping him looking as he should while the impression was making.[10]

Thus did Henry temporarily move out of the Emersons' household.

John's funeral preceded Lidian's second letter to Lucy. The eulogy was given by Barzillai Frost of the First Parish Church. Of John, Frost said,

He had a love of nature, even from childhood amounting to enthusiasm. He spent many of his leisure hours in straying over these hills and along the banks of the streams. There is not a hill, nor a tree, nor a bird, nor a flower of marked beauty in all this neighborhood that he was not familiar with, and any new bird or flower he discovered gave him the most unfeigned delight, and he would dwell with it and seem to commune with it for hours. He spent also many a serene and loving evening gazing upon the still moonlight scene and the blazing aurora, or looking into the bright firmament, radiant with the glory to God. . . .

The benevolence of the deceased appeared in his love of animals, in the pleasure he took in making children happy, and in his readiness to give up his time to oblige all. He had a heart to feel and a voice to speak for all classes of suffering humanity; and the cause of the poor inebriate, the slave, the ignorant and depraved, was very dear to him. . . .

Of his religious opinions I must speak with less confidence. He has been affected no doubt by the revolutionary opinions abroad in society in regard to inspiration and religious instructions, as it is very natural the young should. But there has been a tendency of late in his mind, I have thought, to those views which have fortified the minds of the great majority of the wise and good in all ages. (I may be mistaken in supposing that he adopted the transcendental views to any considerable extent.) But, however his theories *about* religion were unsettled, his principles and religious feelings were always unshaken. The religious sentiment had been awakened, and he manifested it in his tastes, feelings, and conversation.[11]

About a week after her first letter, Lidian reported to Lucy concerning the funeral and Henry:

Seldom has a death caused a more general feeling of regret, every one speaks in praise of the departed, heartily too [,] not in common-place expressions. Mr. [Barzillai] Frost preached last Sunday a funeral sermon in which he portrayed an uncommonly beautiful character and yet did no more than justice as it seemed to me. Henry behaves worthily of himself. He says John is not lost but nearer to him than ever, for he knows him better than he ever did before and to know a friend better leaves him nearer. I asked him if this sudden fate gave any shock to John when he first was aware of his danger. He said "none at all." After J. had taken leave of all the family he said to Henry now sit down and talk to me of Nature and Poetry, I shall be a good listener for it is difficult for me to interrupt you. During the hour in which he died, he looked at Henry with a "transcendent smile full of Heaven" (I think this was H's expression) and Henry "found himself returning it" and this was the last communication that passed between them.[12]

For a week and a half after John's death, Henry maintained his outward composure; in Lidian's words, he did not "give way in the least" even though his "demeanour was that of one struggling with sickness of heart." But this composure was only the calm before the storm. A friend of Edward Emerson's told him that the "shock, the loss, and the sight of his brother's terrible suffering at the end, for a time overthrew Henry so utterly ... that he sat still in the house, could do nothing, and his sisters led him out passive to try to help him."[13] Then on January 22 Henry too developed what seemed to be a case of fatal lockjaw—even though he had not been cut. Emerson reported the occurrence to his brother William in a letter of January 24:

> My pleasure at getting home on Saturday night at the end of my task was somewhat checked by finding that Henry Thoreau who has been at his fathers since the death of his brother was ill & threatened with *lockjaw!* his brother's disease. It is strange—unaccountable—yet the symptoms seemed precise & on the increase. You may judge we were all alarmed & I not the least who have the highest hopes of this youth. This morning his affection be it what it may, is relieved essentially, & what is best, his own feeling of better health established.[14]

As late as March 14, Thoreau wrote to Isaiah Williams, "I have been confined to my chamber for a month with a prolonged shock of the same disorder—from close attention to, and sympathy with him, which I learn is not without precedent."[15] In the same letter, he informed Williams that Waldo, Emerson's oldest child—"a boy of rare promise, who in the expectation of many was to be one of the lights of his generation"—had died of scarlet fever. Undoubtedly the death of Waldo, whom he had become attached to at Emerson's, did nothing to speed up Henry's recovery. Even by the middle of April, Harding tells us, he was still unable to work in the garden. Although he moved back to Emerson's soon thereafter, "he continued silent and depressed and for a long, long while could not be induced to indulge in one of his favorite pastimes—singing." [16]

Grief-Responses

It is important to speculate on the short-term and long-term effects of John's sudden death on Henry. It goes without saying that Thoreau had every right to grieve deeply; he had lost a brother and valued friend. Yet his reaction to the death went beyond the limits of "normal" mourning. Surely, one of the short-term responses which begs for explanation is Henry's extraordinary attack of "sympathetic" (or what would be called today "psychosomatic") lockjaw. It is undeniable that the disease *was* a reaction to his brother's death, as Thoreau—always interested in mind-body relationships—acknowledged. Also clear is that Henry's illness was psychosomatic; had it been an *actual* case of lockjaw, his chances of recovery would have been slight indeed. Such an extreme form of mourning is called a "morbid grief reaction" by Erich Lindemann in his influential study, "Symptomotology and Management of Acute Grief." This "acquisition of symptoms belonging to the last illness of the deceased" is "often labelled hypochondriacal or hysterical." [17] In their study of "Children's Disturbed Reactions to the Death of a Sibling," Cain, Fast, and Erickson indicate that "hysterical" symptoms are by no means uncommon, even in these "enlightened" days: "in approximately 40 per cent of the cases there were either immediate, prolonged, or 'anniversary' hysterical identifications with the dead child's prominent symptoms. These included hysterical pains, convulsivelike attacks, severe asthmatic attacks (the first occurring immediately after a sibling died in such an attack), and apparent almost total motor paralysis, which indeed nearly did lead to death." [18] As in Thoreau's case, these "hysterical" symptoms may be delayed "when there is necessity for maintaining the morale of others." [19] Stoic that he was, Thoreau tried to appear cheerful and "manly"—presumably to lend emotional support to others (Lidian "loved him" for it), but also to protect himself from feelings which, if acknowledged, could have lead to a complete breakdown.

Labelling Thoreau's illness as "psychosomatic," "hysterical," or a "morbid grief reaction" does not of course explain it. One explanation, and the one the victim himself subscribed to, is that Henry so closely sympathized, empathized, and identified with John—indeed, nursed him in his final hours—that he could not avoid experiencing in delayed fashion the same pains that his brother had endured. Another possible explanation is that Thoreau loved and needed his brother so much that when John died, he too wanted to die; there was no longer a reason for living. Surely, the psychosomatic illness was a way of acknowledging with his whole being how much John had (constructively) meant to him, and how helpless he now felt. Along these lines, it might further be argued that the sudden and needless death of so promising a young man left Thoreau despairing, bereft of faith in the meaningfulness of existence. When the universe is no longer meaningful, when one does not "trust" the world to "make sense," one may wish to put an end to one's own meaningless existence.

While all these explanations may contribute to an understanding of Thoreau's grief reaction, it is probable that the illness was in large part the acute expression of a more general torment that would haunt Henry throughout his life. His short-term and long-term responses to John's death cannot be fully explained without reference to guilt, regret, and anxiety. Henry had lost a model and companion whom he deeply loved and respected. But, as has been previously established, his feelings toward his brother had been characterized by hostility and ambivalence as well as abiding love. It has been shown that Thoreau was, at the very least, dimly conscious of the negative feelings he had for John, no matter how hard he tried to repress or sublimate them. He had been put, or put himself, into the position of competing with his brother for parental attention and approval, achievement, student affections, and community approval. As Jules Henry has said in *Culture Against Man*, nothing "has greater potential for creating hostility than competition." [20] Thus the very fact that he had competed with John led to hostility. Moreover, to the extent that Henry did not perceive himself as winning these competitions, he felt even greater hostility. (Or he would try to displace his hostility toward his brother onto those who had found him wanting—parents, students, and community.) Because Henry so loved John, these negative feelings evoked guilt. To the extent that John was, or was imagined to be, his "outer foe," Henry had to contend with the "inward foes." Furthermore, to the extent that he perceived himself as surpassing or defeating his brother, he also experienced guilt. Perhaps Henry could have coped with these unpleasant feelings after John's death had it not been for the all-too-recent eruption of hostility and anxiety during and after the Ellen affair. If the rivalry with John, John's being rejected by Ellen, Henry's own pursuit and proposal, the ensuing "difference with a Friend," and the elder brother's ill health had raised alarmingly the level of Henry's anxiety and guilt, John's death was undoubtedly the most severe and enduring source of guilt.

When a person feels guilty in relation to another person, the latter's death—especially when it is unexpected—can serve greatly to intensify and rigidify the guilt.[21] John's death made it impossible for Henry to make up with him, or to be forgiven for the wrongs he had done (or imagined he had done). The last words had been said. As close as they had been in their youth and early adulthood, the fact remained that in the months before John's death Henry had not been as close to his brother—either physically or emotionally—as previously. No longer did he look up to or depend upon his brother to the extent that he once had. He may well have imagined that John remained suspicious of his motivations, and resentful of his intrusion, in the courtship of Ellen. On January 8, the same day that John noted that his skin had "mortified," Thoreau—who was at home caring for the family—wrote in his journal upon listening to a music box:

> Am I so like thee, my brother, that the cadence of two notes af-
> fects us alike? Shall I not some time have an opportunity to thank
> him who made music? I feel a sad cheer when I hear these lofty
> strains, because there must be something in me as lofty that
> hears. . . . What, then, can I do to hasten that other time, or that
> space where there shall be no time, and these things be a more liv-
> ing part of my life, —where there will be no discords in my life?
> (J, I: 317–18)

Whether "him who made music" can be construed as Thoreau's brother is not clear. If so, then Henry was concerned about whether he would ever have the opportunity to thank him, to be completely reconciled with him. In any case, Henry acknowledges here, in the presence of his ailing brother who had been disabled from his usual work, that he does *not* feel lofty, that there *were* discords in his life. It is quite possible that at this time he was preoccupied with his discord with John. The next day, January 9,[22] when John already had "stiffness of the jaws," Thoreau wrote (presumably while tending to his brother),

> One cannot too soon forget his errors and misdemeanors; for [to]
> dwell long upon them is to add to the offense, and repentance and
> sorrow can only be displaced by somewhat better, and which is
> as free and original as if they had not been. Not to grieve long
> for any action, but to go immediately and do freshly and other-

wise, subtracts so much from the wrong. Else we may make the
delay of repentance the punishment of the sin. (*J*, I: 318)

While nursing his brother, he could seek to make restitution for his
sins, errors, and misdemeanors; it was precisely in his brother's suffering presence that Henry could *not* forget the error, imagined or real,
of his ways. On March 2, Thoreau would write to his confidante Lucy
Brown that "we feel at first as if some opportunities of kindness and
sympathy were lost, but learn afterward that any *pure grief* is ample
recompense for all." [23] Despite his protestations to the contrary, Henry
was always to grieve for the "opportunities of kindness and sympathy"
that had been lost. Moreover, somewhere deep in his being, Thoreau
felt that it was he who was responsible for his brother's death. In many
earlier instances, he had wished his brother out of the way, his "elder
deceased." The most extreme instance had also been the most recent—
during his pursuit of Ellen. As a suitor, he wished to "couch his lance,"
but he had, for a time, been inhibited by John's courtship of Ellen.
As a rival he had stabbed and wounded John and was unable to "draw
the sword straight back out of the wound." Now, to his horror, his
most secret and terrible wishes had come true. John had died, and the
mortal wound had been inflicted by a blade which Henry, on some
level, feared he had wielded. Because he loved his brother so much,
Thoreau experienced unbearable guilt. His psychosomatic illness could
be interpreted as a way of punishing himself and trying to share the
fate of John, thereby relieving his guilt. [24]

On even deeper levels of the psyche, Thoreau may have felt that
he had "killed" John and ought to be punished. The event reverberated
on both conscious and unconscious levels. We may go back as far as
the oedipal situation to explain his grief-reaction. [25] Henry, who had
competed with John for his mother during the oedipal stage, had
defeated his brother in the most emphatic and brutal way, thus provoking enormous guilt. Moreover, John was not, at the oedipal stage,
the *only* elder competitor. As has been argued, Henry was subject
to guilt accompanying the challenging and defeating of his father
in the oedipal project as well as in the real world. Thoreau always
feared that he had been only too successful in winning his mother
away from his father. His brother's death reopened the Pandora's
Box not only of his guilt vis-à-vis John, but also vis-à-vis his
father. To the extent that the elder brother was a father-surrogate for
Henry (and it has been shown that he *had* been, in many ways, a
father to his younger brother), the "killing" of John would be asso-

ciated, by transference, with the imagined defeat of the father. Thus Henry had doubly sinned and the grief-guilt compounded manifold. His superego demanded that he be punished for his transgressions; sympathetic lockjaw was the short-term form of punishment. The fact that, only months before his brother's violent "defeat," Henry had engaged in a rivalry with his brother (father) for the affections of a woman could only have exacerbated the guilt feelings and aroused the wrath of the superego.

But the short-term punishment was not enough to placate the conscience or dissipate grief, guilt, and regret. Erik Erikson speaks of "the curse" as it appears in Gandhi's life. The central event involves the death of Gandhi's father. It seems that he had been nursing his dying father, but had left his father's side to join his own pregnant wife in their bedroom. While he was out of the sickroom, his father had died. For all his attentiveness and care, he had not been "there" with and for his father at the end. Gandhi later wrote that he had "never been able to efface or forget" that "blot." [26] Such a curse "in the lives of spiritual innovators with a similarly precocious and relentless conscience," Erikson observes, "is indicative of an aspect of childhood or youth which comes to represent an account that can never be settled and remains an existential debt all the rest of a lifetime. But it must be clear that one single episode cannot be the *cause* of such a curse; rather, the curse is what we clinicians call a 'cover memory,' that is, a condensation and projection of a pervasive childhood conflict on one dramatized scene." In this case the "pervasive childhood conflict" to which the curse was related was the oedipal conflict, the tension between initiative and guilt. Gandhi's " 'feminine' service to his father would have served to deny the boyish wish to replace the (aging) father in the possession of the (young) mother and the youthful intention to outdo him as a leader in later life." That Gandhi's father died at the very moment when his son was *not* tending him and that the son thus failed "to receive a lasting sanction for his superior gifts" represented a lifelong "curse" on young Gandhi's initiative and ambitions.[27]

How may we relate Gandhi's "curse" to Thoreau's? Unlike Gandhi, Thoreau was nursing his brother rather than his father. Also unlike Gandhi, he was holding John in his arms when the end came. However, it has been indicated that, in many ways, John *was* a father to his younger brother and that their relationship was burdened with oedipal as well as post-oedipal rivalries. In Thoreau's case, the curse was associated less with the moment of death itself, more with events of the two years preceding the death. As much as he loved his brother, he had competed with him, felt hostility towards him. There had been a "difference with a Friend," suspicions, hints of alienation, John's illness which had ended his promising teaching career. Now, in spite of his efforts to make up with John by nursing him, his brother had died before he could feel completely reconciled with him. It is possible that even while tending to him, Henry picked up hints of alienation and accusation. When John, "in the intervals of his suffering," thought he had written something and said, "I will carry it down to Robinson; he will like to read it," it may have seemed to the anxious younger brother that John was saying, "I would prefer that Henry *not* read it. He would *not* like to read it. He does not understand or appreciate me." When John said to Henry, "now sit down and talk to me of Nature and Poetry, I shall be a good listener for it is difficult for me to interrupt you," it may have been interpreted by Henry as meaning, "You have never wanted or allowed me to interrupt you." In any event, there had been enough of a falling out before John's death so that Henry could never dispel his doubts and suspicions about his brother's feelings toward him.

While, "in the hour that he died," John "looked at Henry with a 'transcendent smile full of Heaven,'" Thoreau must have felt that he had one foot in hell. He could never be sure that his brother completely approved of his gifts, aspirations, ambitions. Plagued by a "relentless conscience," Thoreau would desperately search for assurance that his own aspirations were pure and innocent, his gifts never tainted by competitiveness, sinful motivations, forbidden sexual desires. His greatly intensified need to purify himself and expiate guilt would eventually lead him in the direction of Walden and *Walden*. To the extent that Henry was never able to find complete assurance of purity and innocence, he was indeed "cursed." John's death strongly reinforced his distaste for "worldly" ambitions. After informing Isaiah Williams in a March 14 letter of his brother's death and his own sympathetic lockjaw, Thoreau writes, "I must confess I am apt to consider the trades and professions so many traps which the Devil sets to catch men in—and good luck he has too, if one may judge." [28] The pursuit of success became ever more "devilish" for Thoreau. Whenever he thought to "rise to the step above," he would fear "treading hardest on the step below." On that step lay the broken body of his beloved brother.

There is one further point which links Gandhi's experience to Thoreau's. Erikson indicates that Gandhi's solicitous nursing of his father would have enabled him to deny that he wished to take the place of his father and possess his mother, that he desired to surpass his father "as a leader" in adulthood. "Thus," says Erikson, "the pattern would be set for a style of leadership which can defeat a superior adversary only nonviolently and with the express intent of saving him as well as those whom he oppressed." [29]

For Thoreau also, the nursing of a "superior adversary" (his esteemed elder brother) was a way of denying to himself that he had ever intended to hurt, surpass, or defeat John (or, by transference, his father).[30] Thus he had established a pattern whereby a "superior adversary" or authority figure could be defeated only nonviolently. "Civil disobedience" would be a mode of expressing aggression, defying authority, and defeating an adversary by passive resistance, by going to jail. Gandhi's own strategy of "militant nonviolence" would owe a great deal to Thoreau's formulations of civil disobedience. The two men not only embraced remarkably similar public strategies; they also had much in common in terms of the private, psychological roots of those public strategies. They were both "cursed."

Thus far, I have not considered how the responses of *others* to John's death, and the way Thoreau *imagined* that other people responded, may have influenced the surviving brother. Louise Osgood Koopman, a daughter of Ellen Sewall Osgood, writes of her reaction to hearing about the tragedy—long after it happened: "I think I wished that it had been Henry instead of John. I imagined John as a beautiful youth, perhaps because he died so young." [31] At the time of John's untimely death, Henry must have suspected that many wished *him* dead instead of John. Having been thought of as the "less promising," less responsible, and less beloved of the Thoreau brothers by the community-at-large, it is only natural that Henry would imagine his fellow-townsmen whispering among each other, "Why did it have to be John? Why couldn't it have been that irresponsible and defiant younger brother of his, that David Henry?" If Thoreau listened carefully to Barzillai Frost's eulogy, he may have perceived it as an implied judgment on himself and his right to remain alive. John was pictured by Frost as taking pleasure in "making children happy" and being ever ready to "give up his time to oblige all." Henry was not quite the child-pleaser John was (though he did provide his schoolchildren with many happy hours), and he *certainly* was not thought of as a sociable or obliging member of the community. He had been obstinate and unappreciative—especially when compared to his brother. Frost claimed that John "had a heart to feel and a voice to speak for all classes of suffering humanity; and the cause of the poor inebriate, the slave, the ignorant and the depraved was very dear to him." Many townspeople saw the younger brother as having only one cause he believed in: himself. Thoreau would say of himself on March 25, "How can I talk of charity, who at last withhold the kindness which alone makes charity desirable?" (*J*, I: 348). If the preceding remarks by Frost disturbed Henry, the comments about John's "religious opinions" must have felt like stab wounds:

> He has been affected no doubt by the revolutionary opinions abroad in society in regard to inspiration and religious instructions, as it is very natural the young should. But there has been a tendency of late in his mind, I have thought, to those views which have fortified the minds of the great majority of the wise and good in all ages. (I may be mistaken in supposing that he adopted the transcendental views to any considerable extent.)

To Henry, who was the acknowledged "transcendental brother" of John, Frost's remarks were almost surely experienced as direct assaults on his own character, on his own *being*. Frost was telling him that the "wise and good" did not approve of him, that John—less "transcendental" than Henry—was a more worthy person.[32] As much as Thoreau would have liked to ignore community opinion (at least as he imagined it), in this instance he was unable to. When one imagines that an entire community questions one's character and even wishes one dead, instead of a more popular brother, the emotional consequences can be devastating. To the extent that Thoreau *accepted* the damning judgment of the community, he may have wished to comply with the judgment—and die. It is possible that the psychosomatic illness was in part an unconscious attempt to satisfy Concord's wishes as he imagined them.

However, Thoreau's suspicions of persecution by the community, as intensified alarmingly by John's death, also exacerbated the rage and hostility he felt toward the town he could not leave. After all, the community was not only threatening his way of life; it was, in a sense, threatening his *life*. It is therefore not surprising that Thoreau's confrontations with the Concord community often took on the aura of life-and-death struggles. Henry would have to defend himself with even greater vigilance against townspeople whom he always suspected thought of him as "the brother who should have died instead of John." If he was to live, he would have to remain marginal to a community which could so think of him.

Coupled with the sense that the community would have preferred his death to John's, it is probable that Henry also feared that his parents wished he had died rather than his sibling. Cain, Fast, and Erickson submit that the surviving siblings often sense "their parents' basic wish that *they*, not the dead sibling, had died." [33] After all, John, Jr. had brought honor and prestige to the Thoreau household while alive; now that he was gone, the tendency to overidealize him must have been strong for all family members, including Henry himself. All fond memories of John's sociability, gentleness, compassion, and responsibleness could have been interpreted by Henry as implicit comparisons with himself. Compared with that idealized image of his brother, Henry would always come out second-best. Such a situation made Henry resentful of his parents—not to mention his brother. Yet accompanying this rage and resentment was an increased dependence upon the good opinions of his parents. He desperately needed the comfort and affection of his family; he was in no mood to incur the wrath of his parents by any hostile behavior. Left insecure and shaken by John's death (and by the loss of a male figure who had helped him to feel brave and autonomous while living at home), Henry was led to seek reassurance from his parents that he *was* worthy, that they did *not* wish him dead instead of John. While he cursed his parents for invidiously comparing him with his brother, it also became all the more important to receive his parents' blessings. Such dependence made it difficult for him to contemplate such "socially irresponsible" projects as "living away by the pond"; it would be a few years before he could muster up the determination to live fully his *own* life again.

Along these lines, it is crucial to recognize that Henry was now the last surviving male who could carry on the family name after the father's death. John, Jr. would never marry, raise children, become a substantial member of the community; he could neither help with the family business nor establish another school. He would not be there to care for his parents when they grew older. An awareness of these facts imposed an added burden of responsibility on Thoreau. He must have perceived that his parents were now increasingly dependent upon *him* to carry on the family name (in business if not in marriage) and fulfill the expectations they had had for John. If John, Sr. died, Henry would be thrust into the position of head of the household. In effect, it may have seemed to Thoreau that he was being called upon to replace John as well as to be himself. As Cain, Fast, and Erickson have noted, the feeling that one must "replace" the dead sibling can "warp" the replacement's "identity formation." [34] Surely Henry's added responsibilities and his sense that he had to be *two* people in some respects aggravated and prolonged his identity confusion. It became more problematic for him fully to embrace the identity of writer, Transcendentalist, and "forest seer" because he was also expected to take on the socially acceptable character of John. "I am like a feather floating in the atmosphere," he writes on February 21. Frequently, Thoreau must have felt that his identity was at the mercy of an unpredictable and harsh wind. Soon before Henry left for Staten Island in 1843, Hawthorne—to whom he sold the memory-laden boat John and he had used on the Concord-Merrimack trip—observed, "I am glad, on Mr. Thoreau's own account, that he is going away; as he is physically out of health, and, morally and intellectually, seems not to have found exactly the guiding clue." [35]

It should be recognized that, in another sense, John's death may well have made Henry ultimately less sociable than he otherwise would have been. Harding says, "There are those who feel that had John lived, his gaiety and gregariousness would have lightened some of Henry's deep seriousness and involved him more directly in the social life of Concord." [36] However, Edward Emerson argues with much justification that Thoreau's gifts would never have been fully realized had he not lost both Ellen and John:

> He had gone into a Valley of Sorrow, but when, first, the dream of helpmate and guiding presence passed away, and then his nearest companion was taken from him, who shall say but that the presence of these blessings would have prevented his accomplishing his strange destiny? For his genius was solitary, and though his need for friendly and social relation with his kind was great, it was occasional, and to his lonely happiness the world will owe the best gifts he has left.[37]

To lose such "blessings" was indeed a high price for Henry to pay in order to accomplish his "strange destiny."

Grief Work

Erich Lindemann speaks of "grief work" as "the emancipation from the bondage to the deceased, readjustment to the environment in which the deceased is missing, and the formation of new relationships." [38] The journal and letters between February and April of 1842 show Thoreau to be struggling with his grief, trying to make something positive and meaningful out of John's untimely death, seeking to gain restitution for his enormous losses, and to mitigate guilt. The energy he devotes to this struggle reveals the intensity of the underlying sorrow and despair. "Where is my heart gone?" a distraught Thoreau asks himself on March 26. "They say men cannot part with it and live" (J, I: 350). It was Henry's task to recover his heart by any possible psychological means.

Paradoxically, Thoreau could gain emancipation from bondage to the deceased (and emancipation from the guilt and regret accompanying the elder's decease) only by denying the fact of death and by convincing himself that he was closer to John, and more closely identified with him, than ever before. After the funeral Lidian reports Henry as saying, "John is not lost but nearer to him than ever, for he knows him better than he ever did before and to know a friend better brings him nearer." Rather than acknowledging that the deceased was "missing from the environment," he found it necessary to insist that John was to be discovered in every natural scene. Indeed, although he did establish new relationships with people (as, for instance, with Ellery Channing, who became something of a brother-replacement),[39] the death of John strengthened Henry's commitment to a relationship with nature—and with words. Thus if John's death aggravated and prolonged Thoreau's identity confusion, in the long run it also contributed mightily to the further development of his identity as artist and naturalist.

Resuming his journalizing after weeks of apparent silence and debilitation, on February 20 Thoreau writes, "The death of friends should inspire us as much as their lives. If they are great and rich enough, they will leave consolation to the mourners before the expenses of their funerals. It will not be hard to part with any worth, because it is worthy. How can any good depart? It does not go and come, but we" (J, I: 321). The "good" of John remained; therefore, John was not genuinely dead and Henry could not be held responsible for doing away with him. Thoreau sought to see death in cosmic perspective; from such a vantage point there was no such thing as death and no reason to grieve. "Only nature has a right to grieve perpetually," he writes to Lucy Brown on March 2, "for she only is innocent. Soon the ice will melt, and the blackbirds sing along the river which he frequented, as pleasantly as ever. The same everlasting serenity will appear in this face of God, and we will not be sorrowful, if he is not."[40] In the natural order of things, death itself died:

Consider what a difference there is between living and dying. To die is not to *begin* to die, and *continue;* it is not a state of continuance, but of transientness; but to live is a condition of continuance, and does not mean to be born merely. There is no continuance of death. It is a transient phenomenon. Nature presents nothing in a state of death. (*J,* I: 327–28)

To the extent that Thoreau was able to see the world with the "eye of the poet," his own wounds would be healed, he could gain solace. On March 13 he writes,

The sad memory of departed friends is soon incrusted over with sublime and pleasing thoughts, as their monuments are overgrown with moss. Nature doth thus kindly heal every wound. By the mediation of a thousand little mosses and fungi, the most unsightly objects become radiant of beauty. There seem to be two sides to this world, presented us at different times, as we see things in growth or dissolution, in life or death. For seen with the eye of a poet, as God sees them, all are alive and beautiful; but seen with the historical eye, or the eye of memory, they are dead and offensive. If we see Nature as pausing, immediately all mortifies and decays; but seen as progressing, she is beautiful. (*J,* I: 328)

In order to escape the guilt associated with John's death, it became all the more imperative to perceive death and life (including his own) with the "eye of a poet" rather than with the "historical eye."

It is highly suggestive how frequently Thoreau refers to God in the months following his brother's death. Of course, it is natural to turn to God—and to try to accept God's "mysterious ways"—upon the unexpected death of a loved one, just as it is perfectly natural to seek consolation in nature. Henry, however, had not been particularly predisposed to speak of God before John's death; after all, he was the "transcendental brother." Yet Henry's God during the tortured days of February and March was not just a pantheistic "oversoul" or "the gods" to whom he had often referred. He was anthropomorphic—directing and controlling events, personally overseeing Thoreau's situation. It is my belief that Henry sorely needed to see God anthropomorphically during this period, just as he frequently needed to see nature in human terms. On March 11 Thoreau asks, "If Nature is our mother, is not God much more?" (*J,* I: 326). Erikson indicates that

God is first experienced by infants in the image of the personal father,[41] and there may well be transference between the image of God and that of the father. To the extent that Thoreau perceived God anthropomorphically, God came to represent his own father *and* his brother. Henry's allusions to God in February and March can partially be explained in terms of his need to reconcile himself with male-figures (especially his brother) and to yield to them. By yielding to God, Thoreau could deny that he ever meant to destroy his father or brother.

On February 20, Thoreau writes, "My path hitherto has been like a road through a diversified country, now climbing high mountains, then descending into the lowest vales. From the summits I saw the heavens; from the vales I looked up to the heights again. In prosperity I remember God, or memory is one with consciousness; in adversity I remember my own elevation, and only hope to see God again" (*J*, I: 320). "To see God again" was to reconcile himself with his brother; to look into the "face of God" and see serenity was to gain absolution for sins he had committed against John—sins that were not forgiven before John had died. A week later, Henry observes, "Events come out of God, and our characters determine them and constrain fate, as much as they determine the words and tones of a friend to us. Hence are they always acceptable as experience, and we do not see how they could have done without them" (*J*, I: 323–24). A journal entry of March 11 illuminates strikingly Thoreau's perception of God; in submitting his life to God, he is denying any ambition to challenge his brother or father:

> I must receive my life as passively as the willow leaf that flutters over the brook. I must not be for myself, but God's work and that is always good. I will wait the breezes patiently, and grow as Nature shall determine. My fate cannot but be grand so. We may live the life of a plant or an animal, without living an animal life. This constant and universal content of the animal comes of resting quietly in God's palm. I feel as if [I] could at any time resign my life and the responsibility of living into God's hands, and become as innocent, free from care, as a plant or stone. (*J*, I: 326–27)

It will be remembered that when Henry decided to yield Ellen to John he thought of his brother as "necessity." Now, not wishing to feel that he is an arrogant and defiant "sinner," he attempts to be a submissive and accepting "innocent," "resting quietly in God's palm."

However, on the very same day, he reveals the depths of his anxiety, the extent to which he is unable to accept completely his fate:

> My life, my life! Why will you linger? Are the years short and the months of no account? How often has long delay quenched my aspirations! Can God afford that I should forget him? Is he indifferent to my career? Can heaven be postponed with no more ado? Why were my ears given to hear those everlasting strains which haunt my life, and yet to be prophaned much more by these perpetual dull sounds? (*J*, I: 327)

In one respect this passage may reveal Henry's desire to die, as his brother had; in this sense, the question is not unlike that posed by Hamlet when confronted by his father's death and his own guilt: "To be, or not to be—that is the question." However, the passage is also an expression of impatience and resentment against "the fates" (and his brother) for quenching aspirations and postponing the development of his career. At this point Thoreau could clearly see how John's death had shaken his resolve to "live away by the pond," to come into his own inheritance. His brother's decease would prolong his already painfully prolonged moratorium. To be passive like a plant or stone was not to seize the opportunity for greatness when it presented itself. Accompanying the resentment and impatience, nevertheless, is Thoreau's deep desire to be reconciled with God and brother: "Why, God, did you include me in your great scheme? Will you not make me a partner at last?" (*J*, I: 327). If there are any doubts that God and brother are closely associated in Henry's mind, they would seem to be dispelled by what directly follows Henry's expression of the need to be a partner of God. He writes, "My friend, my friend, I'd speak so frank to thee that thou wouldst pray me to keep back some part, for fear I robbed myself. To address thee delights me, there is such cleanness in the delivery. I am delivered of my tale, which, told to strangers, still would linger on my lips as if untold, or doubtful how it ran" (*J*, I: 327). Thoreau here appears to be speaking to John—trying to dispel his older brother's doubts and suspicions. Henry had not had the opportunity to "tell all" to John before he died; now he desperately wants to reconcile himself with John, to end the "difference with a Friend" which haunts his life. Establishing a partnership with God also means reestablishing harmony with his brother.

On March 13, Thoreau remarks, "I am startled that God can make me so rich even with my own cheap stores. It needs but a few wisps of straw in the sun, or some small word dropped, or that has long lain silent in some book. When heaven begins and the dead arise, no trumpet is blown; perhaps the south wind will blow. What if you or I be dead! God is alive still" (*J*, I: 328). Only the "riches" Henry receives from God (rather than by his own ambitiousness) can be accepted without guilt. Furthermore, it is far less guilt-provoking to imagine God (and, by extension, his brother) as outliving him. "I have not succeeded," he says on March 22, "if I have an antagonist that fails. It must be humanity's success" (*J*, I: 342). God, Henry imagined, would not approve of any success which involved triumphing over an adversary.

A crucial part of Thoreau's "grief work" consisted in trying to convince himself that he was closer than ever to his brother and that John in some sense remained alive. Contemplating the nature of friendship, he reflects, "My friend is my real brother. I see his nature groping yonder like my own. Does there go one whom I know? then I go there" (*J*, I: 340). It is, of course, no coincidence that Henry would so intimately associate friendship and brotherhood: his "real brother" had been his best friend. To his "real brother," Thoreau says here, "Whither thou goest, I will go." He will follow in pursuit of that friend whose "nature" is "groping yonder." Yet Henry's best friend had also become (especially in the last few years before his death) an enemy. Thus it is highly significant that Henry, immediately after saying "My friend is my real brother" associates friends with enemies: "The field where friends have met is consecrated forever. Man seeks friendship out of desire to realize a home here. As the Indian thinks he receives into himself the courage and strength of his conquered enemy, so we add to ourselves the character and heart of our friends" (*J*, I: 340). In this passage, Thoreau implicitly identifies himself and his "friend" as Indians who have met on a field of battle. Considering the way Henry had thought of himself and John as "braves" in a land of "squaws," the Indian reference should not be surprising. He perceived that he—an Indian brave—had met his best friend and fellow brave on the field of battle; he had conquered his friend-enemy by outliving him. However, as the passage indicates, Thoreau sought to deny that he had actually killed his friend-foe and to avoid the guilt accompanying his "victory" over his brother by asserting that, like an Indian, he could receive "into himself the courage and strength of his conquered enemy," that he could add to himself "the character and heart of his friend." In this way, it was possible to believe that John continued to live on in the body and spirit of his surviving brother. The only manner in which Henry could recover his own heart was to incorporate John's heart into his being.

A day earlier, on March 19, Thoreau had said,

> Wherever I go, I tread in the tracks of the Indian. I pick up the bolt which he has but just dropped at my feet. And if I consider destiny I am on his trail.... In planting my corn in the same furrow which yielded its increase to his support so long, I displace some memorial of him. (*J*, I: 337)

As has been previously noted, John was an ardent collector of Indian relics, and his enthusiasm for Indian lore had rubbed off on his younger brother. Henry could not remember John without remembering his deep interest in Indians and the sense of Indian fellowship they had enjoyed (as evidenced in the November 11–14, 1837 letter from Henry to John). It can be argued that Henry's preoccupation with, and pursuit of, the Indian after John's death was in fact an attempt to assert identification with his fallen brother and to recapture the sense of Indian fellowship the Thoreau brothers had once shared. With his brother, Henry had been able to feel "wild" and independent even while living under his parents' roof; moreover, Henry could acknowledge his dependence on his brother (who was "good medicine") much more readily than he could acknowledge dependence upon other male or female figures. To "tread in the tracks of the Indian" was to follow in his brother's footsteps and assert intimacy with him. To be "on the trail" of the Indian was to seek restoration of that combination of "wildness" and dependence he had once experienced in John's presence. To "displace some memorial" of the Indian was to find evidence that John somehow remained present in the environment; the growth of corn in "the same furrow which yielded its increase to his support so long" helped to assure Henry that he had John's blessings. To study lovingly and extensively the ways of the Indian was to affirm unambivalent love for his dead brother.

In his relationship with Nathaniel Hawthorne (eleven years his senior), who moved into the Old Manse with his wife in 1842, Thoreau tried to recapture in some small way the camaraderie he had with his elder brother—taking him on boat trips on the Musketaquid (and eventually selling him the boat), hunting for arrowheads with him, sharing with him the beauties of nature. On September 1, 1842, Hawthorne remarked on his friend's preoccupation with Indians: "It is a characteristic trait, that he has a great regard for the memory of the Indian tribes, whose wild life would have suited him so well; and strange to say, he seldom walks over a ploughed field without picking up an arrow-point, a spear-head, or other relic of the red men—as if their spirits willed him to be the inheritor of their simple wealth." [42]

It may be argued that Thoreau's trips to the Maine Woods in part represented an attempt to reestablish intimacy with his brother by relating to and learning about Indians, to feel "wild" and yet dependent upon his Indian guides. Indeed, Henry's relationship with, and vivid portrayals of, Joe Polis—one of the "heroes" of his later life [43]—probably owed much to transference; in Polis, Henry saw John reincarnated. In 1861, suffering from what would be his fatal illness (which may well have had a psychosomatic component), Thoreau would go to Minnesota where he could recuperate and study "the American Indian and the flora and fauna of the Middle West." [44] Surely it is highly suggestive that he spent the final weeks before his death working on his Maine Woods papers [45] and that his last recognizable words were "Moose" and "Indian." [46] Only in death could he truly join his "Indian" friend.

Thoreau turned not only to the Indian but also to nature in order to seek reassurance of his brother's presence and blessings and to assert identification with him. It has already been shown how nature provided consolation and compensation for Henry during a time of extreme distress. Nature also provided opportunities for him to expiate guilt and seek purity. He had turned to nature with great intensity in the aftermath of his guilt-provoking rivalry with John; now, after his death, establishing a relationship with non-human (and thus less emotionally threatening) nature was even more important. However, if in one sense it was less threatening to perceive nature as non-human, it also served Henry to seek John's presence or spirit in the natural world. John had been a nature-lover and ornithologist, and his younger brother must have learned much about nature by walking in the Concord woods with him. Indeed, one way Thoreau managed to identify himself with John and compensate for his loss was to become a more passionate and knowledgeable naturalist himself.

The "Natural History of Massachusetts," which he wrote in 1842, was, as Sherman Paul indicates, a reminder "of his debt to John"; it was "not only an attempt 'to waive disease & pain / And resume new life again,' as he wrote of the hawk, it was his attempt to state his faith in the 'health' of nature." [47] Henry could only regain health by immersing himself in nature and thereby approaching more closely John's spirit: "I tread in the steps of the fox that has gone before me by some hours, or which perhaps I have started, with such a tiptoe

of expectation, as if I were on the trail of the Spirit itself which resides in the wood, and expected to catch it in its lair." [48] Hawthorne
noted Thoreau's extraordinary intimacy with nature in 1842:

> Mr. Thorow is a keen and delicate observer of nature—a genuine
> observer, which, I suspect, is almost as rare a character as even
> an original poet; and Nature, in return for his love, seems to
> adopt him as her especial child, and shows him secrets which few
> others are allowed to witness. He is familiar with beast, fish,
> fowl, and reptile, and has strange stories to tell of adventures, and
> friendly passages with these lower brethren of mortality. Herb
> and flower, likewise, wherever they grow, whether in garden or
> wild wood, are his familiar friends. He is also on intimate terms
> with the clouds, and can tell the portents of storms.[49]

In "Great Friend," probably written in 1842, Henry laments the
loss of friend and brother, who was so closely identified with nature:

> I still must seek the friend
> Who does with nature blend,
> Who is the person in her mask,
> He is the man I ask.
>
> Who is the expression of her meaning,
> Who is the uprightness of her leaning,
> Who is the grown child of her weaning
>
> The center of this world,
> The face of nature....[50]

Thoreau hoped to find his "friend" by looking deeply and persistently
into the face of nature. It may be said that John was the person behind
the "mask" of nature. Henry's desire to find John's presence in nature
is even more apparent in the moving 1843 elegy, "Brother Where Dost
Thou Dwell." With profound yearning, he asks,

> Where chiefly shall I look
>   To feel thy presence near?
> Along the neighboring brook
>   May I thy voice still hear?
>
> Dost thou still haunt the brink
>   Of yonder river's tide?
> And may I ever think
>   That thou art at my side?

What bird wilt thou employ
  To bring me word of thee?
For it would give them joy,
  'Twould give them liberty
To serve their former lord
With wing and minstrelsy.[51]

To the extent that John is *not* present, all nature (and, of course, Henry himself) is in mourning: "A sadder strain has mixed with their song, / They've slowlier built their nests, / Since thou art gone / Their lively labor rests." Only by seeing John as still present in the natural environment may Henry recover joy and faith. The final stanza (which Henry deleted from the published version) is both a wish and an anxious question: "May thy influence prevail / O'er this dull scenery, / To lift the heavy veil / Tween me and thee?" "In both poems," says Sherman Paul, "John is the meaning of nature for Thoreau: he is the 'presence' who has animated it and given it its significance—its tutelary deity, and for Thoreau the prism of his own subjective idealism."[52] It is perhaps more accurate to say that Thoreau *struggled* to gain the reassurance that John was present in nature, that his influence prevailed, that he was "blessed" by nature. Without such assurance, the "heavy veil" would not be lifted, the difference between friends would remain unreconciled.

In a pre-1842 poem, Thoreau had said of (and to) Mount Wachusett, "May I approve myself thy worthy brother." In the fall of 1842 he made an excursion to Wachusett with Richard Fuller—Margaret Fuller's brother—whom he had tutored. The trip must have reminded him of earlier expeditions with John. Moreover, travelling to the mountain seems in some way to have been associated in his mind with gaining his brother's blessing. In his 1843 essay, "A Walk to Wachusett," he repeats the line about being a "worthy brother" to the mountain. Curiously, he does not emphasize his climbing of the mountain with his companion; to stress the climbing or "conquering" of Wachusett would have been to remind himself of surpassing and outliving John. Thoreau speaks of "propitiating the mountain gods";[53] he also speaks of the summit as "a place where gods might wander, so solemn and solitary, and removed from all contagion with the plain."[54] In describing the sunset on the summit, he seems intent on assuring himself that the gods—and his brother—have blessed him:

As we stood on the stone tower while the sun was setting, we saw the shades of night creep gradually over the valleys of the east, and the inhabitants went into their houses, and shut their doors, while the moon silently rose up, and took possession of that part. And then the same scene was repeated on the west side as far as the Connecticut and the Green Mountains, and the sun's rays fell on us two alone, of all New England men.[55]

Such a "blessing" could be perceived as the mountain's (John's) approval of Henry as his worthy brother. Perhaps the presence of a friendly companion made it easier for him to feel that he deserved to be one of the "elect." Yet, try as he might, Thoreau could not forget the "Indian Wars" which were "the dark age of New England" [56] and of his own life. Mountains would not always give him the consolation and assurance Wachusett did. For instance, on the tableland just below the Baxter summit of Mount Katahdin he would find a far more disapproving deity: "Why came ye here before your time. This ground is not prepared for you. Is it not enough that I smile in the valleys? I have never made this soil for thy feet, this air for thy breathing, these rocks for thy neighbors." [57]

On March 11, 1842, Thoreau had revealed the precariousness of his faith and assurance; he had wondered why his life "lingered," lamented how often "long delay" had quenched his aspirations, and asked himself if heaven could "be postponed with no more ado." His brother's death, he realized, would further prolong his moratorium. In order to regain faith and reassurance, Thoreau urgently needed to justify to himself this prolongation of adolescence, his inability to commit himself to an adult identity. Less than a month before John's death, Henry had said, "It is time now that I begin to live" (*J*, I: 299). In the aftermath of the tragedy, he often regressed to his deeply-rooted preference for living on anticipation, rather than seeking immediate fulfillment: "What am I good for now, who am still marching after high things, but to hear and tell the news, to bring wood and water, and count how many eggs the hens lay? In the meanwhile, I expect my life will begin. I will not aspire longer, I will see what it is I would be after. I will be unanimous" (*J*, I: 330). It was never easy for the ambivalent Thoreau to be "unanimous" about, to fully commit himself to, an adult identity; therefore, the stance of *expecting* to live was characteristic—even if this stance was itself ambivalent and accompanied by feelings of impatience and anxiety. On February 21 he writes in his journal, "I was always conscious of sounds in nature which my ears could never hear, —that I caught but the prelude to a strain. She always retreats as I advance. Always behind and behind is she and her meaning. Will not this faith and expectation make to itself ears at length? I never saw to the end; but the best part was unseen and unheard" (*J*, I: 321). The "ears" of faith and expectation, then, can replace the actual experience of seeing or hearing to the end. On January 24, 1843, Thoreau would write to Lucy Brown, "We always seem to be living just on the brink of a pure and lofty intercourse which would make the ills and trivialness of life ridiculous. After each little interval, though it be but for the night, we are prepared to meet each other as gods and goddesses. —I seem to have lodged all my days with one or two persons, and lived on expectation—and so I am content to live." [58]

If Henry was to justify to himself his retreat from the immediate prospect of outwardly living his own life and establishing his own home, he had to convince himself that he was nevertheless inwardly "great," or potentially so. In fact, John's death undoubtedly reinforced his sense that he was "chosen," even while it simultaneously led him to fear that he was damned, his aspirations forever dissipated. When a person feels singled out for intense suffering and misfortune, he often comes to think of himself as "special"; dreams of glory alternate with suspicions of worthlessness and persecution. On March 2, Henry confides to Lucy Brown, "when I realize what has transpired, and the greatness of the part I am unconsciously acting, I am thrilled, and it seems as if there were now a history to match it." [59] To be outwardly passive, rather than actively to "begin to live," is thus to rest in "God's palm" and do "God's work." If he "will wait the breezes patiently, and grow as nature shall determine," his "fate cannot but be grand so."

Thoreau turns to the stars as a metaphor for his own long wait, his seeming uselessness in society's eyes:

> What a consolation are the stars to man!—so high and out of his reach, as is his own destiny. I do not know but my life is fated to be thus low and grovelling always. I cannot discover its use even to myself. But it is permitted to see those stars in the sky equally useless, yet highest of all and deserving of a fair destiny. My fate is in some sense linked with that of the stars, and if they are to persevere to a great end, shall I die who could conjecture it? It surely is some encouragement to know that the stars are my fellow-creatures, for I do not suspect but they are reserved for a high destiny. (*J*, I: 338–39)

On March 20, Thoreau speaks of how his "destiny loiters"; two days later he says, "Nothing is more useful to a man than the determination not to be hurried" (*J*, I: 342). For years Henry had resisted the attempts of his parents and townsmen to hurry him into an identity not of his own choosing, to cut short a much-needed moratorium; now, Thoreau once more found it necessary to assert that a "great man," who would not be hurried into a trival existence, must not measure his progress by society's standards: "Society affects to estimate men by their talents, but really feels, and knows them by their characters. What a man does, compared to what he is, is but a small part" (*J*, I: 352). Henry realized that he must create his own rhythms, his own time scheme, if only so as to do away with time completely. As he says on March 26, "Why did I invent time but to destroy it?" (*J*, I: 349). If the present moment outwardly seemed not to confirm Henry's intimations of immortality, there was still hope for tomorrow. He reminds himself on March 27, "No man knoweth in what hour his life may come. Say not that Nature is trivial, for to-morrow she will be radiant with beauty" (*J*, I: 352). To live in the present meant, paradoxically, to be in a constant state of preparation for that morrow "radiant with beauty."

Even if his outward life remained poor, inactive, and disorganized, Thoreau tried to convince himself that he was inwardly rich and growing richer—a "man in reserve." In the face of loss and emptiness, Henry asks on March 24, "If hoarded treasures can make me rich, have I not the wealth of the planet in my mines and at the bottom of the sea?" (*J*, I: 345). The period of mourning is like a period of hibernation, during which one lives on one's own inner resources: "The weight of present woe will express the sweetness of past experience. When sorrow comes, how easy it is to remember pleasure! When, in winter, the bees cannot make new honey they consume the old" (*J*, I: 358). Yet if this is a period of hibernation, of abstinence, of "consuming the old," it is also a time of secret inward growth. Thoreau inquires, "Are setting hens troubled with ennui? Nature is very kind, does she let them reflect? These long March days, setting on and on in the crevice of a hayloft, with no active employment! Do setting hens sleep?" (*J*, I: 350). The answer, of course, is that hens, while appearing to relax or sleep, are either laying eggs or slowly gathering the materials for further procreation. Thus Thoreau seeks to justify his own seeming inactivity by comparing himself with the hen:

> The really efficient laborer will be found not to crowd his day
> with work, but will saunter to his task surrounded by a wide halo
> of ease and leisure. There will be a wide margin for relaxation

to his day. He is only earnest to secure the kernels of time, and
does not exaggerate the value of the husk. Why should the hen
set all day? She can lay but one egg, and besides she will not have
picked up materials for a new one. (*J*, I: 356–57)

In order to fulfill his destiny as "great man," he must be given (and
give himself) time for his riches, his gifts, to develop and mature like
pearls:

> I must confess I have felt mean enough when asked how I was
> to act on society, what errand I had to mankind. Undoubtedly
> I did not feel mean without a reason and yet my loitering is not
> without defense. I would fain communicate the wealth of my life
> to men, would really give them what is most precious in my gift.
> I would secrete pearls with the shellfish and lay up honey with
> the bees for them. I will sift the sunbeams for the public good.
> I know no riches I would keep back. I have no private good,
> unless it be my peculiar ability to serve the public. This is the
> only individual property. Each one may thus be innocently rich.
> I inclose and foster the pearl till it is grown. (*J*, I: 350)

Presumably the "gift" to which he refers is his writing—one of the
few ways he can be "great," "rich," and "innocent" at the same time—
thereby escaping the guilt associated with conventional success. There
are several references in the journal to writing and the inner richness
it implies. For instance, on March 23, Thoreau says,

> A plain sentence, where every word is rooted in the soil, is indeed
> flowery and verdurous. It has the beauty and variety of mosaic
> with the strength and compactness of masonry. All fullness looks
> like exuberance. We are not rich without superfluous wealth; but
> the imitator only copies the superfluity. If the words were suffi-
> ciently simple and answer to the thing to be expressed, our
> sentences would be blooming as wreaths of evergreen and
> flowers. (*J*, I: 343)

Although the period of "fostering pearls" had been much longer than
he expected, Thoreau continued to hope that he would one day bear,
as he had said in "Sic Vita," "more fruits and fairer flowers." However,
in the short run, his brother's death made the realization of his gifts
more problematic—even if in the long run it deepened and enriched
them.

It is not by accident that Thoreau becomes increasingly interested

in the life and death of Sir Walter Ralegh in the aftermath of John's
death. It will be remembered that Henry first showed an interest in
Ralegh when he wished to justify to himself his aggressive pursuit of
Ellen and his competition with his brother; moreover, Ralegh's name
turned up in his journal on January 5, 1842—long after John had been
forced to give up teaching because of illness and immediately before
the development of his lockjaw symptoms. Thoreau continued to discuss Ralegh in his journal of February and March 1842, and by early
1843 he had gathered enough materials to deliver a biographical lecture on him to the Concord Lyceum. The lecture was not published
during Henry's lifetime. Harding says that it is "chiefly of interest only
because it was Thoreau who wrote it." [60] However, I would argue that
Henry's interest in the famous Elizabethan courtier, soldier, and writer
was therapeutic: that is, by considering the example of Ralegh's life
and death, Thoreau could mitigate his own grief and guilt. He came to
identify Ralegh both with himself and with John. Ralegh had been a
gifted writer, scholar, and adventurer, yet his behavior was by no
means beyond reproach. He had engaged in numerous rivalries for
status and power; moreover, he had dared to approach "forbidden"
women such as Elizabeth Throckmorton, a maid of honor in the
Queen's court—whom he married in spite of the damage it did to his
position. Henry could identify himself with Ralegh—he too had engaged in a most fateful rivalry, and he had dared to pursue the woman
his elder brother loved. In his lecture, Thoreau singles out an example
of Ralegh's competitiveness as worthy of condemnation:

> The base use he made of his recovered influence (after having
> been banished from the court, and even suffered imprisonment
> in consequence of the Queen's displeasure) to procure the dis-
> grace and finally the execution of his rival Essex (who had been
> charged with treason) is the foulest stain upon his escutcheon,
> the one which it is hardest to reconcile with the nobleness and
> generosity which we are inclined to attribute to such a char-
> acter.[61]

On some level Thoreau suspected that he too had been responsible for
the death of a rival, and he felt profound remorse for his actions. It
was, therefore, therapeutic for Thoreau to assert that, in spite of this
"foul stain," Ralegh could be seen as noble, generous, heroic. His gift
for language, his adventurousness, his courage: such qualities of character redeemed Ralegh in Henry's eyes. If Sir Walter's faults could be
overshadowed by his sterling qualities, so could Thoreau minimize his

own transgressions. Although it was *"hard* to reconcile" Ralegh's "foul stains" with "the nobleness and generosity which we are inclined to attribute to such a character," Thoreau believed that the two qualities could be reconciled. It must have severely disturbed the course of Henry's self-therapy when the *Concord Freeman*, reviewing his February 8 lecture, argued that Ralegh could *not* be forgiven his trespasses:

> The public conduct of Raleigh is well known to every historical reader, and no one will be found to question the accuracy of the assertion, that much of it added to the glory of the English name. Yet he had many bad traits of character and is scarcely deserving of the admiration of which he is the object.... Raleigh was a selfish man, and to say that many of his acts were superlatively mean, would be but to utter a simple truth.... His conduct in his last voyage was clearly illegal, and Gondomar was right when he called him and his comrades pirates. He was haughty, insolent, and vindictive, an unchivalrous enemy, and too often a deceitful friend.[62]

Thoreau probably perceived this evaluation as an attack on his own character as well as Ralegh's. He was being told that, on balance, his genius and heroism could not outweigh his general "insolence" or specific deeds (most prominently his competition with, and defeat of, John).

The fact that Ralegh was punished for his most severe transgressions also must have been a salve to Henry's conscience. For his pursuit of forbidden women, as well as for his aggressive attacks on rivals, Sir Walter had been imprisoned for treason and eventually executed. After John's death, Henry had imprisoned himself in his parents' house and had punished himself by developing a near-fatal case of sympathetic lockjaw. That Ralegh could anticipate death with relative equanimity could be well understood by Thoreau; for in his mind, only death could completely wash away the sins he had committed. The peaceful manner of Henry's own death may be partially accounted for by his willingness to absolve sins.

Indeed, if there was anything which helped to redeem Ralegh's transgressions, it was the serene and courageous manner of his dying. The *Freeman* concluded its review of Thoreau's lecture by noting that "the closing scene of his life atoned in the opinion of many for all his errors." [63] In his lecture, Thoreau explains that he has followed Ralegh's life precisely because of the exemplary way in which he died:

"The death scenes of great men are agreeable to consider only when they make another and harmonious chapter in their lives, and we have accompanied our hero thus far because he lived, so to speak, unto the end." [64] It is clear that Thoreau identifies not only himself but also John with Ralegh. When he wrote of Ralegh's last days, he had in mind his own brother's death. John "said from the first he knew he should die, but was perfectly quiet and trustful, saying that God had always been good to him and he could trust Him now. His words and behavior throughout were what Mr. Emerson calls manly, even *great*." By praising Ralegh, Henry could laud John and deny any hostile feelings. If Henry too wished to be great, he needed to follow the example of his brother; he had to be courageous and accepting while living his life and when facing death. John's bravery inspired Henry—already predisposed to Stoicism—to meet life and death bravely, calmly; paradoxically, the memory of John's death—and the loss and guilt associated with it—was itself the ultimate test of his faith and fortitude.

By all accounts, Thoreau continued to mourn the loss of his brother long after the fact. He is known to have dreamed tragic dreams on anniversaries of his brother's death,[65] and many years after the tragedy he "still choked and tears came into his eyes at the mention of John's name." [66] Sanborn remembers hearing a forty-year-old Thoreau sing "his favorite song, *Tom Bowline* by Dibdin, which to Thoreau was a reminiscence of his brother John, so early lost and dearly loved":

> "Here a sheer hulk lies poor Tom Bowline,
>   The darling of our crew;
> No more he'll hear the tempest howlin',
>   For death has broached him to.
> His form was of the manliest beauty,
>   His heart was kind and soft;
> Faithful below he did his duty,
>   But now he's gone aloft.
>
> "Tom never from his word departed,
>   His virtues were so rare;
> His friends were many and true-hearted,
>   His Poll was kind and fair:
> And then he'd sing so blithe and jolly,
>   Ah, many's the time and oft!
> But mirth is turned to melancholy,
>   For Tom has gone aloft.

> "Yet shall poor Tom find pleasant weather,
>   When He who all commands,
> Shall give, to call life's crew together,
>   The word to pipe all hands.
> Thus death, who kings—and tars—despatches,
>   In vain Tom's life has doffed;
> For though his body's under hatches,
>   His soul is gone aloft." [67]

Sanborn remarks that he "never heard Henry speak of this brother except by the parable of this sea-song; his death was a most painful memory, as his life had been sweet and useful, with equal independence of mind, but a less pugnacious turn than his younger brother." [68]

Throughout his life Henry had to struggle not to give in to the feelings associated with his rivalry with John and John's death; to give in to these feelings, to allow the "inward foes" to dominate his consciousness, was to invite breakdown—such breakdown as occurred almost immediately following the tragedy.

There is evidence that Henry had begun writing a book about the Concord-Merrimack trip, the "good week," prior to John's fatal illness. After his brother's death, that book would become ever more difficult and, at the same time, ever more meaningful to complete; for Thoreau could not think of the trip without thinking incessantly of his beloved brother, the "crisis" that probably occurred as they rowed on the placid river, the rivalry for Ellen (who had graced the brothers' boat during the courtship period), the "difference with a Friend," John's illness and his horrible, untimely death. Harding observes that the Concord-Merrimack voyage "through the haze of memory was to become a tangible symbol of Thoreau's love and admiration for his lost brother." [69] But the book was also, I think, an attempt to both expiate and deny guilt.[70] Thoreau went to Walden at least partially to "conduct some unfinished business"—the writing of *A Week*. He could not rest until his memorial to John was completed; it was a form of penitence, just as the period at Walden was itself a kind of penitence. Yet the writing of the book, which demanded that Henry picture himself alongside his brother, was an excruciating task. It was not so much that Henry had to "get away from it all" [71] to write the *Week*, but that he needed to gather his courage to face the project. Although there are significant hidden references to John (and Ellen) in the finished work (such as the account of the dream concerning a "difference with a Friend"), John is not directly discussed; it is as if Henry could not bear fully to confront the memories and feelings associated with his brother.[72] Surely, the writing at Walden of *A Week* was therapeutic "grief work" for Thoreau in that he could remember with fondness his friendship with John, affirm their camaraderie to himself and the public, and edit out most of the negative reminiscences. However, working on *A Week* must also have aroused the very grief and guilt he wished to placate. John's death unquestionably postponed and made more painful the completion of the book, though we cannot know for sure what kind of work it would have been had John *not* died. The first inscription to *A Week* reads, "Where'er thou sail'st who sailed with me, / Though now thou climbest loftier mounts, / And fairer rivers dost ascend, / Be thou my Muse, my Brother—." [73] Henry wanted to believe John was his Muse and that he gave his blessings and inspiration to his surviving brother. But lurking somewhere in the recesses of Thoreau's mind was the fear that his brother refused him this service.

In order to protect himself from being overwhelmed by his grief and guilt, Thoreau could write only obliquely about his brother's death and the issues associated with it. Perhaps the most eloquent example of this indirect approach, and of the lasting influence of John's death, are the opening chapters of *Cape Cod*. Without knowing the biographical background of Henry's first trip to the Cape, one could not fully appreciate the significance of the early chapters. Thoreau left Concord with his companion Ellery Channing on October 9, 1849 and headed for the Cape:

> When they reached Boston, they learned that the Provincetown steamer on which they had planned to sail had not yet reached port because of a violent storm and that a sailing brig, the St. John, filled with immigrants from Ireland, had been wrecked at Cohasset with the loss of 145 lives. Although Thoreau had boasted that he would not go around the corner to see the world blow up, he immediately changed his plans and journeyed down to see the wreck. He called upon Ellen Sewall, now Mrs. Joseph Osgood, and with her husband walked along the shore.[74]

So here was Thoreau seeking out—perhaps ambivalently—Ellen Sewall Osgood and witnessing with her husband the wreckage of the *St. John* on the shores of Cohasset. Characteristically, he does not refer to Ellen or her husband in *Cape Cod*. It seems inconceivable that in the presence of the same woman he and John had both pursued, and while observing the wreckage of the *St. "John,"* Henry could have avoided pondering the death of his brother, as well as his own guilt-provoking courtship of Ellen. Thoughts of John seem to condition his perception of the shipwreck scene and other scenes of the Cape. The sight of bodies wasting on the beach evoked memories of his brother's wasting body. Tom Bowline had died at sea, and so had those on the *St. John*. Looking at the body of a dead girl, Thoreau must have been vividly reminded of the ugliness of John's demise:

> I saw many marble feet and matted heads as the cloths were raised, and one livid, swollen, and mangled body of a drowned girl, — who probably had intended to go out to service in some American family, —to which some rags still adhered, with a string, half-concealed by the flesh, about its swollen neck; the coiled-up wreck of a human hulk, gashed by the rocks or fishes, so that the bone and muscle were exposed, but quite bloodless, —merely red and white, —with wide-open and staring eyes, yet lustreless, dead-lights; or like the cabin windows of a stranded vessel, filled with sand.[75]

This horrifying account is followed by the description of the "morbid grief reaction" of a mother, "who had left her infant behind for her sister to bring"; she "came and looked into these boxes, and saw in one ... her child in her sister's arms, as if the sister had meant to be found thus; and within three days after, the mother died from the effect of that sight." [76] This mother, like Thoreau, had responded "hysterically" to the sight of her dead sibling and child (the deaths of whom she may have felt responsible for). She had died after the death of her loved ones; Thoreau had come close to dying when John had died. Probably the most evident, though indirect, reference to his own brother is his subsequent reflection on the "impressiveness" of the scene—with so many broken bodies cast up upon the shore:

> If I had found one body cast up upon the beach in some lonely place, it would have affected me more. I sympathize rather with the winds and waves, as if to toss and mangle these poor human bodies was the order of the day. If this was the law of Nature, why waste any time in awe or pity? If the last day were come, we should not think so much about the separation of friends or the blighted prospects of individuals. I saw that corpses might be multiplied, as on the field of battle, till they no longer affected us in any degree, as exceptions to the common lot of humanity. Take all the graveyards together, they are always the majority.

> It is the individual and private that demands our sympathy.
> A man can attend but one funeral in the course of his life, can
> behold but one corpse.[77]

Can anyone doubt that the "funeral" and "corpse" Thoreau had in
mind were John's? Certainly no one else's death had affected him so
profoundly.

Just as the outer landscape of Cape Cod was "bleak and cheerless,"
and "barren and desolate," [78] so was Thoreau's inner landscape when
he contemplated John. In order to mitigate his feelings of grief and
guilt, it was necessary for him to continue his "grief work." Thus
Thoreau, soon after his individual and private reference to the one
significant "corpse" in his own life, seeks to deny that there is any
reason for grief, since the dead have only traveled to a brighter shore:

> I saw their empty hulks that came to land; but they themselves,
> meanwhile, were cast upon some shore yet further west, toward
> which we are all tending and which we shall reach at last, it
> may be through storm and darkness, as they did....
>
> The mariner who makes the safest port in Heaven, perchance,
> seems to his friends on earth to be shipwrecked, for they deem
> Boston Harbor a better place; though perhaps invisible to them,
> a skillful pilot comes to meet him, and the fairest and balmiest
> gales blow off that coast, his good ship makes the land in halcyon
> days, and he kisses the shore in rapture there, while his old hulk
> tosses in the surf here.[79]

John, like Tom Bowline, has not truly died. And someday, Henry
urgently hopes, he will gain reconciliation with his brother on that
"shore further west." His desire in later life to "go west" was in part a
desire to join John.

That Thoreau is dealing with private grief and guilt in the early
chapters of *Cape Cod* is suggested by several remarks and observations.
Noting the comment of one writer that the "inhabitants of Sandwich
generally manifest a fond and steady adherence to the manners, employments, and modes of living which characterized their fathers,"
Thoreau says, "No people ever lived by cursing their fathers, however
great a curse their fathers might have been to them." [80] Frequently
given to complaining about the inadequacy of "the fathers" (if not
his own father), Henry here must forswear negative feelings regarding his father—and more particularly, his "fatherly" brother—even if
he acknowledges that he has been "cursed" by them. "Cursing" his

brother had been guilt-provoking when he was alive; after his death, it was an even greater transgression against conscience. Yet at the same time, Thoreau suspects that he has been "cursed" by John for having pursued Ellen, for desiring what we wanted for himself, for competing with and outliving him. Indeed, he speaks later of reading with a "melancholy kind of interest" a "Shipwrecked Seaman's Manual": "for the sound of the surf, or, you might say, the moaning of the sea is heard all through it, as if its author were the sole survivor of a shipwreck himself." [81] The author of *Cape Cod*, he knew, had survived the shipwreck while his brother had been drowned and dashed against the rocks. Having outlived his elder brother and surpassed his father, he feels accursed and accused. It will be remembered that Henry had once imagined that the crows sullenly disapproved of his pursuit of Ellen; in effect, the crows had been the imagined accusation of John incarnate. Thus it is indicative that Henry should allude to the presence of so many blackbirds in *Cape Cod:* "The blackbirds, however, still molest the corn. I saw them at it the next summer, and there were many scarecrows, if not scare-blackbirds, in the fields, which I often mistook for men. From which I concluded, that either many men were not married, or many blackbirds were." [82] Thoreau himself may be taken as both scarecrow and scared of crows. He needed to fend off the accusations, the curses; but sometimes he feared that the blackbirds could not be warded off. One way to ward off guilt and retribution was to emphasize that he was one of those men who was not married; he had not succeeded where his brother had failed. This desire to affirm his bachelorhood may account in part for the many wry, acid comments on marriage and domesticity in *Cape Cod*. Also helping to account for his state of mind was the recent presence of Ellen Sewall Osgood by his side; having so recently been confronted with what he had lost, Henry felt it imperative to claim that he had not lost anything.

Because his sense of sinfulness had been aroused by the wreck of the *St. John*, the sight of dead bodies, and the presence of Ellen Sewall, he welcomed the "dreary" landscape of the Cape as bracing and purifying:

> I was glad to have got out of the towns, where I am wont to feel unspeakably mean and disgraced, —to have left behind me for a season the bar-rooms of Massachusetts, where the full-grown are not weaned from savage and filthy habits, —still sucking a cigar. My spirits rose in proportion to the outward dreariness. The towns need to be ventilated. The gods would be pleased to

see some pure flames from their altars. They are not to be appeased with cigar-smoke.[83]

If nature seems to be feminine in much of Thoreau's writing, in *Cape Cod* it is masculine, forceful, even savage:

> The white breakers were rushing to the shore; the foam ran up the sand, and then ran back as far as we could see—and we imagined how much farther along the Atlantic Coast, before and behind us—as regularly, to compare great things with small, as the master of a choir beats time with his white wand; and ever and anon a higher wave caused us hastily to deviate from our path, and we looked back on our tracks filled with water and foam. The breakers looked like droves of a thousand wild horses of Neptune, rushing to the shore, with their white manes streaming far behind.[84]

It is as if, by acknowledging the wild force of the waves, he is acknowledging the power of the masculine figures in his life—his father and elder brother. By granting them all power, by humbling himself before them, he is able to forswear any desire to challenge or defeat them, thereby diminishing the sense of sinfulness. Moreover, the severity of ocean and storm can be accepted by Thoreau as punishment for transgressions. Thus, he says, "Instead of having a dog to growl before your door, to have an Atlantic Ocean to growl for a whole Cape! On the whole, we were glad of the storm, which would show us the ocean in its angriest mood." [85] If the ocean (and male-figures) can be perceived as gaining just retribution, then Thoreau need no longer feel guilty.[86]

One final indication of how the painful memory of John continued to haunt Henry occurs when he discusses the responses of Cape Cod women "whose husbands and sons are either abroad on the sea, or else drowned, and there is nobody but they and their ministers left behind." One old account, observes Thoreau, says that

> "hysteric fits are very common in Orleans, Eastham, and the towns below, particularly on Sunday, in the times of divine service. When one woman is affected, five or six others generally sympathize with her; and the congregation is thrown into the utmost confusion. Several old men suppose, unphilosophically and uncharitably, perhaps, that the will is partly concerned, and that ridicule and threats would have a tendency to prevent the evil." [87]

It is unlikely that Henry could have read this account without contemplating his own grief-reaction. If there is any doubt that he is
pondering his private grief, it is dispelled by the remarkable passage
which immediately follows:

> We saw one singularly masculine woman, however, in a house on
> this very plain, who did not look as if she was ever troubled with
> hysterics, or sympathized with those who were; or, perchance,
> life itself was to her a hysteric fit,—a Nauset woman, of a hard-
> ness and coarseness such as no man ever possesses or suggests.
> It was enough to see the vertebrae and sinews of her neck, and
> her set jaws of iron, which would have bitten a board nail in two
> in their ordinary action,—braced against the world, talking like
> a man-of-war's-man in petticoats, or as if shouting to you through
> a breaker; who looked as if it made her head ache to live; hard
> enough for any enormity. I looked upon her as one who had
> committed infanticide; who never had a brother, unless it were
> some wee thing that died in infancy,—for what need of him?—
> and whose father must have died before she was born.[88]

By describing this "singularly masculine woman," Thoreau is
able to perform some much-needed "grief work." He manages to deny
that *he* is the enemy of infants, brothers, and fathers—even though he
strongly suspects, on some level of the psyche, that he has been the foe
of masculine figures and has even been responsible for the death of the
male he most loved and respected. He obliquely indicates that it is the
dominating woman, the "man-of-war's-man in petticoats," who is the
enemy of infants, brothers, and fathers; it is she who has "committed
infanticide" and who "defeats" (by outsurviving) the brother and
father.[89] This Nauset woman may have given Thoreau the opportunity
to vent indirectly his hostile feelings toward his much-loved but
emasculating mother. By condemning her lack of response to the death
of brother or father, he also is able to affirm his own love for John
and, more particularly, John, Jr. Unlike the Nauset woman, Henry
had responded "hysterically" to the death of his brother; no "ridicule
or threats" could have prevented his sympathetic lockjaw, his deep
feelings of grief, loss, and guilt at John's passage to a "shore yet
further west." Thoreau would continue to mourn John's passing and
be haunted by his memory. He had lost his brother, and he would never
fully recover from that loss. His life was forever transformed.

Epilogue: "Over Snow-capped Mountains to Reach the Sun"

In the "Natural History of Massachusetts," Thoreau expressed his admiration for how the trees in winter "grow up without forethought, regardless of the time and circumstances." They "do not wait as man does, but now is the golden age of the sapling. . . . The 'winter of *their* discontent' never comes." [1] During the 1842–45 period, a prolonged winter of discontent for Thoreau, he must often have wondered how many more snow-capped mountains he would have to climb before he reached the sun—or if he would ever reach the sun. How much longer would he have to wait, to prepare, before he could seize the opportunity for greatness and enter upon his own "golden age"? As drifts of winter storms gathered about his outward life—at Emerson's in 1842–43, at Staten Island from May to December 1843, at his mother's house and father's pencil factory in 1844—Thoreau turned with a heightened sense of urgency to his inner resources for warmth, hope, and purpose.

Soon after arriving at Staten Island, where he was expected not only to tutor William Emerson's child but also to rub shoulders with New York's prominent literati and thereby advance his own career, Thoreau wrote "A Winter Walk." If the winter of discontent had been cold in Concord, it was like the Arctic on Staten Island. The erstwhile "traveller in Concord" felt homesick and out of place in New York; [2] his essay, an affectionate remembrance of Concord's winter woods, "showed the depth of his need for the Concord environment." [3] However, "A Winter Walk" also shows Thoreau using winter imagery to reassure himself that his inner life was not frozen solid, that he had not lost his potential for greatness, that his gifts were incubating within.

Even if he seems to be making little progress toward the realization of his dreams in these dark hours of his life, the "recent tracks of the fox or otter, in the yard, remind us that each hour of the night is crowded with events, and primeval nature is still working and making tracks in the snow." [4] Just as "corn grows in the night" and "primeval nature" makes "tracks in the snow," so does Thoreau, despite the outer darkness, continue to grow and saunter toward the fulfillment of his aspirations. An "inward heat" survives in the coldest weather: "Meanwhile we step hastily along through the powdery snow, warmed by an inward heat, enjoying an Indian summer still, in the increased glow of thought and feeling." [5] Thoreau speaks of a "subterranean fire in nature which never goes out, and which no cold can chill. It finally melts the great snow, and in January or July is only buried under a thicker or thinner covering." [6] While this "fire" exists in nature, Thoreau also cherishes the belief that he himself, as he trudges over icy hills, is a keeper of the fire: "This subterranean fire has its altar in each man's breast, for in the coldest day, and on the bleakest hill, the traveller cherishes a warmer fire within the folds of his cloak than is kindled on any hearth." [7] The "evergreen" of the pines is "that portion of the summer which does not fade, the permanent year, the unwithered grass"; [8] similarly Thoreau feels that he, too, is evergreen, that he nurtures in his soul a summer which will not fade. He is like the lichen which survives and maintains a green tinge on the coldest of rocks. Imagery of hibernation seems particularly comforting, for he recognizes his own situation as comparable to that of animals who must depend upon their accumulated resources to make it through the winter. He begins "A Winter Walk" with the observation that "the meadow-mouse [mole] has slept in his snug gallery in the sod, the owl has sat in a hollow tree in the depth of the swamp, the rabbit, the squirrel, and the fox have all been housed." [9] Later he explains, "How much more living is the life that is in nature, the furred life which still survives the stinging nights, and, from amidst fields and woods covered with frost and snow, sees the sun rise." [10] The river is compared to a hibernating animal:

> still holding on its way underneath, with a faint stertorous, rumbling sound, as if, like the bear and marmot, it too had hibernated, and we had followed its faint summer-trail to where it earthed itself in snow and ice. At first we should have thought that rivers would be empty and dry in mid-winter, or else frozen solid till the spring thawed them; but their volume is not diminished even, for only a superficial cold bridges their surface. The thousand springs which feed the lakes and streams are flowing still. The issues of a few surface springs only are closed, and they go to swell the deepest reservoirs. Nature's wells are below the frost.[11]

Although his creative river may appear to have frozen over or dried up, Thoreau seeks to assure himself that, under the surface, the river continues to flow, the reservoir of genius is deep and full.

The imagery of hibernation in "A Winter Walk" is a precursor to the memorable passage on artistic self-sufficiency in *A Week*, where Thoreau compares the poet to a hibernating creature:

> The poet is he that hath fat enough, like bears and marmots, to suck his claws all winter. He hibernates in this world and feeds on his own marrow. We love to think in winter, as we walk over the snowy pastures, of those happy dreamers that lie under the sod, of dormice and all that race of dormant creatures, which have such a superfluity of life enveloped in thick folds of fur, impervious to cold. Alas, the poet too is in one sense a sort of dormouse gone into winter quarters of deep and serene thoughts, insensible to surrounding circumstances.[12]

Thoreau himself was a "dormant dreamer" in 1843 and 1844; he was in the process of discovering just how much words and art meant to him, how language provided him with a "superfluity of life" which helped make him "impervious to cold." Erikson speaks of "distantiation," of the readiness of an isolated person, of one who has been unable to achieve interpersonal intimacy, to "fortify" his "territory of intimacy and solidarity."[13] Cut off forever from closeness to his brother, unable and unwilling to become involved in sexual and marital relationships, alienated from the community, uncomfortable with his parents and with Emerson, Thoreau felt a deep need to "fortify" his personal territory. Only by turning inward, by relying on his own resources, by "sucking his claws all winter," could he mitigate his sense of isolation. As the year 1845 approached, he became increasingly cognizant of his need for intimacy with his own language and art (as well as with nature and safely distant readers) as a means of compensating for his lack of interpersonal intimacy. A month before his brother's death, Thoreau perceived the "lichens on the rocks" as "somewhat more of my kith and kin"; he then remarked poignantly in his journal,

> I know of no redeeming qualities in me but a sincere love for some things, and when I am reproved I have to fall back on this ground. This is my argument in reserve for all cases. My love is invulnerable. Meet me on that ground, and you will find me strong. When I am condemned, and condemn myself utterly, I think straightway, "But I rely on my love for some things." Therein am I God-propped. (*J*, I: 296)

As long as he remained enveloped in the "thick folds" of his art and consciousness, he would not be vulnerable, he would not have to de-

pend upon mutuality and reciprocation. One-way passions would preserve Thoreau in his loneliest moments. Words, especially in the form
of a poetic prose, became the medium through which he could express
most eloquently his invulnerable love.

Through his art, moreover, he could gain some measure of "generative" fulfillment without depending upon other people. "Generativity," says Erikson, is "primarily the concern for establishing and guiding the next generation," but he acknowledges that having and caring
for one's own children is not the only mode of generativity, that gifted
people, for instance, may in part satisfy their need to be "parents"
through "other forms of altruistic concern and creativity." [14] Thoreau
knew by 1843 that he would have no children of his own. However,
through his writings he could seek to be a "maker," a father (and perhaps a mother) to his contemporaries and to future generations. He
could affirm his concern for nature and for humankind; he could establish a caring relationship with his reading audience while keeping
them at a safe distance. Furthermore, the writings, the words themselves, would become "children" which he "spontaneously generated,"
and in which he had a "libidinal investment." Struggling painfully
against "stagnation," [15] against the fear of inner sterility, Thoreau
needed to feel pregnant and fertile, independently of others, to experience a sense of inner richness and fecundity. Although "inner
space" may apply especially to a woman's sense of harboring (or potentially harboring) new life within her body, Erikson says it also can
refer to gifted and creative persons who "specialize" in "inwardness . . .
and sensitive indwelling" and who "are prone to cyclic swings of mood
while they carry conceived ideas to fruition and toward the act of
disciplined creation." [16] Thoreau was coming to realize that, through
his art, he could feel inwardly rich, that he could be one of those men
"who have the seeds of life in them" (*J*, IV: 478).[17] In 1843–44 he
wished to believe that within "thick folds of fur" new life was stirring.
The gift lay incubating in his "winter quarters," waiting for the
warmth of spring to release it. Soon, he hoped, the gestation period
would end and the metamorphosis would take place, as it does for the
caddice-worms (the larvae of the Plicippenes) depicted in "A Winter
Walk": "Their small cylindrical cases built around themselves, composed of flags, sticks, grass, and withered leaves, shells, and pebbles, in
form and color like the wrecks which strew the bottom. . . . Anon they
will leave their sunken habitations, and, crawling up the stems of
plants, or to the surface, like gnats, as perfect insects henceforth,
flutter over the surface of the water." [18]

Thoreau ended his disappointing Staten Island sojourn in December 1843, moved in with his family, and resumed work in his father's pencil factory. He had come full circle; having tried to break away from home and mother, from being an Apollo serving an Admetus and at the same time surpassing Admetus, he now found himself, at least outwardly, back where he had begun in 1837–38. With his brother gone, there was even more pressure on Henry to be economically responsible and socially acceptable. It was at this juncture, in April 1844, that he and Edward Hoar, the son of Judge Samuel Hoar, went fishing, started to cook the fish, and set fire to the Concord woods—a fire which made the winter of discontent even colder. Not until six years later, in his 1850 journal, did Thoreau describe the occurrence:

> I once set fire to the woods. Having set out, one April day, to go to the sources of the Concord River in a boat with a single companion, meaning to camp on the bank at night or seek a lodging in some neighboring country inn or farmhouse, we took fishing tackle with us that we might fitly procure our food from the stream, Indian-like. At the shoemaker's near the river, we obtained a match, which we had forgotten. Though it was thus early in the spring, the river was low, for there had not been much rain, and we succeeded in catching a mess of fish sufficient for our dinner before we had left the town, and by the shores of Fair Haven Bay we proceeded to cook them. The earth was uncommonly dry, and our fire, kindled far from the woods in a sunny recess in the hillside on the east of the pond, suddenly caught the dry grass of the previous year which grew about the stump on which it was kindled. We sprang to extinguish it with our hands and feet, and then we fought it with a board obtained from the boat, but in a few minutes it was beyond our reach; being on the side of a hill, it spread rapidly upward, through the long, dry, wiry grass interspersed with bushes.
>
> "Well, where will this end?" asked my companion. I saw that it might be bounded by Well Meadow Brook on one side, but would, perchance, go to the village side of the brook. "It will go to town," I answered. While my companion took the boat back down the river, I set out through the woods to inform the owners and to raise the town. The fire had already spread a dozen rods on every side and went leaping and cracking wildly irreclaimably toward the wood. That way went the flames with wild delight, and we felt that we had no control over the demonic creature

to which we had given birth. We had kindled many fires in the woods before, burning a clear space in the grass, without ever kindling such a fire as this. (*J*, II: 21–22)

Thoreau ran toward the town and finally met the "owner of the field, with whom [he] returned at once to the woods, running all the way." While others in the vicinity, now aware of the fire, went to town for more help, Thoreau—instead of making efforts to put out the conflagration—set out for the highest rock on Fair Haven Cliff:

I . . . sat down upon it to observe the progress of the flames, which were rapidly approaching me, now about a mile distant from the spot where the fire was kindled. . . . It was a glorious spectacle, and I was the only one there to enjoy it. The fire now reached the base of the cliff and then rushed up its sides. The squirrels ran before it in blind haste, and three pigeons dashed into the midst of the smoke. The flames flashed up the pines to their tops, as if they were powder. (*J*, II: 23–24)

Only when Thoreau "was about to be surrounded by the fire" did he retreat from Olympus and help his fellow townsmen put out the flames.

On May 3, 1844 the *Concord Freeman* reported the fire as having consumed not less than 300 acres and having cost $2000 in damages. It was finally extinguished by "trenching, beating the fire with pine branches, and lighting 'back fires,' all of which was done cooly and systematically." In the concluding paragraph of the report, the *Freeman* did not hesitate to place the blame:

The fire, we understand, was communicated to the woods through the thoughtlessness of two of our citizens, who kindled it in a *pine stump*, near the Pond, for the purpose of making a chowder. As every thing around them was as combustible almost as a fireship, the flames spread with rapidity, and hours elapsed before it could be subdued. It is to be hoped that this unfortunate result of sheer carelessness will be borne in mind by those who may visit the woods in future for recreation.[19]

Thoreau himself reports that, while some owners "bore their loss like men, . . . other some declared behind my back that I was a 'damned rascal;' and a flibbertigibbet or two, who crowed like an old cock, shouted some reminiscences of 'burnt woods' from safe recesses for some years after" (*J*, II: 25). Harding says, there was talk of court prosecution of the two young men and were it not for the fact that Hoar was a son of the town's leading citizen, something might have been made of it. As it was, Hoar's father is said to have paid some damages to the Hubbards and the Wheelers.... Even on into the twentieth century one of the Wheeler girls was frequently heard to say, "Don't talk to me about Henry Thoreau. Didn't I all that winter have to go to school with a smootched apron or dress because I had to pitch in and help fill the wood box with partly charred wood?" [20]

It is evident that the woods-burning episode had deep and long-lasting repercussions for Thoreau. That he denies any great perturbation six years after the event only serves to emphasize how disturbing it was. To Thoreau, who wished to be considered a nature-lover and naturalist, setting fire to the woods must have caused him to feel much shame and guilt.[21] As if to minimize the enormity of his offense, he speaks in his journal of having burned over a hundred acres when the actual extent of the damage, as reported by the *Freeman*, was "not less" than three hundred acres. He seeks to avoid guilt by equating his own act with any act of nature:

Hitherto I had felt like a guilty person, —nothing but shame and regret. But now [sitting on Fair Haven Cliff] I settled the matter with myself shortly. I said to myself: "Who are these men who are said to be the owners of these woods, and how am I related to them? I have set fire to the forest, but I have done no wrong therein, and now it is as if the lightning had done it. These flames are but consuming their natural food." (It has never troubled me from that day to this more than if the lightning had done it. The trivial fishing was all that disturbed me and disturbs me still.) (*J*, II: 23)

Thoreau also tries to mitigate his chagrin by pointing to the offenses of the train:

The locomotive engine has since burned over nearly all the same ground and more, and in some measure blotted out the memory of the previous fire. For a long time after I had learned this lesson I marvelled that while matches and tinder were contemporaries the world was not consumed; why the houses that have hearths were not burned before another day; if the flames were not as hungry now as when I waked them. I at once ceased to regard the owners and my own fault, —if fault there was any in the matter, —and attended to the phenomenon before me, determined to make the most of it. (*J*, II: 25)

There can be little doubt that Thoreau, despite his disclaimers (and because he so obviously *needed* to disclaim), was profoundly ashamed and that, moreover, he perceived his community as intent upon shaming him. If townspeople had felt sympathy toward him after John's death and approved of his recent attempts to shoulder responsibility in the parental home and business, they now had reverted to regarding him as "irresponsible." The cold stares Thoreau received (or *thought* he received) from Concordians may well have provided him with renewed impetus to "live away by the pond."

So far, it has been suggested that the incident itself was "purely" an accident. Yet, as Edel has observed, Thoreau was one of the least likely people in Concord, given his knowledge of the outdoors and his presumable experience in fire-building, to let a fire get out of control completely by accident.[22] It is possible that, on some level of the psyche, Thoreau *wanted* to start a fire which would burn all "houses that have hearths" in Concord. The fire may have represented not only an expression of hostility toward a town which did not appreciate him and wished to ensnare him but also an attempt to destroy those in Concord who wished him dead instead of his brother.[23] In a sense, allowing the fire to run rampant may have been Thoreau's way—however "unconscious"—of protecting his own life and of eliminating those he perceived as deadly enemies. In his self-defense six years after the fact, Thoreau expressed great hostility toward the townspeople: "I could not help noticing that the crowd who were so ready to condemn the individual who had kindled the fire did not sympathize with the owners of the wood, but were in fact highly elated and as it were thankful for the opportunity which had afforded them so much sport" (*J*, II: 24). Though he speaks sympathetically of some of the owners who "bore their loss like men," he condemns those who condemned him. One farmer who, upon first hearing from Henry of the fire had said, "Well, it is none of my stuff," is described with some glee by Thoreau as later "striving earnestly to save his corded wood, his stuff, which the fire had already seized and which it after all consumed" (*J*, II: 24). In another sense, the fire may have been a form of *self*-punishment, a way of courting both physical and emotional disaster. It will be remembered that Thoreau stayed on top of Fair Haven Hill until the last possible moment, when he "was about to be surrounded by the fire." Something self-hating and self-destructive in Thoreau may have led him to feel that he should be fully surrounded and consumed by the fire.

An even more plausible, if partial, explanation of the fire—and most particularly of the clearly non-accidental behavior *after* the fire had spread—is that Thoreau somehow wanted to insure that he would not be well accepted by the community. To be accepted by the community as the responsible, hardworking son of John and Cynthia was threatening to the sense of unique identity he fostered within. The situation was in some respects similar to the one that he faced when he returned to Concord after graduation and was confronted with the prospect of "success without identity." In 1844 it was once again necessary to preserve his moratorium at any cost, so that he could still be in a position to seize the opportunity for greatness. Speaking of the fire six years later, Thoreau said, "To be sure, I felt a little ashamed when I reflected on what a trivial occasion this had happened, that at the time I was no better employed than my townsmen" (*J*, II: 25). The fire, and his "superior" behavior after it had started, established once and for all that he was different from his townsmen. At the time he was discontent with the knowledge that he was "no better employed" than they; the fire incident protected Henry from being considered, or considering himself, "one of them." By alienating his neighbors, by keeping them at a distance, he could reassure himself that he *would* be "better employed" someday. Moreover, his actions would cause his parents discomfort; perhaps he may have felt it would be easier to escape the household and the pencil factory if his parents were embarrassed and upset by his behavior. In short, starting the fire and then—more obviously—withdrawing to Fair Haven Cliff while his townsmen toiled to extinguish it may have been an attempt, albeit not fully conscious, to keep his "inward fire" burning. The colder his community's response to him, the more certain he could be that the "subterranean fire" smoldering within his breast would eventually be ignited in the open air.

The opportunity for greatness came just in the nick of time. Had Thoreau waited much longer, the flame of genius might have flickered out, the creative garden would have died with the weeds, the gift would have been stillborn. When Emerson bought land on Walden Pond's shore in autumn 1844, potential intersected with opportunity; the eventual result would be the emergence of the "great man" who would write *Walden* and "Civil Disobedience," whose presence would be felt by the nation long after his passing. Remembering the example

214 YOUNG MAN THOREAU

of his college roommate Stearns Wheeler, who had died in 1843, encouraged by his friend Ellery Channing to "build yourself a hut, & there begin the grand process of devouring yourself alive," [24] and impelled by profound personal needs and aspirations, Thoreau received permission from Waldo to "live away by the pond." So it was that, by his own account, in late March 1845 the long winter of discontent seemed to be coming to an end:

> I borrowed an axe and went down to the woods by Walden Pond, nearest to where I intended to build my house, and began to cut down some tall arrowy white pines, still in their youth, for timber.... They were pleasant spring days, in which the winter of man's discontent was thawing as well as the earth, and the life that had lain torpid began to stretch itself.[25]

On July 4, Independence Day, Thoreau finally moved into a home of his own [26] and reported, on July 5, that it "makes me think of some mountain houses I have seen, which seemed to have a fresher auroral atmosphere about them, as I fancy of the halls of Olympus" (*J*, I: 361).

At Walden Thoreau came as close as he ever would in real life to reaching the sun, to achieving a satisfying identity. There he was better able to believe in his heroism and independence while still living close to, and remaining dependent upon, home, mother, and local associations.[27] He could consider himself a "traveller in Concord." Feeling hostility toward and from the town, he could aggressively set himself apart at Walden as superior, as distant from the "triviality" and materialism of Concordians.[28] He was able to perceive himself as living "sincerely" in a "distant land" which was only a short walk from the village; his neighbors were sure to hear his message, to hear him "brag as lustily as Chanticleer in the morning," yet he was protected from their barbs at "Walled In" Pond.

Years earlier he had associated the pond with purity. Living there, he could devote each day to purifying himself, to washing away his guilt, to contrition and asceticism, to reassuring himself of piety. He could finally come to terms with his grief, recover from the loss of "hound, bay horse, and turtle dove," and regain health. Returning to Walden was in some respects like returning to the pre-oedipal, pre-rivalry past, to the maternal breast, to the womb. To penetrate the transparent waters and plumb the pure depths of the pond; to cut through its ice and sound its bottom; to stare lovingly into the pond which was itself "earth's eye"; to revel in its risings and fallings, its "undulations," the "heaving of its breast"; to possess the pond in his imagination: these activities helped him to sublimate his libidinal longings.

While strategically withdrawing himself from society and embracing solitude, Thoreau found himself capable of establishing a compensatory intimacy with nature, himself, and his art; he grew firmer in his conviction that he was inwardly fertile. In the sunlight of Walden, the period of artistic incubation and gestation ended. Talent was at long last transformed to a genius which burst from the coccoon and took flight. Thoreau was able to complete *A Week on the Concord and Merrimack Rivers;* he also wrote voluminously in his journal, composed lectures, and finished the first of many drafts of *Walden.*[29]

The writing and seven years of revising *Walden* was Thoreau's way of assuring himself that he could continue to live in the sunlight of his Walden experience even after he had left the pond. The book emerged out of his desperate need to keep away the shadows of identity confusion, shame, and guilt—shadows which continued to hover threateningly over him in the post-Walden years.[30] Thoreau's intensely desired self-conception was precarious; the man who in the 1854 edition of *Walden* had proposed not "to write an ode to dejection, but to brag as lustily as Chanticleer in the morning" had, in the fragment of an earlier inscription to *Walden* (which he crossed out) admitted, "I could tell a pitiful story respecting myself . . . with a sufficient list of failures, and flow as humbly as the very gutters." [31] It thus became imperative for Thoreau to cling to his Walden identity—indeed, to create and believe in a persona who was more independent and purer than the real man who had lived by the pond. It is this persona, this "presence"—rather than the historical Thoreau—which has captured the imagination of so many Americans.[32] In writing *Walden,* Thoreau created a myth of personality and experience which helped to sustain him, and which has given inspiration and hope to others.

Walden was, moreover, Thoreau's final proof that the Walden experience had been successful, that his commitment to ideals and art—in the face of much temptation, opposition, bewilderment, and waiting—had been worth it. The story of the artist in the city of Kouroo is a metaphor for his own commitment and artistic achievement:

> There was an artist in the city of Kouroo who was disposed to strive after perfection. One day it came into his mind to make a staff. Having considered that in an imperfect work time is an ingredient, but into a perfect work time does not enter, he said to himself, It shall be perfect in all respects, though I should do

nothing else in my life. He proceeded instantly to the forest for
wood, being resolved that it should not be made of unsuitable
material; and as he searched for and rejected stick after stick,
his friends gradually deserted him, for they grew old in their
works and died, but he grew not older by a moment. His single-
ness of purpose and resolution, and his elevated piety, endowed
him, without his knowledge, with perennial youth. As he made
no compromise with Time, Time kept out of his way, and only
sighed at a distance because he could not overcome him. Before
he had found a stock in all respects suitable the city of Kouroo
was a hoary ruin, and he sat on one of its mounds to peel the
stick. Before he had given it the proper shape the dynasty of the
Candahars was at an end, and with the point of the stick he wrote
the name of the last of that race in the sand, and then resumed
his work. By the time he had smoothed and polished the staff
Kalpa was no longer the pole-star; and ere he had put on the
ferule and the head adorned with precious stones, Brahma had
awoke and slumbered many times. But why do I stay to mention
these things? When the finishing stroke was put to his work, it
suddenly expanded before the eyes of the astonished artist into
the fairest of all the creations of Brahma. He had made a new
system in making a staff, a world with full and fair proportions; in
which, though the old cities and dynasties had passed away, fairer
and more glorious ones had taken their places. And now he saw
by the heap of shavings still fresh at his feet, that, for him and
his work, the former lapse of time had been an illusion, and that
no more time had elapsed than is required for a single scintilla-
tion from the brain of Brahma to fall on and inflame the tinder of
a mortal brain. The material was pure, and his art was pure; how
could the result be other than wonderful? [33]

The "staff" was *Walden*—in which he succeeded in making a "new system," a "world with full and fair proportions; in which, though the
old cities and dynasties had passed away, fairer and more glorious ones
had taken their places." The "result" was indeed wonderful.

If at Walden and in writing *Walden* Thoreau was committed to
his art, he was also committed to non-commitment. "As long as possible
live free and uncommitted," he said.[34] In his own life he had followed
this advice, and it had brought him both pain and pleasure. He had
often seemed to prefer the moratorium, "perennial youth," waiting,
and preparation to adulthood and consummation. Walden and *Walden*

made it possible for him to see the moratorium as fulfilling in itself, as perhaps the most constructive mode of living. In the experience at Walden and in the book, Thoreau provided Americans with the archetype, in deed and word, of a psychosocial moratorium. He speaks eloquently of each person's need, at some stage of his or her life, to refrain from commitments and escape entanglements, to retreat from "busi-ness" and the demands and expectations of other people, to get in touch with the self, to experiment with fresh ideas and identities. Just as *Walden* suggests how Thoreau struggled to resist "success without identity" and "other-directedness," so does it call on each individual to resist anything short of personal authenticity. To accept what is not authentic, what is not autonomously determined, was to doom oneself to a "life of quiet desperation." [35] Only by means of a moratorium, which is itself a "crisis in our lives," can one discover or recover oneself; only by "internal industry and expansion" can the metamorphosis occur. Thoreau says in *Walden:*

> Perhaps we should never procure a new suit, however ragged or dirty the old, until we have so conducted, so enterprised or sailed in some way, that we feel like new men in the old, and that to retain it would be like keeping new wine in old bottles. Our moulting season, like that of the fowls, must be a crisis in our lives. The loon retires to solitary ponds to spend it. Thus also the snake casts its slough, and the caterpillar its wormy coat, by an internal industry and expansion: for clothes are but outmost cuticle and mortal coil. Otherwise we shall be found sailing under false colors, and be inevitably cashiered at last by our own opinion, as well as that of mankind. [36]

As Thoreau indicates, each person must find his or her own time and space for internal growth, his or her own Walden. "I would not," he says, "have any one adopt *my* mode of living on any account; for, beside that before he has fairly learned it I may have found out another for myself, I desire that there may be as many different persons in the world as possible; but I would have each one be very careful to find out and pursue *his own* way, and not his father's or his mother's or his neighbor's instead." [37]

Implicit in *Walden* is the belief that one must create one's own moratorium since family, society, and community have not permitted or institutionalized a satisfactory "moulting period" for individuals who need it. The book is in one sense an urgent plea for community encouragement and establishment of a moratorium as well as for more meaningful identity alternatives; [38] in another sense, it is pervaded by the recognition that society and community will not provide constructive moratoria and identity-choices, that individuals must depend only upon themselves if they are to achieve personal authenticity. Indeed, *Walden* may also be said to be an eloquent and poignant lament of America's lost opportunity for a moratorium. By the time the book was completed, Thoreau perceived that there was no turning back, that America was headed irrevocably toward an adulthood of which he did not fully approve. Only through his art and in his consciousness could the juggernaut of undesirable social and technological change be resisted and immobilized. Leo Marx observes, "For Thoreau the realization of the golden age is, finally, a matter of private and, in fact, literary experience. . . . In the end Thoreau restores the pastoral hope to its traditional location. He removes it from history, where it is manifestly unrealizable, and relocates it in literature, which is to say, in his own consciousness, in his craft, in *Walden*." [39] To relocate the pastoral hope in one's consciousness was to maintain an internal moratorium, a "middle landscape" between childhood and adulthood, in the face of hard historical fact.

Walden concludes with spring and dawn rather than with summer and day. The Walden experience and the writing of *Walden* were Thoreau's nearest approaches to the summer; if like the "strong and beautiful bug which came out of the dry leaf of an old table of apple-tree wood" [40] he had emerged from his dark cave into action and achievement at Walden, he still preferred—and needed—to believe that the "perfect summer" was yet to come:

> Who knows what beautiful and winged life, whose egg has been buried for ages under many concentric layers of woodenness in the dead dry life of society, deposited at first in the alburnum of the green and living tree, which has been gradually converted into the semblance of its well-seasoned tomb,—heard perchance gnawing out now for years by the astonished family of man, as they sat round the festive board,—may unexpectedly come forth from amidst society's most trivial and handselled furniture, to enjoy its perfect summer life at last! [41]

He knew nature's summer was not what he was waiting for and could not satisfy him; in June, the "season of hope and promise is past; already the season of small fruits has arrived. The Indian marked the midsummer as the season when berries were ripe. We are a little saddened, because we begin to see the interval between our hopes and their fulfillment. The prospect of the heavens is taken away, and we are presented only with a few small berries" (*J*, VI: 363–64). Living at Walden and in *Walden*, he caught glimpses of the "perfect summer"; the sun of that summer was both blinding and revelatory. Thoreau preferred to wait, to prepare himself, for that true summer rather than be content with "a few small berries." He always wished to have the "prospect of the heavens" before him. In one of his final essays, "Walking," he would still see himself as sauntering toward the Holy Land, "till one day the sun shall shine more brightly than ever he has done, shall perchance shine into our minds and hearts, and light up our whole lives with a great awakening light, as warm and serene and golden as on a bankside in autumn." [42] Even if the "winter of discontent" seemed to be thawing in the spring of 1845, winter would always be a dominant season in his soul. He would say in 1856, when the warmth and illumination of Walden had faded, when despair and dejection often threatened to overcome faith, "Our eyes go searching along the stems for what is most vivacious and characteristic, the concentrated summer gone into winter quarters. For we are hunters, pursuing the summer on snow-shoes and skates, all winter long" (*J*, IX: 164). Thoreau had gone over many snow-capped mountains to reach the sun, but the sun itself, he discovered, was but a morning star.

Notes

Introduction

1. Walter Harding, "Thoreau's Life," *A Thoreau Handbook* (New York: New York University Press, 1959), p. 31. This chapter contains a helpful review of previous biographical work on Thoreau.
2. Raymond D. Gozzi, "Tropes and Figures: A Psychological Study of David Henry Thoreau" (Diss., New York University, 1957), p. vi.
3. Ibid., p. xvi.
4. Ibid., p. xv.
5. Carl Bode, "The Half-Hidden Thoreau," in *Thoreau in Our Season*, ed. John H. Hicks (Amherst: University of Massachusetts Press, 1962), pp. 104–116.
6. Ibid., p. 112.
7. Perry Miller, *Consciousness in Concord* (Boston: Houghton Mifflin Company, 1958), pp. 33–34. It should be noted that Miller had read at least a "digest" of Gozzi's thesis (p. 227 n.) and seems to have been influenced by his work.
8. See Quentin Anderson, "Thoreau on July 4," *The New York Times Book Review*, 4 July 1971, p. 17.
9. Leon Edel, *Henry D. Thoreau* (Minneapolis: University of Minnesota Press, 1970), p. 43.
10. Ibid.
11. Anderson, "Thoreau on July 4," p. 18.
12. Harding, "Thoreau's Life," p. 31. It should be noted that Canby's *Thoreau* (1939) was the first full-scale biography to probe deeply and with some psychological acuity into the romantic involvement of Henry and John Thoreau with Ellen Sewall.
13. Erik Erikson, *Young Man Luther* (New York: W.W. Norton & Company, 1958), p. 15.
14. Ibid., p. 18.
15. See Lionel Trilling, "Art and Neurosis," in *Art and Psychoanalysis*, ed. William Phillips (New York: The World Publishing Company, 1957), p. 518.
16. Erik Erikson, "The Life Cycle: Epigenesis of Identity," *Identity: Youth and Crisis* (New York: W.W. Norton & Company, 1968), p. 96. See this chapter for a full discussion of stages in the life cycle.
17. Ibid., p. 94.
18. Robert Coles, *Erik Erikson: The Growth of His Work* (Boston: Little, Brown, and Company, 1970), p. 136.
19. Ralph Waldo Emerson, "Fate," *Selected Writings of Ralph Waldo Emerson* (New York: New American Library, 1965), p. 379.
20. See Anderson, "Thoreau on July 4," p. 18, for a similar appraisal of Thoreau's limitations.

21. Henry David Thoreau, "Life Without Principle," *Walden and Other Writings*, ed. Brooks Atkinson (New York: The Modern Library, 1950), p. 717.

Chapter 1

1. Walter Harding, *The Days of Henry Thoreau* (New York: Alfred A. Knopf, 1965), p. 51.
2. Ralph Waldo Emerson, "The American Scholar," *Selected Writings of Ralph Waldo Emerson* (New York: New American Library, 1965), p. 238.
3. Ibid.
4. See Quentin Anderson, *The Imperial Self* (New York: Alfred A. Knopf, 1971), p. 40. He suggests that "identity crisis" is a more attractive model for the era than the "Adamic metaphor."
5. Ralph Waldo Emerson, "Lecture on the Times," *Nature, Addresses, and Lectures* (1903; rpt. New York: AMS Press, 1968), p. 261.
6. Emerson, "The American Scholar," p. 224.
7. Emerson, "Lecture on the Times," p. 285.
8. See the section on Concord and Chapter 3, "The Graduate," for a further discussion of the "moratorium" concept.
9. Leo Marx speaks of the period between 1840 and 1860 as that time when "the nation reached that decisive stage in its economic development which W.W. Rostow called the 'take off.' In his study of the more or less universal stages of industrial growth, Rostow defines the take-off as the 'great watershed in the life of modern societies' when the old blocks and resistances to steady development are overcome and the forces of economic progress 'expand and come to dominate society.'" See *The Machine in the Garden* (New York: Oxford University Press, 1964), pp. 26–27.
10. Henry David Thoreau, *The Writings of Henry David Thoreau*, ed. F. B. Sanborn (Cambridge, Mass.: Houghton Mifflin and Company, 1906), VI: 9.
11. Henry David Thoreau, "Paradise (To Be) Regained," *The Writings of Henry David Thoreau* (1906; rpt. New York: AMS Press, 1968), pp. 302–3.
12. See R. W. B. Lewis, *The American Adam* (Chicago: University of Chicago Press, 1955) for the classic use of the "Adamic" metaphor in portraying nineteenth-century America.
13. See Alice Felt Tyler's *Freedom's Ferment* (New York: Harper & Row, 1944); also Frederick Jackson Turner, *The United States, 1830–1850* (New York: Henry Holt and Company, 1935).
14. Ralph Waldo Emerson, "Man the Reformer," *Nature, Addresses, and Lectures* (1903; rpt. New York: AMS Press, 1968), p. 249.
15. Emerson, "Lecture on the Times," p. 275.
16. Ibid., p. 260.
17. Ibid.
18. Alexis de Tocqueville, *Democracy in America*, ed. Phillips Bradley (New York: Vintage Books, 1945), II: 145.

19. Emerson, "Man the Reformer," p. 232.

20. David Riesman says that the "other-directed" persons of today are in some respects "strikingly similar" to those described by Tocqueville and other visitors from Europe. See *The Lonely Crowd* (Garden City, N.Y.: Doubleday & Company, 1955), pp. 34–35.

21. Ralph Waldo Emerson, "The Young American," *Nature, Addresses, and Lectures* (1903; rpt. New York: AMS Press, 1968), p. 388.

22. Emerson, "The American Scholar," p. 224.

23. Emerson, "Man the Reformer," pp. 230–31.

24. Emerson, "The American Scholar," p. 233.

25. See Chapter 3, "The Graduate."

26. Hendrik Ruitenbeek, *The Individual and the Crowd: A Study of Identity in America* (New York: The New American Library, 1964), p. 15.

27. Ralph Waldo Emerson, "Historic Notes of Life and Letters in New England," in *The American Transcendentalists*, ed. Perry Miller (Garden City, N.Y.: Doubleday & Company, 1957), p. 5.

28. Ibid.

29. Emerson, "The American Scholar," pp. 237–38.

30. Ibid.

31. Ralph Waldo Emerson, "Self-Reliance," *Selected Writings of Ralph Waldo Emerson* (New York: New American Library, 1965), p. 269.

32. Emerson, "Lecture on the Times," pp. 287–88.

33. Ibid., p. 281.

34. Ibid., p. 279.

35. Ibid., p. 278.

36. Ibid., p. 283.

37. Emerson, "Man the Reformer," p. 256.

38. Emerson said prophetically in "Lecture on the Times" that "all the children of men attack the colossus [of Conservatism] in their youth, and all, or all but a few, bow before it when they are old" (p. 260).

39. Emerson, "Historic Notes of Life and Letters in New England," p. 5.

40. Probably several members of the class of '37 at Harvard were in the general predicament described by David Donald in his analysis of abolitionists; while growing up they saw their fathers—the preachers, doctors, teachers, farmers, and merchants who had been leaders in their communities—displaced by a new breed of capitalists, lawyers, and industrialists: "The bustling democracy of the 1830's had passed them by; as the Reverend Ludovicus Weld lamented to his famous son Theodore: 'I have . . . felt like a stranger in a strange land.'" See *Lincoln Reconsidered* (New York: Vintage Books, 1956), pp. 80–81.

41. Emerson, "Historic Notes," p. 5.

42. Anderson, *The Imperial Self*, p. 40.

43. De Tocqueville, *Democracy in America*, II: 202–8.

44. Emerson, "Historic Notes," p. 7.

45. Emerson, "Man the Reformer," p. 250.

46. See Anderson, *The Imperial Self*, p. 40.

47. Erik Erikson, *Gandhi's Truth* (New York: W. W. Norton & Company, 1969), p. 129.

48. Helene Deutsch, *Selected Problems of Adolescence* (New York: International Universities Press, Inc., 1967), p. 61. It should be emphasized that pointing out the familial roots of rebellion does not necessarily make the rebellious youth's criticisms of society invalid.

49. See Chapter I of Anderson, *The Imperial Self*, "The Failure of the Fathers," pp. 3–58, to which my own argument is clearly indebted.

50. For a further discussion of guilt in father-son relations, see Chapter 2, "Roots of Identity and Identity Confusion in Family and Childhood."

51. Henry David Thoreau, *The Variorum Walden* (New York: Washington Square Press, 1963), pp. 5–6.

52. See Erikson, *Gandhi's Truth*, p. 102.

53. I am indebted to Richard Bushman's seminar, "Social Change in Concord," for information and insights used in this section.

54. Richard Bushman has suggested that the "sermon" form was giving way to "debates."

55. Townsend Scudder, *Concord: American Town* (Boston: Little, Brown, and Company, 1947), p. 150.

56. Ruth Wheeler, *Concord: Climate for Freedom* (Concord: Concord Antiquarian Society, 1967), pp. 156–57.

57. Scudder, *Concord: American Town*, p. 151.

58. Ralph Waldo Emerson, "Divinity School Address," *Selected Writings of Ralph Waldo Emerson* (New York: New American Library, 1965), p. 250.

59. Wheeler, *Concord: Climate for Freedom*, p. 165.

60. Ruth Wheeler, "Thoreau's Concord," in *Henry David Thoreau: Studies and Commentaries*, eds. Walter Harding, George Brenner, and Paul Doyle (Rutherford, N.J.: Fairleigh Dickinson University Press, 1972), p. 27.

61. F. B. Sanborn, *The Life of Henry David Thoreau* (Boston: Houghton Mifflin Co., 1917), p. 38.

62. Wheeler, *Concord: Climate for Freedom*, pp. 170–71.

63. Ibid.

64. For Concord, the "big city" was Boston; there may well have been hostility toward Boston as a threat to Concord's self-image, economy, and autonomous culture, but there was probably also a desire on the part of some Concordians to emulate Bostonians.

65. See Chapter 1, "Sleepy Hollow, 1844," *The Machine in the Garden*.

66. Wheeler, *Concord: Climate for Freedom*, p. 169.

67. Wheeler, "Thoreau's Concord," p. 27.

68. Ibid.

69. Ralph Waldo Emerson, "Historical Discourse at Concord," *The Complete Works of Ralph Waldo Emerson (Miscellanies)*, (Boston: Houghton Mifflin Co., 1911), XI: 84–85.

70. Other—less sociological and philosophical—reasons for Thoreau's dissatisfac-

tion with, and hostility toward Concord will be discussed in subsequent chapters.

71. Lemuel Shattuck published the first full-scale history of Concord in 1835— thus heightening Concord's consciousness of itself and its identity.

72. Emerson, "Historical Discourse at Concord," pp. 30–31.

73. Ibid., p. 67.

74. Ibid., pp. 72–73, 75–76.

75. Thoreau, *The Variorum Walden*, p. 128.

76. See Chapter 2.

77. Thoreau, *The Variorum Walden*, p. 88.

78. These people may justifiably be called "other-directed," although not to the extent described by Reisman in *The Lonely Crowd*. In modern times, for instance, the mass media have been a far more powerful influence than they were in Thoreau's day.

79. See Chapters 2 and 3.

80. Stanley Cavell, *The Senses of Walden* (New York: The Viking Press, 1972), p. 10.

81. Thoreau, *The Variorum Walden*, p. 130.

82. See Chapter 2.

83. Sherman Paul, *The Shores of America* (Urbana: University of Illinois Press, 1958), pp. 24–25.

84. See Chapters 2 and 3.

85. De Tocqueville, *Democracy in America*, II: 202.

86. See Chapter 3.

87. Erik Erikson, "Reflections on the American Identity," *Childhood and Society*, rev. ed. (New York: W. W. Norton & Company, 1963), p. 293.

88. See the final section of Chapter 3, "A Traveller in Concord."

Chapter 2

1. Harding, *The Days of Henry Thoreau*, p. 8.

2. Ibid.

3. For purposes of simplicity and recognition, I shall refer to "David Henry" as "Henry" in this chapter.

4. Harding, *The Days of Henry Thoreau*, p. 11.

5. Ibid.

6. Ibid., p. 13.

7. Thoreau, *Journal*, eds. Bradford Torrey and Francis H. Allen, (1906; rpt. New York: Dover Publications, Inc., 1962), XI: 436.

8. Thoreau, *The Correspondence of Henry David Thoreau*, eds. Walter Harding and Carl Bode (New York: New York University Press, 1958), p. 546.

9. Harding, *The Days of Henry Thoreau*, p. 16.

10. Ibid.

11. Ibid., p. 57.

12. Harding is reasonably certain that John did not stop "moonlighting" *completely* until at least the late 1840s.

13. Edward Emerson, *Henry Thoreau as Remembered by a Young Friend* (Boston: Houghton Mifflin Company, 1917), p. 13.

14. F. B. Sanborn, *The Life of Henry David Thoreau*, p. 43.

15. F. B. Sanborn, *The Personality of Thoreau* (1901; rpt. Folcroft, Pa.: The Folcroft Press, 1969), pp. 12–13.

16. Mrs. W. S. Robinson, *"Warrington" Pen-Portraits* (Boston: Mrs. W. S. Robinson, 1877), p. 68.

17. S. A. Jones, *The Inlander*, February, 1893, as quoted in Henry S. Salt, *Life of Henry David Thoreau* (London: Walter Scott, Limited, 1896), p. 21.

18. Harding, *The Days of Henry Thoreau*, p. 8.

19. Ibid., pp. 8–9.

20. Cf. Miller, *Consciousness in Concord*, p. 8; Leon Edel, *Henry D. Thoreau*, p. 11. Both Miller and Edel agree that the Thoreau home was "dominated" by females.

21. Harding, *The Days of Henry Thoreau*, p. 9.

22. George Frisbie Hoar, *Autobiography of Seventy Years* (New York: Charles Scribner's Sons, 1903), I: 57.

23. I am indebted to Walter Harding for pointing out this ambiguity to me.

24. Cf. Gozzi, "Tropes and Figures," p. 57. Gozzi uses this story to suggest that Henry's unconscious perception of his father as a man of violence "was not just oedipally motivated but had some basis in fact too."

25. Helene Deutsch, *Selected Problems of Adolescence*, p. 61. Speaking of alienated youth, she says, "The chief reason . . . for the boy's resentment against the father is the fact that the latter was too weak to protect the boy against dependency upon the mother. . . ."

26. Bruno Bettelheim, "The Problem of Generations," in *The Challenge of Youth*, ed. Erik Erikson (Garden City, N.Y.: Doubleday & Co., 1963), p. 85.

27. Sanborn, *Life*, p. 6.

28. Harding, *The Days of Henry Thoreau*, p. 6.

29. Ibid.

30. Sanborn, *Life*, pp. 19–20.

31. Harding, *The Days of Henry Thoreau*, p. 6.

32. Henretta's data indicate that, in Hingham, Massachusetts (1800–1815), the rate of premarital conception was close to 30%—and between 15% and 20% for children born less than six months after marriage (pp. 132–34). The rate was gradually declining in the 1800–1850 period. Henretta comments, "The decline in the frequency of arranged marriages during the eighteenth century had already decreased the power of the father over his female offspring, and had given to the woman herself a somewhat greater role in the determination of her own future. This emancipation from the paternal will was, at best, an ambiguous legacy from the colonial period; for, if marriage based on romantic love gave women a wider choice of partners, it also introduced the blinding and often irrational impulse of sexual passion into the selective

process." James A. Henretta, *The Evolution of American Society, 1700–1815: An Interdisciplinary Analysis* (Lexington, Mass.: D. C. Heath and Company; 1973), pp. 171–72.

33. Edward Emerson, *Thoreau as Remembered*, pp. 13–14.
34. Annie Russell Marble, *Thoreau: His Home, Friends and Books* (1902; rpt. New York: AMS Press, 1969), p. 44.
35. Harding, *The Days of Henry Thoreau*, p. 9.
36. Ellery Channing, *Thoreau, the Poet-Naturalist*, ed. F. B. Sanborn (Boston: Charles E. Goodspeed, 1902), p. 5.
37. Sanborn, *Life*, p. 320.
38. Sanborn, *The Personality of Thoreau*, pp. 12–13.
39. Robinson, *"Warrington" Pen-Portraits*, p. 68.
40. Marble, *Thoreau*, pp. 40–41.
41. Irving Allen, *The Independent*, July 25, 1895, as quoted by Marble, *Thoreau*, p. 42.
42. Edward Emerson, *Thoreau as Remembered*, p. 13.
43. Marble, *Thoreau*, p. 43.
44. Harding, *The Days of Henry Thoreau*, p. 10.
45. Marble, *Thoreau*, pp. 38–39.
46. Edward Emerson, *Thoreau as Remembered*, p. 14.
47. Erik Erikson, "Identity Confusion in Life History and Case History," *Identity: Youth and Crisis* (New York: W. W. Norton & Co., 1968), pp. 176–77.
48. Thoreau, *Journal*, II: 307.
49. Erik Erikson, *Gandhi's Truth*, p. 132.
50. Erik Erikson, "Reflections on the American Identity," p. 312.
51. Ibid., pp. 312–13.
52. See the section on "The Elder Brother" for a full discussion.
53. Marble, *Thoreau*, p. 60.
54. Channing, *Thoreau, the Poet-Naturalist*, p. 13.
55. Harding, *The Days of Henry Thoreau*, p. 32.
56. Krutch thinks it obvious that Henry "was regarded as the genius of the family." Joseph Wood Krutch, *Henry David Thoreau* (New York: Dell Publishing Co., 1948), p. 21.
57. Edward Emerson, *Thoreau as Remembered* pp. 16–17.
58. Washington Irving's "Rip Van Winkle" (1819), which portrays Rip as a "hen-pecked husband," may be seen as in part a recognition of this developing social trend as well as an indication that *some* families in earlier America had also been "dominated" by women.
59. Erik Erikson, *Young Man Luther* (New York: W. W. Norton & Co., 1958), p. 65.
60. Erikson, "Identity Confusion in Life History and Case History," p. 151.
61. Carl Bode, "Making a Home," *American Life in the 1840's* (New York: New York University Press, 1967), pp. 55–56.
62. Erikson, "Reflections on the American Identity," p. 293.
63. Isaac Hecker, as quoted by Marble, *Thoreau*, p. 44.

64. Such biographers as Krutch, *Henry David Thoreau*, p. 20 and Edel, *Henry D. Thoreau*, p. 12 have also surmised that Thoreau was overly dependent upon his mother.
65. Priscilla Rice Edes, as quoted by Raymond Adams, "Thoreau and His Neighbors," *Thoreau Society Bulletin* 44 (Summer, 1953): 2.
66. Ibid.
67. Channing, *Thoreau, the Poet-Naturalist*, p. 18.
68. Ibid., p. 21.
69. Harding, *The Days of Henry Thoreau*, p. 184.
70. Thoreau's sisters (especially Sophia) made many sacrifices for him and were somewhat less threatening "mother-figures" than Cynthia.
71. I am not suggesting here that "radical" life-styles and views are not in themselves legitimate—only that Thoreau's eventual identity was in part rooted in his private conflicts.
72. Cf. Gozzi, "Tropes and Figures," p. 32. Much of the data used previously in this chapter to understand the sources of Thoreau's identity crisis was interpreted by Gozzi as evidence that Thoreau had deep, unresolved oedipal conflicts.
73. Sanborn, *Life*, pp. 35–36.
74. F. B. Sanborn, *Henry D. Thoreau* (Boston, 1882), pp. 270–71, as quoted by Gozzi, "Tropes and Figures" p. 3.
75. Gozzi, "Tropes and Figures," pp. 4–5.
76. See Erik Erikson, "The Life Cycle: Epigenesis of Identity," p. 97.
77. Thoreau, *Journal*, I: 380–81.
78. See Erikson, "The Life Cycle: Epigenesis of Identity," p. 103–7.
79. Channing, *Thoreau, the Poet-Naturalist*, p. 19.
80. Erikson, "The Life Cycle: Epigenesis of Identity," pp. 106–7.
81. Thoreau, *Correspondence*, p. 75.
82. Thoreau, *Journal*, II: 306–7.
83. Channing, *Thoreau, the Poet-Naturalist*, p. 5.
84. Perhaps this indicates that his ideal image of the father had not yet been shattered.
85. See Gozzi, "Tropes and Figures," Chapter 1, for a useful discussion of Thoreau's childhood "traumas."
86. Thoreau, *Journal*, VIII: 93–94.
87. Gozzi, "Tropes and Figures," p. 11. One key bit of evidence to which Gozzi refers is an account of Edward Emerson's: "John and Henry slept together in the trundlebed, that obsolete and delightful children's bed, telescoping on large castors under the parental four-poster. John would go to sleep at once, but Henry often lay long awake. His mother found the little boy lying so one night, long after he had gone upstairs, and said, 'Why, Henry dear, why don't you go to sleep?' 'Mother,' said he, 'I have been looking through the stars to see if I could n't see God behind them.'" (Edward Emerson, *Thoreau as Remembered*, pp. 14–15). Gozzi believes it probable that Thoreau slept in

this trundle-bed in the parental bedroom until approximately the age of five and that he was awake more than once when his parents were having intercourse.

88. Channing, *Thoreau, the Poet-Naturalist*, p. 6.

89. Ibid., p. 18.

90. Harding, *The Days of Henry Thoreau*, p. 19.

91. Channing, *Thoreau, the Poet-Naturalist*, p. 5.

92. Erikson, "The Life Cycle: Epigenesis of Identity," p. 108.

93. Ibid.

94. Ibid., p. 109.

95. Ibid., pp. 109–110.

96. Ibid., p. 111.

97. Ibid.

98. Ibid., p. 114.

99. Erikson, *Gandhi's Truth*, pp. 125–26.

100. See Erikson, "The Life Cycle: Epigenesis of Identity," pp. 115–19.

101. Thoreau, *Journal*, IX: 210–11.

102. Gozzi argues that, to Thoreau's unconscious at least, John Thoreau was a wild, violent force who threatened castration (p. 57). I would agree with Gozzi that fear was one important component of Henry's response to oedipal conflict. However, I would contend that to the extent that Henry sensed he had defeated his father and turned him irrevocably into a weak, passive figure, he did not feel fear as strongly as he felt guilt.

103. In a more general sense, the development of public schooling served to diminish the sense of paternal authority and increase the possibility of son surpassing father.

104. Harding, *The Days of Henry Thoreau*, p. 57.

105. Gozzi at one point hypothesizes that Thoreau's response to the "success" of *Walden*—as indicated in journal entries and his illness of 1855–57—reveals that he had an "unconscious" fear of success (pp. 140ff.). While I do not wholly agree with this particular example, I do agree that Thoreau had a fear of success. Gozzi does not (as I do) stress how the fear of success influenced the development of Thoreau's adult identity.

106. Kenneth Keniston, *The Uncommitted: Alienated Youth in American Society* (New York: Dell Publishing Co., 1965), p. 154.

107. See Gozzi, "Tropes and Figures," p. 36; Bode, "The Half-Hidden Thoreau," p. 111.

108. Thoreau, *Collected Poems*, ed. Card Bode (Baltimore: Johns Hopkins University Press, 1965), p. 42.

109. Horace Hosmer, as quoted by Edward Emerson, *Thoreau as Remembered*, p. 125.

110. Harding, *The Days of Henry Thoreau*, pp. 11–12.

111. Marble, *Thoreau*, p. 48.

112. Sanborn, *Life*, p. 216.

113. Harding, *The Days of Henry Thoreau*, p. 87.

114. Thoreau, *The Correspondence of Henry David Thoreau*, p. 18. This letter will be discussed later in more detail.

115. Thoreau, *Collected Poems*, p. 314.

116. John Thoreau, as quoted by Sanborn, *Life*, p. 216.

117. See Gozzi, "Tropes and Figures," p. 278.

118. Thoreau, *Journal*, VIII: 94.

119. See Wilbert E. Moore, *The Impact of Industry* (Englewood Cliffs, N.J.: Prentice-Hall, 1965), p. 88.

120. Robinson, *"Warrington" Pen-Portraits*, p. 12.

121. Priscilla Rice Edes, as quoted by Adams, "Thoreau and his Neighbors," p. 2.

122. See Erikson, "The Life Cycle: Epigenesis of Identity," pp. 123–24.

123. Harding, *The Days of Henry Thoreau*, p. 17.

124. Alfred Munroe, as quoted by Harding, *The Days of Henry Thoreau*, p. 18.

125. Ibid., p. 31.

126. That he almost failed the entrance examination might indicate, among other things, an ambivalence about being the hope of the family. Harding has suggested to me that one important factor in sending Henry rather than John to Harvard might have been that the family was more prosperous when Henry reached college age. Even if this is true, it seems to me that John—only two years older—*could* have been chosen at that time. In any case, the fact that Henry *did* go to college (and John did not) must have had significant psychological consequences.

Chapter 3

1. Thoreau, *Collected Poems*, p. 81. See pages 81–82 for the entire poem.

2. Bode, *Collected Poems of Henry Thoreau*, p. 351 n.

3. Erikson, "Identity Confusion in Life History and Case History," pp. 156–57.

4. Thoreau, *Journal*, I: 299.

5. Erik Erikson, "Youth: Fidelity and Diversity," *The Challenge of Youth* (Garden City, N.Y.: Doubleday & Co., 1963), p. 10.

6. Erikson, "Identity Confusion in Life History and Case History," p. 171.

7. Gozzi argues in his thesis that Thoreau's illnesses had a psychic, as well as physical, component.

8. Emerson had written to Quincy in order to recommend financial aid for his fellow Concordian (Harding, *The Days of Henry Thoreau*, p. 47).

9. Josiah Quincy, letter cited by Harding, p. 47.

10. John Weiss, "Cold and Unimpressible," *Henry David Thoreau: A Profile*, ed. Walter Harding (New York: Hill and Wang, 1971), pp. 36–38.

11. See Harding, *The Days of Henry Thoreau*, pp. 40–44.

12. Ibid, p. 44.

13. Thoreau, Letter to Orestes Brownson, December 30, 1837, *Correspondence*, p. 19.

14. Sanborn, *The Life of Henry David Thoreau*, p. 84. See Sanborn, pp. 54–189, for a discussion of Thoreau's college writing.

15. Marble, *Thoreau*, p. 77.

16. Miller, *Consciousness in Concord*, p. 9.

17. Marble, *Thoreau*, p. 65.

18. Harding, *The Days of Henry Thoreau*, p. 52.

19. James Richardson, Jr., in Thoreau, *Correspondence*, p. 11.

20. Channing, *Thoreau, the Poet-Naturalist*, pp. 32–33.

21. Edward Emerson, *Thoreau as Remembered*, p. 21.

22. Cf. Erikson, *Gandhi's Truth*, p. 153.

23. Erikson, *Young Man Luther*, p. 43.

24. Cf. Erikson, "Youth: Fidelity and Diversity," pp. 5–6.

25. Sherman Paul, *The Shores of America* (Urbana: University of Illinois Press, 1958), pp. 24–25. See "Concord: Choice and Limitation." It will be remembered that Paul, quoting Henry James, observed that there was a "terrible paucity of alternatives" in New England towns of Thoreau's time.

26. See Gozzi, "Tropes and Figures," p. 267.

27. Thoreau, *Correspondence*, p. 17.

28. Thoreau, *Journal*, I: 37.

29. Thoreau, *Correspondence*, pp. 16–17. This passage could be read differently: the Dundee were cowardly ("women"). In either reading, Thoreau's hostility toward women and what he perceived to be "womanly" qualities is evident. If the life of the women was in some way "cowardly," there was all the more reason not to surrender to their way of life.

30. Harding, *The Days of Henry Thoreau*, p. 54

31. Priscilla Rice Edes, as quoted by Adams, "Thoreau and his Neighbors," p. 2.

32. Mrs. Daniel Chester French, as quoted by Adams, "Thoreau and his Neighbors," p. 3.

33. Channing (*Thoreau, the Poet-Naturalist,*—p. 18) sets the time as earlier ("before leaving college"), but Harding (*The Days of Henry Thoreau,* —p. 55) apparently thinks that it makes more sense to place the event after Thoreau's graduation and his resignation from the Center School. In either case, Mrs. Thoreau's words to Henry, and his response to them, are revealing.

34. Channing, *Thoreau, the Poet-Naturalist*, p. 18.

35. Erikson, *Young Man Luther*, p. 46.

36. Ibid., p. 99.

37. Helen Merrell Lynd, *On Shame and the Search for Identity* (New York: Harcourt, Brace and Co., 1958), pp. 204–210. Like Erikson she believes that an analytic distinction can be made between shame and guilt (which "is more related to specific acts, going against specific taboos").

38. Thoreau, *Journal*, I: 3. Because the *Journal* will be alluded to frequently, references henceforth will be included in the body of the text. The Dover edition (1962) is a republication in two large volumes of the fourteen volume Houghton Mifflin edition (1906—Bradford Torrey and Francis Allen, editors). Volume and page numbers in the text will refer to the 1906 edition.

39. Thoreau, *Correspondence*, pp. 12–13.
40. Henry Vose, in Thoreau, *Correspondence*, p. 14
41. Ibid., p. 15.
42. Indeed, Gozzi argues that nature was an "alternative mother" for Henry; his love for nature was an expression of his "unconscious mother-fixation and defense against that fixation." See the chapter on "Mother-Nature" in Gozzi's thesis.
43. See Erikson, "Identity Confusion in Life History and Case History," p. 169. According to Erikson, this fluctuating sense of time is a frequent characteristic of identity confusion.
44. Thoreau, *Correspondence*, p. 19.
45. Ibid., p. 24.
46. Prudence Ward, as quoted by Sanborn, *Life*, p. 200.
47. See the next section, "In Search of a 'Great Man,'" for a discussion of why his relationship with Emerson and his developing sense of himself as a writer and Transcendentalist also made him reluctant to leave. Certainly, if he *had* left, the development of his identity would have been modified.
48. Prudence Ward, as quoted by Sanborn, *Life*, pp. 200–201.
49. Josiah Quincy, in Thoreau, *Correspondence*, pp. 25–26.
50. Prudence Ward, as quoted by Sanborn, *Life*, p. 201.
51. Ibid., p. 200.
52. At the same time, Thoreau might have been flattered by recognition from someone of Quincy's status, by a father-figure (who probably did not know the circumstances of his resignation from the Concord position).
53. Thoreau, *Correspondence*, p. 25.
54. Erikson, *Young Man Luther*, p. 44.
55. See Erikson, "Youth: Fidelity and Diversity," pp. 1–28.
56. Harding, *The Days of Henry Thoreau*, pp. 60–61. We do know that Emerson wrote a June 1837 letter to the President of Harvard, in which he recommended Thoreau for a scholarship.
57. See Erikson, *Gandhi's Truth*, p. 74 for a helpful definition of "transference."
58. Cf. Gozzi, "Tropes and Figures" pp. 329–30.
59. See Gozzi, "Tropes and Figures" pp. 329ff. for an incisive psychoanalytical discussion of the Emerson-Thoreau relationship and an effective presentation of the argument that Thoreau and Lidian were "attracted" to each other. Canby (pp. 155–63) had earlier argued in his biography that Henry "loved" Lidian. A letter which Henry wrote from Staten Island on June 20, 1843—at the height of his homesickness—certainly suggests that his feelings for Mrs. Emerson could be intense. He says, among other things, "My friend, I have read your letter as if I was not reading it. After each pause I could defer the rest forever. The thought of you will be a new motive for every right action. You are another human being whom I know, and might not our topic be as broad as the universe" (*Correspondence*, p. 120). While Lidian seems to have discouraged Thoreau from further passionate expression of his affection (as evidenced by the tone of his subsequent letters—see *Correspondence*, pp. 123–

25, for instance), it is likely that there was some attraction between Thoreau and Mrs. Emerson and that it caused them both—*and* Mr. Emerson—some discomfort and anxiety. However, it is my belief that, although the relationship may have had romantic and oedipal *overtones,* the overt quality of the relationship hovered between that of elder sister-brother and mother-son. In a May 22, 1843 letter, for example, Thoreau had addressed Lidian as "some elder sister of mine, whom I could not have avoided" (*Correspondence,* p. 103). It would, I think, be blowing the matter out of proportion to call their relationship a "romance." By 1843, I would submit, Thoreau had lost any conscious inclination to be "romantically" (and, more emphatically, sexually) involved with a woman.

60. Gozzi, "Tropes and Figures," p. 399.
61. Ralph L. Rusk, *The Life of Ralph Waldo Emerson* (New York: Charles Scribner's Sons, 1949), pp. 20–21.
62. Ibid., p. 206.
63. Ibid., p. 231.
64. Ibid., p. 230.
65. See Chapter 6, "The Death of a Brother," for an extended discussion of the possible psychodynamics involved in the untimely death of a brother.
66. R. W. Emerson, *The Journals and Miscellaneous Notebooks of Ralph Waldo Emerson,* ed. Merton M. Sealts, Jr. (Cambridge, Mass.: Belknap Press, 1965), V: 456.
67. Ibid., ed. Ralph H. Orth, VI: 255.
68. Ibid., p. 258.
69. Ibid., ed. Sealts, V: 459.
70. Rusk, *Emerson,* p. 237.
71. R. W. Emerson, "Thoreau," *The Selected Writings of Ralph Waldo Emerson* (New York: New American Library, 1965), p. 427.
72. Cf. Erikson, *Young Man Luther,* p. 165.
73. See Sanborn, *Life,* pp. 54–189.
74. Ibid., pp. 128–29.
75. James Russell Lowell, as quoted in Bode, "The Half-Hidden Thoreau," p. 112.
76. See Henry Seidel Canby, *Thoreau* (Boston: Houghton Mifflin Co., 1939), p. 90; Harding, *The Days of Henry Thoreau,* p. 64.
77. Henry David Thoreau, "Thomas Carlyle and his Works," *The Writings of Henry David Thoreau* (1906; rpt. New York: AMS Press, 1968), IV: 333–34.
78. Ibid., p. 336.
79. Erik Erikson, "Human Strength and the Cycle of Generations," *Insight and Responsibility* (New York: W. W. Norton & Company, 1964), p. 115. See the entire chapter, pp. 111–57.
80. See Erikson, "Human Strength and the Cycle of Generations," p. 125.
81. Emerson, *Journal,* ed. Sealts, V: 452.
82. Ibid., pp. 453–54.
83. Ibid., p. 460.
84. Ibid., p. 480.

85. Harding, *The Days of Henry Thoreau*, p. 63. In 1840, he became particularly friendly with Bronson Alcott; this would prove to be one of Thoreau's most enduring and least ambivalent friendships.

86. Ibid., p. 70.

87. Once again, he was dependent upon the approval of a domineering, talkative, often rejecting woman, a situation that unquestionably upset him.

88. See the next section, "In Search of an Ideology."

89. Erikson, *Young Man Luther*, p. 22.

90. Ibid., p. 41.

91. Ibid.

92. See Octavius Brooks Frothingham, *Transcendentalism in New England* (1876; rpt. Philadelphia: University of Pennsylvania Press, 1972); Harold Clarke Goddard, *Studies in New England Transcendentalism* (New York: Columbia University Press, 1908); Perry Miller, *The Transcendentalists* (Cambridge, Mass.: Harvard University Press, 1950); George Hochfield, "Introduction," *Selected Writings of the American Transcendentalists* (New York: New American Library, 1966), pp. ix–xxviii; Brian Barbour, ed., *American Transcendentalism—An Anthology of Criticism* (Notre Dame: University of Notre Dame Press, 1973); Lawrence Buell, *Literary Transcendentalism: Style and Vision in the American Renaissance* (Ithaca: Cornell University Press, 1973); Paul F. Boller, *American Transcendentalism 1830–1860: An Intellectual Inquiry* (New York: G. P. Putnam's Sons, 1974).

93. Emerson, "Divinity School Address," *The Selected Writings of Ralph Waldo Emerson* (New York: The Modern Library, 1950), pp. 76–77.

94. Erikson, "Youth: Fidelity and Diversity," pp. 14–15.

95. Emerson, "Self-Reliance," *Selected Writings* (New York: New American Library, 1965), p. 272.

96. Emerson, "The Young American," p. 379.

97. Emerson, "The Transcendentalist," *Selected Writings* (New York: The Modern Library, 1950), p. 103.

98. See Perry Miller, "From Edwards to Emerson," *Errand Into the Wilderness* (New York: Harper & Row, 1956), p. 200.

99. Emerson, "The Transcendentalist," p. 96.

100. Emerson, "Self-Reliance," p. 260.

101. Emerson, "The Transcendentalist," p. 90.

102. See "Life Without Principle," one of Thoreau's most concentrated and eloquent Transcendentalist statements, in *Walden and Other Writings*, ed. Brooks Atkinson (New York: The Modern Library, 1950), pp. 711–32.

103. Emerson, "The Transcendentalist," p. 91.

104. It will be remembered that Thoreau wrote a poem, "Conscience is instinct bred in the house." See the discussion of conscience in the second section of Chapter 2, "Childhood—from Eriksonian Perspectives."

105. Emerson, "The Transcendentalist," p. 92.

106. Emerson, "Self-Reliance," pp. 259–60.

107. Cf. Erikson, *Young Man Luther*, p. 43.
108. Emerson, "The Transcendentalist," p. 93.
109. Emerson, "The Transcendentalist," p. 99. See Chapter I, section 1, "The Age of Revolution," for other statements by Emerson affirming the legitimacy and frequent preferability of waiting.
110. Emerson, "Self-Reliance," p. 263.
111. Harding, *The Days of Henry Thoreau*, p. 75.
112. Thoreau, *Correspondence*, p. 27.
113. It is possible that Emerson encouraged Henry to think in these terms; after all, he would say in "Self-Reliance," "The soul is no traveler; the wise man stays at home" (p. 275).
114. Harding, *The Days of Henry Thoreau*, p. 75.
115. Erikson, *Young Man Luther*, p. 157.
116. Ibid., p. 207
117. Harding, *The Days of Henry Thoreau*, p. 75.
118. Thoreau, *Correspondence*, p. 656.
119. Harding, *The Days of Henry Thoreau*, p. 76.
120. Ibid.
121. Ibid.
122. Paul, *The Shores of America*, pp. 65–67, 70.
123. Emerson, *Journal*, ed. Sealts, V: 473.
124. Harding, *The Days of Henry Thoreau*, p. 94.
125. Miller, *Consciousness in Concord*, p. 153. References to page numbers from the "Lost Journal" (as it appears in Miller's book) will be included in the body of the text.
126. See, for instance, Joseph J. Moldenhauer, "Paradox in *Walden*," in *Twentieth Century Interpretations of Walden*, ed. Richard Ruland (Englewood Cliffs, N.J.: Prentice-Hall, Inc., 1968), pp. 73–84. Moldenhauer traces Thoreau's use of paradox back to Donne, Brown, metaphysical poetry, and Emerson.
127. Krutch, *Henry David Thoreau*, p. 286.

Chapter 4

1. The relative sparseness of journal entries during the first few months of the joint teaching venture *may* indicate that he was indeed kept busy with his teaching. However, it is also possible that Thoreau simply cut out many of the entries during this period (as he may have done often in his early journal).
2. Harding, *The Days of Henry Thoreau*, p. 81.
3. *Yeoman's Gazette*, February 9, 1839, in Harding, p. 76.
4. Edward Emerson, *Thoreau as Remembered*, p. 23.
5. Horace Hosmer, as quoted by Edward Emerson, *Thoreau as Remembered*, p. 22.
6. Sanborn, *The Life of Henry David Thoreau*, p. 209.

7. Ibid., p. 204.

8. George Keyes, as quoted by Edward Emerson, *Thoreau as Remembered*, p. 129.

9. Harding, *The Days of Henry Thoreau*, p. 88.

10. Ibid., p. 73.

11. Sanborn, *Life*, p. 218.

12. Horace Hosmer, as quoted by Edward Emerson, *Thoreau as Remembered*, p. 125.

13. Ibid., p. 127.

14. Harding, *The Days of Henry Thoreau*, p. 87.

15. Harding citing George Hoar, *The Days of Henry Thoreau*, p. 87.

16. Harding citing John S. Keyes, Letter to F. H. Underwood, November 15, 1886, *The Days of Henry Thoreau* p. 87.

17. Sanborn, *Life*, p. 209.

18. Horace Hosmer, as quoted by Edward Emerson, *Thoreau as Remembered*, p. 125.

19. Robinson, *"Warrington" Pen-Portraits*, p. 21.

20. Harding, *The Days of Henry Thoreau*, p. 77.

21. In his thesis, Gozzi argues (on the basis of passages in *A Week*, journal entries, and his attitudes toward friendship and friends) that Thoreau had an "unconscious homoerotic orientation."

    See Harding's "Afterword" in *Henry David Thoreau: A Profile* (pp. 246–47) for a brief evaluation of this question. Given his fears of women and his ambivalence about, and discomfort with, heterosexuality, it is not unlikely that Thoreau did have a stronger than "normal" *"unconscious* homoerotic orientation." I am inclined to agree with Harding that if he had such an orientation, he was "apparently successful in supressing or sublimating" it. Having said this, I must add that I have not found this "homoerotic" factor particularly salient or helpful to my understanding of young man Thoreau.

22. Marble, *Thoreau*, p. 87.

23. Harding, *The Days of Henry Thoreau*, p. 79.

24. Louise Osgood Koopman, a daughter of Ellen Sewall, says, "I must mention here that my mother, according to all accounts was a beautiful girl. As she was over forty when I was born the youngest of ten children—I am now 98 years old—I can speak only of her sympathy and imagination, and of course, to me she was beautiful. I know that we five sisters, a good looking lot, were always told we were not as pretty as our mother." "The Thoreau Romance," in *Thoreau in our Season*, ed. John H. Hicks (Amherst: University of Mass. Press, 1962), p. 98.

25. Harding, *The Days of Henry Thoreau* p. 94.

26. See, for instance, Miller, *Consciousness in Concord*, p. 86.

27. See Erikson, "The Life Cycle: Epigenesis of Identity," p. 132.

28. In his biography, Harding presents a cogent description of Thoreau's romance with Ellen, well-documented with letters of Prudence Ward, Ellen Sewall, and others; second-hand reports from friends and relatives; and readings from

the *Journal*. Because of the unavailability to me of some primary sources, Harding's description wll be relied upon whenever appropriate.

29. Henry Seidel Canby, *Thoreau* (Boston: Houghton Mifflin Co., 1939), p. 116. See pp. 106–127 for an in-depth discussion of the "Transcendental Triangle."

30. Koopman, "The Thoreau Romance," p. 99.

31. Elizabeth Osgood Davenport and Louise Osgood Koopman, "Henry D. Thoreau 1839–1840." MS, George L. Davenport, Jr., in Harding, p. 96.

32. Ibid., pp. 96–97.

33. Margaret Fuller, in Thoreau, *Correspondence*, p. 57.

34. Thoreau, *A Week*, p. 255.

35. Harding (based on Davenport and Koopman), *The Days of Henry Thoreau*, p. 97.

36. Ellen Sewall, in Harding, *The Days of Henry Thoreau*, p. 97.

37. By July of 1840, in fact, Thoreau had written an essay on the "brave man"— "The Service"—which was largely based on his journal entries beginning the previous December; he submitted it to *The Dial*, but Margaret Fuller rejected it. Only in 1902 was it posthumously published by Sanborn.

38. Emerson, "Thoreau," *Selected Writings of Ralph Waldo Emerson* (New York: New American Library, 1965), p. 414.

39. Emerson, "Heroism," *Selected Writings of Ralph Waldo Emerson* (New York: The Modern Library, 1950), p. 252.

40. See Sherman Paul, *The Shores of America*, pp. 80–89.

41. Erikson, "The Life Cycle: Epigenesis of Identity," p. 136.

42. Sanborn, *Life*, p. 245.

43. Indeed, in "The Service" (Sanborn, *Life*, pp. 245–48), Thoreau identifies with the aggressive elder brother, thereby perhaps giving vent to his hostility: "The brave man is the elder son of creation, who has stept buoyantly into his inheritance; while the younger, who is the coward, waiteth patiently till he decease." The possible ambiguities of the "coward" passage suggest the ambivalence with which Henry confronted his elder brother's pursuit of Ellen. See also "The Service" as it appears in *The Writings of Henry David Thoreau* (1906; rpt. New York: AMS Press, 1968), IV: 277–79.

44. Ellen Sewall, Letter to Prudence Ward, December 26, 1839. MS, George Davenport, Jr., in Harding, *The Days of Henry Thoreau*, p. 98.

45. Harding, *The Days of Henry Thoreau*, p. 98.

46. Canby, *Thoreau*, p. 113.

47. Parts of this poem were later published in *A Week* as "The Poet's Delay."

48. Harding, *The Days of Henry Thoreau*, p. 99.

49. Ibid.

50. Canby, *Thoreau*, pp. 115–16.

51. Harding, *The Days of Henry Thoreau*, pp. 99–100.

52. Thoreau, *A Week*, pp. 252–53.

53. Thoreau's fascination with, and identification with, Ralegh will be discussed further in Chapter 6, "The Death of a Brother."

54. It is also possible, though I think not likely, that he cut out all writings from

the *Journal* during this period for reasons unrelated to his preoccupation with, and feelings about, Ellen.

55. Harding, *The Days of Henry Thoreau*, p. 101.

56. Henry David Thoreau, "Natural History of Massachusetts," *Excursions* (1863; rpt. New York: Corinth Books, 1962), p. 49.

57. Canby, *Thoreau*, p. 117.

58. Ellen Sewall, Letter to Prudence Ward of October 26, 1840. MS, George Davenport, Jr., in Harding, *The Days of Henry Thoreau*, p. 101.

59. Koopman, "The Thoreau Romance," p. 100.

60. Harding, *The Days of Henry Thoreau*, p. 101.

61. Ibid, p. 102.

62. Thoreau, *Collected Poems*, p. 124.

63. Thoreau may have been thinking of this letter when he wrote in *Walden*, "To speak critically, I never received more than one or two letters in my life— I wrote this some years ago—that were worth the postage" (p. 69).

64. Harding, *The Days of Henry Thoreau*, p. 101.

65. Ellen Sewall, Letter to Prudence Ward, November 18, 1840. MS, George Davenport, Jr., in Harding, *The Days of Henry Thoreau*, pp. 101–2.

66. Koopman, "The Thoreau Romance," p. 102.

67. Harding suggests (*The Days of Henry Thoreau*, pp. 107–110) that Henry became romantically interested in Mary Russell of Plymouth, but the evidence for any serious interest is skimpy indeed.

68. *Hamlet*, act 2, sc. 2. See also Erikson, "Youth: Fidelity and Diversity," pp. 5–6. Erikson speaks of Ernest Jones' contention that Hamlet "is unable to avenge his father's recent murder, because as a child he had himself betrayed him in phantasy, and wished him out of the way."

69. Canby, *Thoreau*, pp. 124–25.

70. Thoreau, *Correspondence*, p. 39.

71. There are no recorded journal entries between November 15 and December 2, 1840; this *may* indicate that this was a period during which Thoreau was trying to catch his breath, regain his poise, recoup his losses. It may also suggest that, if he did write anything personal in his journal in this period, he chose to leave it out, or cut it out, of the public record.

72. See Epilogue, " 'Over Snow-capped Mountains to Reach the Sun' " for a discussion of Thoreau's compensatory intimacy with words and what words came to mean to him.

73. Miller, *Consciousness in Concord*, p. 209.

74. Thoreau, *A Week*, p. 255.

75. Canby, *Thoreau*, pp. 124–25.

76. In a way, Henry may have suspected that he had wished to "castrate" his brother by depriving him of his mate. Moreover, just as "the scythe that cuts will cut our legs," so might Henry have feared that he would himself be castrated as punishment for his sinful intentions.

77. Harding, *The Days of Henry Thoreau*, p. 122.

78. Ibid.

Chapter 5

1. Gozzi ("Tropes and Figures," p. 81) thinks it likely that Cynthia's "sharp tongue" was one of the factors that led Henry to move to the Emersons' home.
2. Harding, *The Days of Henry Thoreau,* p. 106.
3. Ibid., p. 122.
4. George Ward, Letter to his mother, in Canby, *Thoreau,* p. 176.
5. Harding, *The Days of Henry Thoreau,* p. 125.
6. Ibid., pp. 87–88.
7. On the other hand, the substantial members of the community might have questioned Henry's motivation in completely giving up school teaching; thus, he was again courting community censure by discontinuing his teaching duties.
8. Harding, *The Days of Henry Thoreau,* p. 123.
9. Rusk, *The Life of Emerson,* pp. 289–90.
10. Canby, *Thoreau,* p. 142.
11. Paul, *The Shores of America,* p. 99.
12. Though there would be some hints of a cooling off in the friendship before the year was out, not until 1842 and 1843 did a serious rift begin to develop between the two Transcendentalists.
13. Thoreau, *Correspondence,* p. 45.
14. It might be said that this characterization reveals not only Henry's fear of commitment, but also the anal-retentive side of his personality.
15. Thoreau, *Correspondence,* p. 46.
16. Ibid., p. 45.
17. Ibid., p. 47.
18. Margaret Fuller, in Thoreau, *Correspondence,* p. 57.
19. Ibid., p. 53.
20. Isaiah Williams, in Thoreau, *Correspondence,* p. 58.
21. Harding, *The Days of Henry Thoreau,* p. 123.

Chapter 6

1. See, for instance, Harding, *The Days of Henry Thoreau,* pp. 134–37; Paul, *The Shores of America,* pp. 103–5; Canby, *Thoreau,* pp. 177–79.
2. Canby says (*Thoreau,* p. 177): "they went on no more excursions together, and do not seem to have spent much time in each other's company; nor are there references to John in Henry's letters."
3. Harding, *The Days of Henry Thoreau,* p. 134.
4. Robinson, *"Warrington" Pen-Portraits,* letter of February 2, 1842, pp. 12–13.
5. Thoreau, *Collected Poems,* p. 151.
6. Davenport and Koopman, in Harding, *The Days of Henry Thoreau,* p. 134.
7. Harding, *The Days of Henry Thoreau,* p. 134.
8. Joel Myerson, "More Apropos of John Thoreau," *American Literature,* 45 (March, 1973): 104–6.

9. Letter of Lidian Emerson, in Myerson, "More Apropos of John Thoreau," p. 105.

10. Ibid.

11. Barzillai Frost (Funeral sermon for John Thoreau, Jr.), MS, George Davenport, Jr., in Harding, *The Days of Henry Thoreau*, p. 135.

12. Letter of Lidian Emerson, in Myerson, "More Apropos of John Thoreau," p. 106.

13. Edward Emerson, *Thoreau as Remembered*, p. 26.

14. Emerson, *Letters of Ralph Waldo Emerson*, ed. Ralph Rusk (New York: Columbia University Press, 1939), III: 4.

15. Thoreau, *Correspondence*, p. 66.

16. Harding and S. E. Rena, "Thoreau's Voice," *Boston Transcript*, February 15, 1896, in Harding, *The Days of Henry Thoreau*, p. 136.

17. Erich Lindemann, "Symptomotology and Management of Acute Grief," in *Death and Identity*, ed. Robert Fulton (New York: John Wiley & Sons, 1965), p. 194. Reprinted from *American Journal of Psychiatry*, 101 (1944): 141–48.

18. A. C. Cain, I. Fast, and M. E. Erickson, "Children's Disturbed Reactions to the Death of a Sibling," *American Journal of Orthopsychiatry*, 34 (1964): 747.

19. Lindemann, "Acute Grief," p. 192.

20. Jules Henry, *Culture Against Man* (New York: Random House, 1963), p. 296.

21. Although Cain, Fast, and Erickson discuss children's responses to the death of a sibling, their description may well be said to apply to Thoreau:

> We found, of course, a heavy accent on guilt-laden reactions. In approximately half our cases, guilt was rawly, directly present. So, too, was trembling, crying, and sadness upon mention of the sibling's death, with the guilt still consciously active five years or more after the sibling's death. Such children felt responsible for the death, sporadically insisted it was all their fault, felt they should have died too, or should have died *instead* of the dead sibling. They insisted they should enjoy nothing, and deserved only the worst. Some had suicidal thoughts and impulses, said they deserved to die, wanted to die—this also being motivated by a wish to join the dead sibling. They mulled over and over the nasty things they had thought, felt, said, or done to the dead sibling, and became all the guiltier. They also tried to recall the good things they had done, the ways they had protected the dead sibling, and so on. The guilt was variously handled by each child in accord with his unique personality structure, with reactions including depressive withdrawal, accident-prone behavior, punishment-seeking, constant provocative testing, exhibitionistic use of guilt and grief, massive projection of superego accusations, and many forms of acting out. ("Children's Reactions," p. 743)

22. The next date of journal entry would not be until February 19, 1842.

23. Thoreau, *Correspondence*, p. 62.

24. The argument could also be made that the sympathetic lockjaw was a way

of *denying* guilt: "in all those who have developed symptoms of hysteria as a protection against the pain of grief there is the strongest denial of an unconscious conviction of personal responsibility for the loss, for the murder of the object. I think these hysterical reactions are an attempt to ward off something worse, a depressive attack, and that a part of the organism is killed (and yet nursed and kept alive) to save the whole organism from self-destruction; a desperate quasi-suicide is enacted instead.—See Charles Anderson, "Aspects of Pathological Grief and Mourning," *International Journal of Psychoanalysis*, 30 (1949): 50.

25. See Gozzi, "Tropes and Figures," pp. 278–79. Gozzi does not discuss in depth, as I have, the more "conscious" reasons for hostility between the two brothers. He also minimizes the possible significance of the rivalry for Ellen. However he does observe that Thoreau felt intense guilt when his brother died because of his unconscious hatred of John as an oedipal foe and as a competitor for maternal love. Henry had unconsciously wished his brother dead, and, when he *did* die, his superego was convinced that he had been the *cause*. As a consequence, Gozzi says, of "identification ('I am like John in loving mother') and the lex talionis principle ('I deserve what I wish on others')," Thoreau duplicated the symptoms of lockjaw and seemingly came close to dying himself.

26. Gandhi, as quoted by Erikson, *Gandhi's Truth*, p. 128

27. See Erikson, *Gandhi's Truth*, pp. 123–33 for a full discussion of the "curse" in Gandhi's life.

28. Thoreau, *Correspondence*, p. 68.

29. Erikson, *Gandhi's Truth*, p. 129.

30. When John Thoreau, Sr. was dying in the late 1850s, Henry would once more be a devoted and attentive nurse; again, such "feminine service" could also be construed as a denial of impure or evil motives. Yet the denial was not successful. Bode, commenting on Gozzi's findings, says that after the father had died, "Henry's Oedipal foe was gone. The son had triumphed, the mother was his. He had become head of the house and was responsible for conducting the family business as well. His feeling of guilt, though, at replacing his father must have been severe" (Bode, "The Half-Hidden Thoreau," p. 115). After his father's death, Gozzi believes, Thoreau on some level wished to die himself—and did soon thereafter. What Gozzi fails to recognize is that Thoreau had been "cursed" by his brother's death long before his father's death. By the late 1850s he was, then, *doubly* cursed.

31. Koopman, "The Thoreau Romance," p. 101.

32. A passage in the "Natural History of Massachusetts" may well have been Thoreau's response to Frost's sermon: "Cannot these sedentary sects do better than prepare the shrouds and write the epitaphs of those other busy living men? The practical faith of all men belies the preacher's consolation" (p. 40).

33. Cain, Fast, and Erickson, "Children's Reactions," p. 748.

34. Ibid., pp. 747–48.

35. Nathaniel Hawthorne, *The American Notebooks*, ed. Claude M. Simpson, Centenary Edition of the Works of Nathaniel Hawthorne, Vol. VIII (Columbus, Ohio: Ohio State University Press, 1972), p. 369.

36. Harding, *The Days of Henry Thoreau*, p. 136.

37. Edward Emerson, *Thoreau as Remembered*, p. 27.

38. Lindemann, "Acute Grief," p. 190.

39. See Gozzi, "Tropes and Figures," pp. 303–319; Paul, *The Shores of America*, pp. 104–5 for a discussion of Channing as brother-substitute for Thoreau.

40. Thoreau, *Correspondence*, p. 62.

41. Erikson, *Gandhi's Truth*, p. 129. For a further psychological discussion of God as father, see Sigmund Freud, *The Future of an Illusion*, trans. W. D. Robson-Scott, ed. James Strachey (Garden City, N.Y.: Doubleday & Co., 1964).

42. Hawthorne, *The American Notebooks*, p. 354.

43. See F. B. Sanborn, quoting Emerson, in *The Writings of Henry David Thoreau*, ed. Sanborn (Cambridge, Mass.: The Riverside Press, 1906), VI: 290.

44. Harding, *The Days of Henry Thoreau*, p. 445.

45. Ibid., p. 466.

46. Channing, *Thoreau, the Poet-Naturalist*, p. 319.

47. Paul, *The Shores of America*, p. 105.

48. Thoreau, "Natural History of Massachusetts," p. 54.

49. Hawthorne, *The American Notebooks*, p. 354.

50. Thoreau, *Collected Poems*, p. 144.

51. Ibid., pp. 151–52; p. 315.

52. Paul, *The Shores of America*, p. 104.

53. Henry David Thoreau, "A Walk to Wachusett," *Excursions* (1863; rpt. New York: Corinth Books, 1962), p. 84.

54. Ibid., p. 87.

55. Ibid., pp. 87–88.

56. Ibid., p. 93.

57. Henry David Thoreau, *The Maine Woods*, ed. Dudley Lunt (New York: Bramhall House, 1950), p. 271.

58. Thoreau, *Correspondence*, p. 75.

59. Ibid., p. 62.

60. Harding, *The Days of Henry Thoreau*, p. 144.

61. Henry David Thoreau, *Sir Walter Raleigh*, ed. Henry A. Metcalf (Boston: Bibliophile Society, 1905), p. 29.

62. *Concord Freeman*, February 10, 1843, in Harding, *The Days of Henry Thoreau*, p. 144.

63. Ibid., p. 144.

64. Thoreau, *Sir Walter Raleigh*, p. 46.

65. Harding, *The Days of Henry Thoreau*, p. 136; Hildegarde Hawthorne, *Concord's Happy Rebel* (New York, 1940), p. 73.

66. Harding, *The Days of Henry Thoreau*, p. 136.

67. Sanborn, *The Personality of Thoreau*, pp. 38–39.

68. Ibid., p. 39.

69. Harding, *The Days of Henry Thoreau*, p. 93.

70. That Henry could have achieved success through this book by using the trip with his brother to gain fame for himself, might have troubled his conscience.

71. Harding, *The Days of Henry Thoreau*, p. 179.

72. It may be that he was following the convention of not naming the deceased in an elegy, but it may also be that he chose to follow this convention mostly *because* it allowed him to avoid confronting associations with his brother.

73. Thoreau, *A Week*, p. 16.

74. Harding, *The Days of Henry Thoreau*, p. 270.

75. Henry David Thoreau, *Cape Cod* (New York: Bramhall House, 1951), p. 16.

76. Ibid., p. 17.

77. Ibid., pp. 20–21.

78. Ibid., p. 34.

79. Ibid., pp. 21–22.

80. Ibid., p. 31

81. Ibid., p. 64.

82. Ibid., pp. 47–48.

83. Ibid., p. 51.

84. Ibid., p. 59.

85. Ibid., p. 49.

86. It might be hypothesized that Thoreau in one sense sought out Ellen Sewall and the wreckage of *St. John* as a form of self-punishment.

87. Thoreau, *Cape Cod*, pp. 55–56.

88. Ibid., p. 56.

89. Indeed, Mrs. Thoreau would outlive all the males in her immediate family.

Epilogue

1. Henry David Thoreau, "Natural History of Massachusetts," *Excursions* (1863; rpt. New York: Corinth Books, 1962), p. 64.

2. His homesickness and dependency is clearly revealed in his letters. He wrote to Lidian on May 22, "I carry Concord ground in my boots and in my hat, — and am I not made of Concord dust? I cannot realize that it is the roar of the sea I hear now, and not the wind in Walden woods" (*Correspondence,* pp. 103–4). He confided to his mother, "I am chiefly indebted to your letters for what I have learned of Concord and family news, and am very glad when I get one. I should have liked to be in Walden woods with you. . . . Methinks I should be content to sit at the back-door in Concord, under the poplar-tree, henceforth forever" (*Correspondence*, p. 131). Thoreau's fervent declaration of affection for Lidian in a June 20, 1843 letter may have been largely a consequence of his homesickness and gratefulness for her comforting words.

3. Sherman Paul, *The Shores of America*, p. 166.

4. Henry David Thoreau, "A Winter Walk," *Excursions* (1863; rpt. New York: Corinth Books, 1962), p. 111.

5. Ibid., p. 113–14.

6. Ibid., p. 115.

7. Ibid., p. 116.

8. Ibid., p. 117.

9. Ibid., p. 109.

10. Ibid., pp. 117–18.

11. Ibid., pp. 129–30.

12. Thoreau, *A Week on the Concord and Merrimack Rivers*, p. 91.

13. Erikson, "The Life Cycle: Epigenesis of Identity," pp. 135–36.

14. Ibid., p. 138.

15. See "The Life Cycle: Epigenesis of Identity," pp. 138–39. Thoreau's sense of generativity was precarious. In later life he was haunted by the fear of sterility; he feared, for instance, that his imaginative powers were drying up when he began to look at nature too scientifically. Frequently threatened by a sense of stagnation as he grew older, Thoreau had to struggle mightily to avoid physical and psychological invalidism.

16. Erik Erikson, "Womanhood and the Inner Space," *Identity: Youth and Crisis* (New York: W. W. Norton & Company, 1968), p. 282.

17. It should be acknowledged that Thoreau's "generativity" was not turned exclusively inward. He did care for children in the real world, as a teacher, as a substitute father for Emerson's children, as a "nurse" for both his brother and father, as captain of many a huckleberry party. When his father fell ill—and finally died—he became head of the household. We also should not forget that Thoreau had "disciples" and followers (such as Blake, Brown, Ricketson, and Cholmondeley) in later life. One further manifestation of his generative impulses was his increasing concern and active involvement in social and political issues, especially Abolitionism and the John Brown controversy. His interest in conservation and the "succession of forest trees" can also be perceived as an expression of the generative urge.

18. Thoreau, "A Winter Walk," pp. 118–19.

19. "Fire in the Wood," *Concord Freeman*, in *Thoreau Society Bulletin*, 32 (July, 1950): 1.

20. Harding, *The Days of Henry Thoreau*, p. 161.

21. Miller speaks uncharitably of Henry as being compelled, in his journal to "vomit forth the cancer of his guilt." See *Consciousness in Concord*, pp. 119–21.

22. Edel, *Henry D. Thoreau*, p. 20.

23. The fire could also be construed as an expression of hostility against his Admetus-like father who, Harding tells us, "was active in the Concord Fire Society, a volunteer fire company, and in the early 1840s acted as its secretary" (*The Days of Henry Thoreau*, p. 8). To start a runaway fire was to get back at the father by causing him great embarrassment. Thoreau's behavior must also have caused his prestige-conscious mother much embarrassment and consternation.

24. Ellery Channing, in Thoreau, *Correspondence*, p. 161.

25. Thoreau, *The Variorum Walden*, p. 29.

26. Harding informs us that "by the late summer of 1844 Mrs. Thoreau was convinced the family could afford a house of their own. She had long since tired of living in rented houses" (*The Days of Henry Thoreau*, p. 177). Thoreau went to Walden soon after his family had moved from the Parkman house to the "Texas house" which he had helped to build.

27. Channing says in *Thoreau, the Poet Naturalist*, "Some have fancied because he moved to Walden he left his family. He bivouacked there, and really lived at home, where he went every day" (p. 24). Harding indicates that Thoreau visited the village, or was visited at Walden, almost every day. Such people as Emerson, the Alcotts, and the children of Concord visited often. Some Concordians, says Harding, "claimed that 'he would have starved, if it had not been that his sisters and mother cooked up pies and doughnuts and sent them to him in a basket.' . . . The Emersons, too, frequently invited him to dinner, as did the Alcotts and the Hosmers. They had all done so before he went to Walden Pond and continued the custom after he left. Rumor had it that every time Mrs. Emerson rang her dinner bell, Thoreau came bounding through the woods and over the fences to be the first in line at the Emerson dinner table" (p. 184). For a full discussion of the historical Thoreau's life at Walden, see Harding, *The Days of Henry Thoreau*, pp. 179-98.

28. The one night Thoreau did admit in *Walden* to spending in the village—in jail—only served to emphasize his moral distance from the town and its "dirty institutions."

29. Harding, *The Days of Henry Thoreau*, pp. 187-88; see also James Lyndon Shanley, *The Making of Walden* (Chicago: University of Chicago Press, 1957).

30. That Thoreau worked on the book for so long may indicate his reluctance to give up immersion in the Walden experience and identity.

31. Huntington Library MS, 924, as quoted in Quentin Anderson, "Thoreau on July 4," p. 17.

32. See Gozzi, "Tropes and Figures," p. iv, and Quentin Anderson, "Thoreau on July 4," *The New York Times Book Review*, 4 July 1971, pp. 1, 16-18 for discussions of Thoreau's "self-image" and "persona."

33. Thoreau, *The Variorum Walden*, p. 247.

34. Ibid., p. 62. In the end, Thoreau did not think it wise to commit himself to living at Walden: "I left the woods for as good a reason as I went there. Perhaps it seemed to me that I had several more lives to live, and could not spare any more time for that one. It is remarkable how easily and insensibly we fall into a particular route, and make a beaten track for ourselves. I had not lived there a week before my feet wore a path from my door to the pondside" (p. 244).

35. Maurice Stein, discussing Erikson's work, uses Thoreau's very words to characterize what may happen to individuals who do not have an opportunity for a constructive moratorium: "They suffer both from 'identity diffusion,'

not being certain who they are, and from 'identity foreclosure,' the hasty espousal of self-conceptions to avoid the anxieties of diffusion without satisfactorily determining whether the identities so adopted are suitable for their unique capacities. In an earlier formulation, Erikson referred to the psychic condition of the American adolescent as one of 'ego restriction' arising as a defense against the demands made by parents and society. Living in an utterly discontinuous culture, confronted by irrational demands from his parents, unaided by any significant rituals of transition, and deprived of adult roles which promise satisfactions in depth, affect is withdrawn from any of the alternatives and a life of quiet desperation accepted" *The Eclipse of Community* (Princeton, New Jersey: Princeton University Press, 1960), p. 265.

See also Richard Sennett's discussion in *The Uses of Disorder* (New York: Alfred A. Knopf, 1970) of adolescents who, in the face of the ambiguities, pluralism, and anxieties of their life-stage, develop a strong need for "purity and coherence." The "grown up" community, argues Sennett, has perpetuated and codified this desire rooted in adolescence to "escape from freedom." Thus, the community imposes a "voluntary slavery" on its members. While, as Leo Marx has suggested to me, Thoreau, along with Luther and Gandhi, all had a strong need for a "purified identity" and imposed some forms of voluntary restriction on themselves, it must be emphasized that each had the fortitude to resist premature and irrevocable commitment to an unsuitable (and externally imposed) identity.

36. Thoreau, *The Variorum Walden*, p. 16.
37. Ibid., p. 52.
38. Stein says, "Exceptional individuals establish their own moratorium, and Erikson has shown how this worked in the case of George Bernard Shaw and Sigmund Freud. Most people, however, require a socially established moratorium. . . . The human life cycle is a social as well as a biological fact. Only the most gifted and courageous are able to carve out their own. Unless the groundwork for identity elaboration is laid in adolescence, the adult is condemned to permanent confusion. A community must then provide its members with, at the least, meaningful sexual and work identities if it is to ensure its own continuity, as well as the psychic integrity of its members" *The Eclipse of Community*, pp. 265–66.

Of course, it may be argued that in one sense America has now institutionalized a moratorium—in the form of prolonged schooling—and that this prolongation of adolescence has by no means been an unmixed blessing for those who experience it. It should be emphasized that an extended period of schooling is certainly not a satisfactory moratorium for everyone, that different people need different *kinds* of moratoria. Moreover, it must be recognized that, for some people, a prolonged adolescence can have destructive as well as constructive consequences, that some are ready for productive adulthood sooner than others and should not be "held up" if they *are* ready, and that prolonged adolescence (or moratorium) should not be so unreservedly glorified that it becomes an end in itself. Those people who prolong adolescence indefinitely may also lead "lives of quiet desperation."

39. Marx, *The Machine in the Garden,* pp. 264–65.
40. Thoreau, *The Variorum Walden,* p. 251.
41. Ibid., p. 252.
42. Henry David Thoreau, "Walking," *Excursions* (1863; rpt. New York: Corinth Books, 1962), p. 214.

Selected Bibliography

Adams, Raymond. "Thoreau and His Neighbors." *Thoreau Society Bulletin,* 44 (Summer 1953): 1–4.

Anderson, Charles. "Aspects of Pathological Grief and Mourning." *International Journal of Psychoanalysis,* 30 (1949): 48–55.

Anderson, Charles R. *The Magic Circle of Walden.* New York: Holt, Rinehart, and Winston, 1968.

————, ed. *Thoreau's World, Miniatures From His Journal.* Englewood Cliffs, N.J.: Prentice-Hall, Inc., 1971.

Anderson, Quentin. *The Imperial Self.* New York: Alfred A. Knopf, 1971.

————. "Thoreau on July 4." *The New York Times Book Review,* 4 July 1971, pp. 1, 16–18.

Bettelheim, Bruno. "The Problem of Generations." In *The Challenge of Youth,* edited by Erik Erikson, pp. 76–109. Garden City, N.Y.: Doubleday & Company, 1963.

Bode, Carl. "The Half-Hidden Thoreau." In *Thoreau in Our Season,* edited by John Hicks, pp. 104–116. Amherst: University of Massachusetts Press, 1962.

————, ed. *American Life in the 1840's.* New York: New York University Press, 1967.

Bushman, Richard L. "Jonathan Edwards as Great Man: Identity, Conversion and Leadership in the Great Awakening." *Soundings, An Interdisciplinary Journal,* 52 (Spring, 1969): 15–46.

Cain, A. C., Fast, I., and Erickson, M. E. "Children's Disturbed Reactions to the Death of a Sibling." *American Journal of Orthopsychiatry,* 34 (1964): 741–52.

Canby, Henry Seidel. *Thoreau.* Boston: Houghton Mifflin Company, 1939.

Cavell, Stanley. *The Senses of Walden.* New York: The Viking Press, 1972.

Channing, Ellery. *Thoreau, the Poet-Naturalist.* Edited by F. B. Sanborn. Boston: Charles E. Goodspeed, 1902.

Coles, Robert. *Erik Erikson: The Growth of His Work.* Boston: Little, Brown, and Company, 1970.

————. "Shrinking History—Part I." *The New York Review of Books,* 22 February 1973, pp. 15–21.

————. "Shrinking History—Part II." *The New York Review of Books,* 8 March 1973, pp. 25–29.

Concord Freeman. "Fire in the Woods." *Thoreau Society Bulletin,* 32 (July 1950): 1.

Cook, Reginald L. *Passage to Walden.* Boston: Houghton Mifflin and Company, 1949.

Cosman, Max. "Apropos of John Thoreau." *American Literature,* 12 (1940): 241–43.

Derleth, August. *Concord Rebel.* Philadelphia: Chilton Company, 1962.

De Tocqueville, Alexis. *Democracy in America.* Edited by Phillips Bradley. 2 vols. New York: Vintage Books, 1945.

Deutsch, Helene. *Selected Problems of Adolescence.* New York: International Universities Press, Inc., 1967.

Donald, David. *Lincoln Reconsidered.* New York: Vintage Books, 1956.

Edel, Leon. *Henry D. Thoreau.* Minneapolis: University of Minnesota Press, 1970.

Emerson, Edward. *Henry Thoreau as Remembered by a Young Friend.* Boston: Houghton Mifflin Company, 1917.

Emerson, Ralph Waldo. "The American Scholar." *Selected Writings of Ralph Waldo Emerson.* Edited by William H. Gilman. New York: New American Library, 1965.

———. "The Conservative." *Nature, Addresses, and Lectures,* 1903. Reprint. New York: AMS Press, 1968.

———. "Divinity School Address." *Selected Writings of Ralph Waldo Emerson.* Edited by William H. Gilman. New York: New American Library, 1965.

———. "Fate." *Selected Writings of Ralph Waldo Emerson.* Edited by William H. Gilman. New York: New American Library, 1965.

———. "Heroism." *The Selected Writings of Ralph Waldo Emerson.* Edited by Brooks Atkinson. New York: The Modern Library, 1950.

———. "Historic Notes of Life and Letters in New England." In *The American Transcendentalists,* edited by Perry Miller, pp. 5–20. Garden City, N.Y.: Doubleday & Company, 1957.

———. "Historical Discourse at Concord." *Miscellanies.* Boston: Houghton Mifflin Company, 1876.

———. *The Journals and Miscellaneous Notebooks of Ralph Waldo Emerson.* Edited by Merton M. Sealts, Jr. Vol. v. Cambridge: Belknap Press, 1965.

———. *The Journals and Miscellaneous Notebooks of Ralph Waldo Emerson.* Edited by Ralph H. Orth. Vol. vi. Cambridge: Belknap Press, 1965.

———. "Lecture on the Times." *Nature, Addresses and Lectures.* 1903. Reprint. New York: AMS Press, 1968.

———. *Letters of Ralph Waldo Emerson.* Edited by Ralph Rusk. New York: Columbia University Press, 1939.

———. "Man the Reformer." *Nature, Addresses, and Lectures.* 1903. Reprint. New York: AMS Press, 1968.

———. "Nature." *Nature, Addresses, and Lectures.* 1903. Reprint. New York: AMS Press, 1968.

———. "New England Reformers." *The Selected Writings of Ralph Waldo Emerson.* Edited by Brooks Atkinson. New York: The Modern Library, 1950.

———. "Self-Reliance." *Selected Writings of Ralph Waldo Emerson.* Edited by William H. Gilman. New York: New American Library, 1965.

———. "Thoreau." *Selected Writings of Ralph Waldo Emerson.* Edited by William H. Gilman. New York: New American Library, 1965.

————. "The Transcendentalist." *The Selected Writings of Ralph Waldo Emerson.* Edited by Brooks Atkinson. New York: The Modern Library, 1950.

————. "The Young American." *Nature, Addresses, and Lectures.* 1903. Reprint. New York: AMS Press, 1968,

Erikson, Erik H. *Childhood and Society.* Rev. ed. New York: W. W. Norton & Company, 1963.

————. *Dimensions of a New Identity.* New York: W. W. Norton & Company, 1974.

————. *Gandhi's Truth.* New York: W. W. Norton & Company, 1969.

————. "Human Strength and the Cycle of Generations." *Insight and Responsibility.* New York: W. W. Norton & Company, 1964.

————. "Identity Confusion in Life History and Case History." *Identity: Youth and Crisis.* New York: W. W. Norton & Company, 1968.

————. *Identity: Youth and Crisis.* New York: W. W. Norton & Company, 1968.

————. *Insight and Responsibility.* New York: W. W. Norton & Company, 1968.

————. "The Life Cycle: Epigenesis of Identity." *Identity: Youth and Crisis.* New York: W. W. Norton & Company, 1968.

————. "Reflections on the American Identity." *Childhood and Society.* Rev. ed. New York: W. W. Norton & Company, 1963.

————. "Womanhood and the Inner Space." *Identity: Youth and Crisis.* New York: W. W. Norton & Company, 1968.

————. *Young Man Luther.* New York: W. W. Norton & Company, 1958.

————. "Youth: Fidelity and Diversity." In *The Challenge of Youth,* edited by Erik Erikson, pp. 1–28. Garden City, N.Y.: Doubleday & Company, 1963.

————, ed. *The Challenge of Youth.* Garden City, N.Y.: Doubleday & Company, 1963.

Freud, Sigmund. *The Basic Writings of Sigmund Freud.* Edited by Dr. A. A. Brill. New York: The Modern Library, 1938.

————. *Civilization and Its Discontents.* Edited by James Strachey. New York: W. W. Norton & Company, 1961.

————. *The Future of an Illusion.* Translated by W. D. Robson-Scott. Edited by James Strachey. Garden City, N.Y.: Doubleday & Company, 1964.

————. *A General Introduction to Psychoanalysis.* New York: Washington Square Press, Inc., 1952.

Frost, Ruth Hallingby. "Thoreau's Worcester Associations." Worcester, Mass.: American Antiquarian Society, 1943.

Frothingham, Octavius Brooks. *Transcendentalism in New England.* 1876. Reprint. Philadelphia: University of Pennsylvania Press, 1972.

Fulton, Robert, ed. *Death and Identity.* New York: John Wiley & Sons, 1965.

Goddard, Harold Clark. *Studies in New England Transcendentalism.* New York: Columbia University Press, 1908.

Gozzi, Raymond Dante. "Tropes and Figures: A Psychological Study of David Henry Thoreau." Dissertation, New York University, 1957.

————. "Tropes and Figures: A Psychological Study of David Henry Thoreau— A Summary." *Thoreau Society Bulletin,* 58 (Winter 1957): 1–2.

Hall, Calvin S. *A Primer of Freudian Psychology*. New York: New American Library, 1954.

Harding, Walter. *The Days of Henry Thoreau*. New York: Alfred A Knopf, 1965.

————. *A Thoreau Handbook*. New York: New York University Press, 1959.

————, ed. *Henry David Thoreau: A Profile*. New York: Hill and Wang, 1971.

————, ed. *Thoreau: A Century of Criticism*. Dallas: Southern Methodist University Press, 1954.

————, Brenner, George, and Doyle, Paul A., eds. *Henry David Thoreau: Studies and Commentaries*. Rutherford, N.J.: Fairleigh Dickinson University Press, 1972.

Hawthorne, Nathaniel. *The American Notebooks*. Edited by Claude M. Simpson. Centenary Edition of the Works of Nathaniel Hawthorne, Vol. VIII. Columbus, Ohio: Ohio State University Press, 1972.

————. "The Old Manse." In *American Poetry and Prose*, edited by Norman Foerster, pp. 596–609. Boston: Houghton Mifflin Company, 1957.

Henretta, James A. *The Evolution of American Society, 1700–1815: An Interdisciplinary Analysis*. Lexington, Mass.: D. C. Heath and Company, 1973.

Henry, Jules. *Culture Against Man*. New York: Random House, 1963.

Hicks, John H., ed. *Thoreau in Our Season*. Amherst: University of Massachusetts Press, 1962.

Hoar, George Frisbie. *Autobiography of Seventy Years*. Vol. 1. New York: Charles Scribner's Sons, 1903.

Hochfield, George, ed. *Selected Writings of the American Transcendentalists*. New York: New American Library, 1966.

Jones, Ernest. "The Death of Hamlet's Father." In *Art and Psychoanalysis*, edited by William Phillips. Cleveland: The World Publishing Company, 1957.

Kalman, David. "A Study of Thoreau." *Thoreau Society Bulletin*, 58 (Winter 1948): 1–2.

Keniston, Kenneth. *The Uncommitted: Alienated Youth in American Society*. New York: Dell Publishing Company, 1965.

————. *Young Radicals: Notes on Committed Youth*. New York: Harcourt, Brace, and World, Inc., 1968.

Koopman, Louise Osgood. "The Thoreau Romance." In *Thoreau in Our Season*, edited by John Hicks, pp. 97–103. Amherst: University of Massachusetts Press, 1962.

Krutch, Joseph Wood. *Henry David Thoreau*. New York: Dell Publishing Company, 1948.

Kutscher, Austin H., ed. *Death and Bereavement*. Springfield, Illinois: Charles C. Thomas, 1969.

Lewis, R. W. B. *The American Adam*. Chicago: University of Chicago Press, 1955.

Lindemann, Erich. "Symptomotology and Management of Acute Grief." In *Death and Identity*, edited by Robert Fulton. New York: John Wiley & Sons, 1965; reprinted from *American Journal of Psychiatry*, 101 (1944): 141–48.

Lynd, Helen Merrell. *On Shame and the Search for Identity*. New York: Harcourt, Brace, and Company, 1958.

Mannheim, Karl. *Ideology and Utopia*. New York: Harcourt, Brace, & World, Inc., 1936.

Marble, Annie Russell. *Thoreau: His Home, Friends, and Books*. 1902. Reprint. New York: AMS Press, 1969.

Marx, Leo. *The Machine in the Garden*. New York: Oxford University Press, 1964.

———. Introduction to *Excursions*, by Henry David Thoreau. New York: Corinth Books, pp. v–xiv, 1962.

Matthiessen, F. O. *American Renaissance*. London: Oxford University Press, 1941.

Mazlish, Bruce, ed. *Psychoanalysis and History*. New York: Grosset & Dunlap, 1971.

Miller, Perry. *Consciousness in Concord*. Boston: Houghton Mifflin Company, 1958.

———. "From Edwards to Emerson." *Errand into the Wilderness*. New York: Harper & Row, 1956.

———, ed. *The American Transcendentalists*. Garden City, N.Y.: Doubleday & Company, Inc., 1957.

———, ed. *The Transcendentalists*. Cambridge, Mass.: Harvard University Press, 1950.

Moldenhauer, Joseph J. "Paradox in Walden." In *Twentieth Century Interpretations of Walden*, edited by Richard Ruland, pp. 73–84. Englewood Cliffs, N.J.: Prentice-Hall, Inc., 1968.

Moore, Wilbert E. *The Impact of Industry*. Englewood Cliffs, N.J.: Prentice-Hall, 1965.

Myerson, Joel. "More Apropos of John Thoreau." *American Literature*, 45 (March 1973): 104–6.

Paul, Sherman. "Resolution at Walden." *Accent*, 12 (1953): 101–113.

———. *The Shores of America*. Urbana: University of Illinois Press, 1958.

———, ed. *Thoreau: A Collection of Critical Essays*. Englewood Cliffs, N.J.: Prentice-Hall, Inc., 1962.

Pearson, Leonard, ed. *Death and Dying*. Cleveland: The Press of Case Western Reserve University, 1969.

Phillips, Wiiliam, ed. *Art and Psychoanalysis*. Cleveland: The World Publishing Company, 1957.

Porte, Joel. *Emerson and Thoreau*. Middletown, Connecticut: Wesleyan University Press, 1965.

Riesman, David, Glazer, Nathan, and Denney, Reuel. *The Lonely Crowd*. Garden City, N.Y.: Doubleday & Company, 1955.

Robinson, Mrs. W. S. *"Warrington" Pen-Portraits*. Boston: Mrs. W. S. Robinson, 1877.

Ruitenbeek, Hendrik. *The Individual and the Crowd: A Study of Identity in America*. New York: New American Library, 1964.

Ruland, Richard, ed. *Twentieth Century Interpretations of Walden*. Englewood Cliffs, N.J.: Prentice-Hall, Inc., 1968.

Rusk, Ralph L. *The Life of Ralph Waldo Emerson*. New York: Charles Scribner's Sons, 1949.

Salt, Henry S. *Life of Henry David Thoreau*. London: Walter Scott, Limited, 1896.

Sanborn, F. B. *The Life of Henry David Thoreau*. Boston: Houghton Mifflin Company, 1917.

———. *The Personality of Thoreau*. 1901. Reprint. Folcroft, Pa: The Folcroft Press, 1969.

Scudder, Townsend. *Concord: American Town*. Boston: Little Brown, and Company, 1947.

Sennett, Richard. *The Uses of Disorder*. New York: Alfred A. Knopf, 1970.

Seybold, Ethel. *Thoreau: The Quest and the Classics*. New Haven: Yale University Press, 1951.

Shanley, James Lyndon. *The Making of Walden*. Chicago: University of Chicago Press, 1957.

Slater, Philip. *The Pursuit of Loneliness*. Boston: Beacon Press, 1970.

Stein, Maurice R. *The Eclipse of Community: An Interpretation of American Studies*. Princeton, New Jersey: Princeton University Press, 1960.

Stoller, Leo. *After Walden: Thoreau's Changing Views on Economic Man*. Stanford, Calif.: Stanford University Press, 1957.

Thoreau, Henry David. *Cape Cod*. Edited by Dudley Lunt. New York: Bramhall House, 1951.

———. "Civil Disobedience." *Walden and Other Writings*. Edited by Brooks Atkinson. New York: The Modern Library, 1950.

———. *Collected Poems of Henry Thoreau*. Edited by Carl Bode. Baltimore: Johns Hopkins Press, 1965.

———. *The Correspondence of Henry David Thoreau*. Edited by Walter Harding and Carl Bode. New York: New York University Press, 1958.

———. *Excursions*. 1863. Reprint. New York: Corinth Books, 1962.

———. *The Journal of Henry D. Thoreau*. Edited by Bradford Torrey and Francis H. Allen. 1906. Reprint. (14 vols. bound as 2). New York: Dover Publications, Inc. 1962.

———. "The Landlord." *Excursions*. 1863. Reprint. New York: Corinth Books, 1962.

———. "Life Without Principle." *Walden and Other Writings*. Edited by Brooks Atkinson. New York: The Modern Library, 1950.

———. *The Maine Woods*. Edited by Dudley Lunt. New York: Bramhall House, 1950.

———. "Natural History of Massachusetts." *Excursions*. 1863. Reprint. New York: Corinth Books, 1962.

———. "Paradise (To Be) Regained." *The Writings of Henry David Thoreau*. Vol. IV. 1906. Reprint. New York: AMS Press, 1968.

———. "The Service: Qualities of the Recruit." *The Writings of Henry David Thoreau*, Vol. IV. 1906. Reprint. New York: AMS Press, 1968.

———. *Sir Walter Raleigh*. Edited by Henry A. Metcalf. Boston: Bibliophile Society, 1905.

———. "Thomas Carlyle and His Works." *The Writings of Henry David Thoreau*, Vol. IV. 1906. Reprint. New York. AMS Press, 1968

———. *The Variorum Walden*. New York: Washington Square Press, Inc., 1963.

———. *Walden and Other Writings*. Edited by Brooks Atkinson. New York: The Modern Library, 1950.

———. "Walking" *Excursions*. 1863. Reprint. New York: Corinth Books, 1962.

———. "A Walk to Wachusett." *Excursions*. 1863. Reprint. New York: Corinth Books, 1962.

———. *A Week on the Concord and Merrimack Rivers*. New York: New American Library, 1961.

———. "A Winter Walk." *Excursions*. 1863. Reprint. New York: Corinth Books. 1962.

———. *The Writings of Henry David Thoreau*. Edited by F. B. Sanborn. Vol. VI. Cambridge: The Riverside Press, 1906.

Thoreau Society Bulletin, 1–100 (October 1941-Summer 1967). New York: Johnson Reprint Corporation, 1970.

Trilling, Lionel. "Art and Neurosis." In *Art and Psychoanalysis*, edited by William Phillips, pp. 502–520. New York: The World Publishing Company, 1957.

Turner, Frederick Jackson. *The United States, 1830–1850*. New York: Henry Holt and Company, 1935.

Tyler, Alice Felt. *Freedom's Ferment*. New York: Harper & Row, 1944.

Van Doren, Charles. *Henry David Thoreau, A Critical Study*. New York: Russell and Russell, 1916.

Weiss, John. "Cold and Unimpressible." In *Henry David Thoreau: A Profile*, edited by Walter Harding, pp. 36–43. New York: Hill and Wang, 1971.

Wheeler, Ruth. *Concord: Climate for Freedom*. Concord: Concord Antiquarian Society, 1967.

———. "Thoreau's Concord." In *Henry David Thoreau: Studies and Commentaries*, edited by Walter Harding, George Brenner, and Paul Doyle, pp. 25–33. Rutherford, N.J.: Fairleigh Dickinson University Press, 1971.

Whicher, Stephen E. *Freedom and Fate: An Inner Life of Ralph Waldo Emerson*. Philadelphia: University of Pennsylvania Press, 1953.

Index

Thoreau, Henry David (*Cont.*)
102; as "traveller in Concord," 27, 46,
99, 106, 107, 108, 138, 156–57, 214;
trip to Cape Cod of, 199–204, 243 n.
102; as writer, 4, 5, 56, 64, 66, 74–75,
79, 88, 89, 106, 117, 129, 134, 156, 159,
163, 181, 182, 185, 194, 207, 208, 213,
215. Works: "The Assabet," 115;
"The Bluebirds," 78; "The Breeze's
Invitation," 115; "Brother Where
Dost Thou Dwell," 168, 189–90; *Cape
Cod*, 5, 199, 201, 202; "Chapter on
Bravery," 123–24; "Civil Disobedience," 2, 5, 213; "Cliffs," 99; "The
Commercial Spirit," 10–11, 66; "Conscience is instinct," 58, 234 n.104;
Correspondence, 5, passim; "Fair Haven," 103; "The Fisher's Son," 125;
"A Freshet," 126; "Friendship," 76;
"Great Friend," 189; *Journal*, passim;
"Life Without Principle," 8, 234 n.
102; "The Literary Life," 65; "The
Lost Journal" (as it appears in Miller's *Consciousness in Concord*), 106,
passim; *Maine Woods*, 5, 188; "Natural History of Massachusetts," 134,
188, 205, 241 n.32; "The Peal of Bells,"
106; "The Poet's Delay," 126; "The
Service," 122, 237 nn.37, 43; "Sic Vita,
63, 64, 78, 79, 84, 194; "Sir Walter
Raleigh," 195; "Society," 76, 89;
"Sound and Silence," 105; "Sympathy," 113, 114; "The Thaw," 101;
"Thomas Carlyle and His Works,"
86; "Wachusett," 117, 161; *Walden*,
1, 2, 5, 9, 17–18, 22, 24–25, 129, 142,
167, 177, 215, 216, 217, 219; "Walking," 219; "A Walk to Wachusett,"
190; "A Week on the Concord and
Merrimack Rivers," 5, 117, 118, 198,
199, 207, 215; "A Winter Walk,"
205–6, 208
Thoreau, John (brother): birth of, 30;
as buffer, 59, 152; with children, 169,
170; death of, 58, 59, 116, 117, 140,
166, 167–81, 194, 201; education of,
59; and Ellen Sewall, 116–21, 122, 129,
130, 140, 155–56; as father-figure (*see*
Father-figure); health of, 59, 149, 155,

156, 173, 181; as inadequate, 152; interest in nature of, 58, 133, 170, 188,
189; as model for HDT (*see* Identity
model); as mountain, 190–91; power
of, 203; sociability of, 60–62, 110; as
teacher, 59, 61, 62, 71, 75, 77, 104, 109,
111, 177; Transcendentalism of, 130,
140, 170, 179. *See also* HDT, relationship of, with JT
Thoreau, John (father): absence of,
54–55; as cause of identity confusion,
34–36; in debt, 29–30, 33, 164; early
life of, 20, 29–33; as father, 34, 40, 228
n.84; honesty of, 29–30, 32, 33, 35;
identification of HDT with, 35; as inadequate, 34, 35, 45, 54–55, 105, 151–
53; as model for HDT (*see* Identity
model); passiveness of, 32, 34, 43; as
pencil maker, 20, 31, 33; power of,
203; as protector, 50; as provider, 30,
40, 226 n.14; silence of, 31, 32, 35, 39,
58; violence of, 34–35, 68, 226 n.24,
229 n.102
Thoreau, Sarah (aunt), 47
Thoreau scholarship, 2–5, 115, 167, 228
n.64
Thoreau, Sophia (sister), 30, 76, 139,
228 n.70
Tocqueville, Alexis de, 12, 16, 26, 223 n.
20
Toilet training, 51–52
"Tom Bowline," 197–98, 200, 201
Transcendental Hedge Club, 81, 88
Transcendentalism, 65, 79, 81, 85, 89,
91–98, 159
Trinitarian Society, 19
Tucker, Ellen, 82

Unitarianism, 19, 91

Van Buren, Martin, 16
Very, the Rev. Jones, 88, 125
Vose, Henry, 71, 72, 77

Wachusett, Mount, 160, 190–91
Walden, 1, 2, 5, 9, 17–18, 22, 24–25, 129,
142, 167, 177, 215, 216, 217, 219

Library of Congress Cataloging in Publication Data
Lebeaux, Richard, 1946–
Young man Thoreau.

Bibliography: p.
Includes index.
1. Thoreau, Henry David, 1817–1862—Biography—
Character. 2. Authors, American—19th century—
Biography. I. Title.
PS3053.L37   818'.3'09 [B]   76-44851
ISBN 0–87023–231–2

10   1/08

8 12/99

9/96 7